THE
SHAMANIC WISDOM
OF THE
HUICHOL

"I am happy to learn that your work with entheogens continues. It is and will be an important contribution to the aims to convince the health authorities to loosen the ban that inhibits the legal use of entheogens. Entheogens must become available legally for meaningful use in psychiatry and for healing."

ALBERT HOFFMAN, SWISS SCIENTIST
AND DISCOVERER OF LSD-25

"In this absorbing account of his initiations with the Huichol, Tom Pinkson helps us to reconnect with the teachings of our indigenous American ancestors. This is healing Earth-wisdom for our fractured civilization, and inspiration to honor the creative forces inherent in the land, the plants, the animals, and the people."

RALPH METZNER, PH.D., AUTHOR OF
GREEN PSYCHOLOGY AND SACRED MUSHROOM OF VISIONS

"Tom Pinkson's fascinating journey into Huichol shamanism and how he applies this ancient tradition to healing others as well as the crises that our modern world now faces is a must read for anyone searching to raise consciousness for the betterment of both humanity and our Mother Earth."

JAMES ENDREDY, AUTHOR OF BEYOND 2012:
A SHAMAN'S CALL TO PERSONAL CHANGE
AND THE TRANSFORMATION OF GLOBAL CONSCIOUSNESS

"Indigenous wisdoms offer ways we can learn from both the seen and unseen worlds. Thomas Pinkson shares more than 20 years of experience and wisdom he has garnered from the Huichol Indians of Central America. This book is very relevant to fostering interdependence and re-visioning healing possibilities for restoring environment, communities, and humanity."

ANGELES ARRIEN, PH.D.,
CULTURAL ANTHROPOLOGIST
AND AUTHOR OF *THE FOUR-FOLD WAY*

"Tom's book is well written, like creating a finely woven basket, the kind our ancestors in northern California tribes used to receive the gifts of Nature. Thus it is that Tom has provided modern people in search of a soul with a basket full of ancient flowers. I really enjoyed reading the book; it is, indeed, a good teaching and gift to the people."

BOBBY "MEDICINE GRIZZLY BEAR" LAKE-THOM,
TRADITIONAL NATIVE HEALER AND SPIRITUAL TEACHER
AND AUTHOR OF *CALL OF THE GREAT SPIRIT*

"Seeing beyond the constrictions of our present ways is critical for our survival. Tom Pinkson's story sheds light on the potential in each one of us to change the current channels of our perceptions in order to live a more expansive, sacred, and compassionate life. His encouragement for us to walk our path with ceremonial gratitude grew from his apprenticeship with Huichol shamans and is medicine for our times."

MARION WEBER, FOUNDER OF
THE ARTS AND HEALING NETWORK
AND THE FLOW FUND CIRCLE

THE
SHAMANIC WISDOM
OF THE
HUICHOL

Medicine Teachings
for Modern Times

TOM SOLOWAY PINKSON, PH.D.

Destiny Books
Rochester, Vermont • Toronto, Canada

Destiny Books
One Park Street
Rochester, Vermont 05767
www.DestinyBooks.com

Destiny Books is a division of Inner Traditions International

Originally published in 1995 by Wakan Press under the title *Flowers of Wiricuta:
A Gringo's Journey to Shamanic Power*
Published in 1997 by Destiny Books under the title *The Flowers of Wiricuta: A
Journey to Shamanic Power with the Huichol Indians of Mexico*

Library of Congress Cataloging-in-Publication Data
Pinkson, Tom Soloway, 1945–
  The shamanic wisdom of the Huichol : medicine teachings for modern times /
Tom Soloway Pinkson. — [New ed.].
    p. cm.
  Rev. ed. of: The flowers of Wiricuta . c1995.
  Summary: "True account of a decade-long apprenticeship with Huichol shamans
in the Mexican Sierra Madre"—Provided by publisher.
  ISBN 978-1-59477-349-5 (pbk.)
  1. Shamanism—Mexico. 2. Huichol Indians—Religion. 3. Pinkson, Tom
Soloway, 1945– I. Pinkson, Tom Soloway, 1945– Flowers of Wiricuta. II. Title.
  BF1622.M6P56 2010
  299.7'84544—dc22
                                                              2009044884

Printed and bound in the United States by Lake Book Manufacturing

10 9 8 7 6 5 4 3 2 1

Text design and layout by Virginia Scott Bowman
This book was typeset in Garamond Premier Pro with Gil Sans, Minion, and
Helvetica Neue as display typefaces

Photos of original artwork by Michael St. James
Title page photo by Maria Rosa Kauffman

This book is dedicated to my friends:

Ruck
Claude Nelson Rucker III
Cola—the Tail
Untamed Mountain-Magnificent Liberation

Marsha Richman
A Flower of Beauty and Strength

Tom *Grandfather* Dunphy
A For-Real Brother
Healer
and Friend

and to

Ben Dickson
Who Taught Me How to Grow Roses.

Their lives live on in the hearts of all who knew them.

Contents

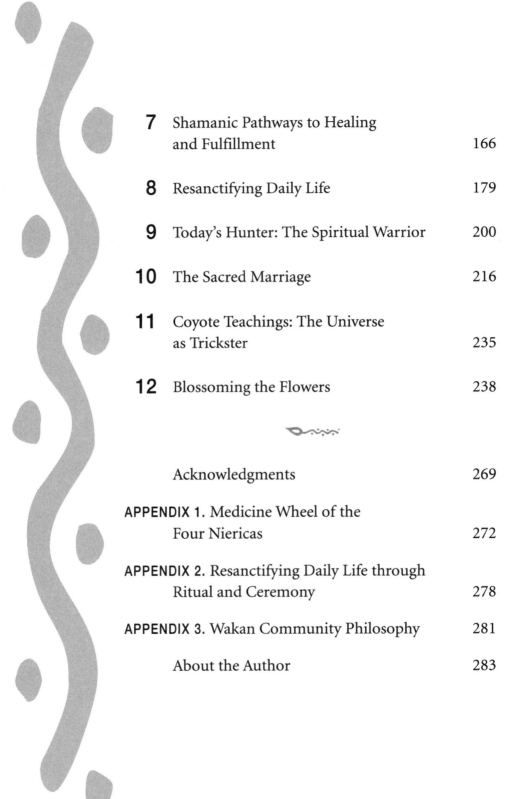

꞉ᷧᷧ꞉

The Transmission of Wisdom across Cultures

The transmission of a religious and spiritual tradition to a new culture can be an event of historic proportions, an event that transforms both the tradition and the culture. To take but one example, consider Buddhism. Over centuries, as it wended its way around the world, it changed much of Asia. In the process, it morphed into multiple novel forms, such as Vajrayana in Tibet, Chan and Hua Yen in China, and Zen and Pure Land in Japan. Now it has arrived in the West, and once again both it and its new host are adapting to each other.

But in today's world, not just one, but multiple traditions are crossing cultures. Our contemporary world is more than a melting pot of the world's religious and spiritual traditions; it is an alchemical cauldron that is yielding unprecedented cross-fertilization and creative emergence.

How the world and its religious traditions will be transformed we cannot know. However, already we are seeing signs that the effects will be far reaching. For example, consider meditation and yoga. Once little known in the West, they have now spread worldwide and are practiced by millions of Westerners, studied by thousands of scientists, and used by many thousands of health practitioners. In the process, they have demonstrated the mind's remarkable potentials and healing powers, changed our understanding of the human psyche, and become a standard part of health care.

How does the transmission of traditions to new cultures occur? In the modern world, academics and anthropologists have often made the initial studies. Academics have pored over foreign texts while anthropologists have braved foreign lands. The knowledge they glean is invaluable. However, it is usually limited to knowledge. That is, it is theoretical rather than experiential, and observational rather than participatory.

However, for the transmission of spiritual wisdom and practices, something further is required. That something is personal practice of the disciplines, and a direct realization of the experiences and understandings they produce. Only in this way can the disciplines' deeper wisdom—what philosophers call their "higher grades of significance"—be fully grasped.

So to bring spiritual traditions and their experiential wisdom and practices to a new culture requires academics and anthropologists *and practitioners*. These practitioners can become what are called *gnostic intermediaries*—direct transmitters of transpersonal, gnostic wisdom.

This is certainly true of shamanism, the world's oldest religious/spiritual tradition. We owe an enormous debt to the pioneering work of early investigators—such as the religious scholar Mircea Eliade and the anthropologist Knud Rasmussen—as well as to the detailed studies of contemporary scholars and anthropologists.

But we also owe a great debt to the pioneers who not only studied, but actually took up the practices of shamanism. It is they who introduced the practices and their fruits to the West. These practitioners include anthropologists such as Michael Harner and Barbara Tedlock, as well as psychologists such as Larry Peters, Bradford Keeney, and Tom Pinkson.

It requires a great deal—courage, dedication, endurance, and more—to penetrate deeply into any authentic spiritual discipline. It requires even more to brave a foreign culture and to be one of the first to offer oneself fully to its spiritual practices, with all their belief-shattering and life-altering implications.

Tom Pinkson did just that, and it is our good fortune that he has chronicled his pilgrimage in *The Shamanic Wisdom of the Huichol*. It is a wonderful story—an autobiography of a superb spiritual warrior who dedicated and surrendered his life to serving the highest Good, in whatever forms that Good took. This dedication led him to follow unfamiliar paths, explore his inner depths, face his deepest fears, and open to the fundamental questions and mysteries of life. The fruits of these explorations include a depth of love and wisdom that shine forth from this book, and that Tom Pinkson now uses to guide students, heal patients, and comfort the dying.

This book is impressive in recounting a spiritual warrior's pilgrimage and describing Huichol practices. But it is also impressive in transmitting the purity of heart, the sacredness of vision, and the depth of wisdom that these practices can produce—qualities which our imperiled world desperately needs, and needs to learn how to cultivate.

Through Tom Pinkson, a taste of the Huichol's precious wisdom—hard won by thousands of people across hundreds of years—is made available to us and to the world.

ROGER WALSH

Roger Walsh, M.D., Ph.D., is a professor in the department of psychiatry and human behavior at the University of California College of Medicine at Irvine. He is the author of *The World of Shamanism: New Views of an Ancient Tradition* and *Essential Spirituality: The 7 Central Practices to Awaken Heart and Mind.*

Ceremonial objects gathering spiritual power near the summit of Mt. Shasta.
Photo by Mike Lerner

Preface
to the New Edition

If there is to be any hope whatsoever of living well on this earth, we have to take the ancient root and put new sap in it. That doesn't mean we need to do something new, but to do something old in a new way, which takes great courage.

MARTIN PRECHTEL

When the first edition of this book came out in 1995, as *The Flowers of Wiricuta,* I eagerly took a number of copies on my next visit to the Huichol. Sitting around Sacred Grandfather Fire, Tatewari, in the rancho of my spiritual grandmother, Guadalupe de la Cruz—a *cantadora,* or singing shaman who heals with her songs, prayers, and ceremonies—I brought forth my book. I showed the twenty-five assembled Huichol their photos, taken on previous visits with their permission. They were delighted, joking and laughing about how they looked. Sections of the book were then read out loud in Spanish as we sat together listening under the stars.

I hoped for Guadalupe's approval of the book so I could share it with the world having her and the other Huichol's blessings. Nervously I awaited her response at the end of the reading. Taking her time, she looked intently into the flames that danced brightly before us. Finally she raised her head, looked directly at me, and smiled. *"Si, es bueno."* "It is good." With a release of accumulated tension, I rejoiced in relief.

"You have completed a covenant with my words in your book. Now it is up to you to carry the seeds of Wiricuta and the guidance from Tatewari al Norte," she said. The medicine teachings given by her and the other shamans I had worked with over the years of my apprenticeship were to be shared with others. The book was a tool to raise awareness about the wisdom of Huichol spirituality along with the teachings it held for mainstream Western culture.

Many years ago Guadalupe told me Father Sun was coming closer to the Earth because people in the North had forgotten how to live. The Sun was coming closer to purify and cleanse the toxic ways of living that disrespected life and the spirits of nature. Decades before the notion of global warming, a Huichol shaman in the remote mountains of Mexico was warning of dangers to come while giving me a loving boot to let others know what was coming if we didn't change our ways.

Now, with my book completed, Guadalupe and I wrote up a contract that was solemnized by each of us in front of Grandfather Fire and Guadalupe's extended family. The contract stipulated a percentage of book sale profits would go to her and, when she died, on to her family. I then placed a copy of the book into the heart of the Fire expressing my gratitude for all I had been given. Later that evening while watching the logs burn down I wondered what the future held in store as I went forward with my task of "bringing the medicine to the North."

Fortunately I was able to have three more pilgrimages with Guadalupe to Wiricuta, the Huichol Holy Land where the sacred peyote cactus grows, before she left this world. This woman who was childless but mother to so many died on Mother's Day May 9, 1999. A few weeks earlier a handful of fellow gringo pilgrims accompanied me to Mexico for a final visit with our beloved elder before she died. Along with her extended family and other shamans, we stayed with her for a week as she moved closer into her "Death Lodge." Numerous ceremonies took place during this time but knowing that we would not see her again in this world, Grandmother took time to share with each one of us her final medicine gifts. Today her body lies buried at her rancho outside Tepic, two and a half hours north of Puerto Vallarta in the foothills of the mountains from which she came.

With the natural reflection that comes as I approach my sixty-sixth year, I have a growing appreciation and understanding of what I was so fortunate to receive from Guadalupe and the Huichol people. I see with increasing clarity how shamanic medicine ways have integrated their way into my own life and how they can benefit the larger Western culture.

The shamanic wisdom of the Huichol provides time-tested methods for opening the mind to a wider range of awareness than the materialistic-based understanding of the West. It offers an understanding of health and well-being based on "finding your life" through an archetypal vision quest premised on the belief that you are a sacred being, not here by accident but with sacred purpose to find your heart path and the power to walk it all the days of your life so that you might attain "completion."

Huichol shamans keep the channels of communication open to the spirit world by working reverently with Tatewari who reminds us that we are luminous beings with love at the core of our being. The Huichol perform their ceremonies for all of life, not just for themselves, and they call us to reinvent an Earth-honoring way of joining them in working for the survival of all beings—not just the ones who walk on two legs. They call out to us to create our own ceremonies to thank the forces of nature for their life-giving gifts, which we are dependent upon for our lives.

The Huichol shamanic worldview is obtained experientially through intimate relationship and exploration with the invisible spirit powers of nature and the cosmology of altered states. All aspects of creation are perceived as conscious, alive, containing power, purpose, intelligence, with importance and meaning—the earth, fire, sun, ocean, deer and other animals, plants, rain, rocks, trees, and rivers. Huichol shamanic wisdom recognizes the sacredness of reciprocity with nature, the lack of which puts us on a destructive path whose impact we experience today. Their medicine teachings offer an understanding that reciprocal gift exchange with the spirit powers of nature forms the basis of sustainability through a balance of right relationship between giving and receiving. Rather than a fear-based, control-with-force patriarchy emphasizing masculine sky-gods running the show, Huichol cosmology honors the Great Cosmic Mother as integral to life and its maintenance.

Western mainstream culture needs to overcome its learned description of reality that projects misguided notions of separation, premised on ego-based identity and personal history, onto the cosmic soup of what some call "a field of plenty." The Western mindset limits itself to a very tight culturally determined, socially reinforced bandwidth of knowing, which provides our description of who we are and what is real. In our smug egocentrism we believe that what we see is the totality of what is, which constricts our understanding that evolution is an exploration of what is possible and that we can play a more skillful and conscious role in it than we have done so far.

We desperately need to learn what the Huichol know so well— how to interact with the net of power that animates the universe we are embedded within, a field of infinite possibilities and mysterious workings. Huichol traditional ways provide a model of inspiration to reweave our connections with this web of life, moving us from alienation to cooperative partnership.

The Huichol teachings have served me well in the fifteen years since I finished my apprenticeship with Guadalupe and the other Huichol shaman. I have stayed in touch with Guadalupe's extended family and the shamanic teachings that today are a vital presence in how I live my life. When you enter my office there is the sacred fire in the center of the room (as a candle). The walls are filled with Huichol art and symbols. I continue to honor my commitments and my assignments, bringing the Huichol medicine teachings to the North, integrated in my yearly vision quest retreats in the Sierra Nevada, my monthly weekend shamanic retreats, pilgrimages to places of power in the United States, my work with totemic animal spirits, equinox and solstice ceremonies, marriages, baby-blessings, initiatory rites of passage for youth, work with the terminally ill, memorial services, along with helping people work shamanically with the unplanned misfortunes that life can periodically serve up. I repeatedly hear from participants how meaningful this work is to them as they learn about growing their own spiritual intelligence to face the challenges of their lives.

One of the most rewarding developments that grew out of my work with the Huichol is helping people develop and be part of a committed spiritual community. Just these past two weeks the Wakan community, which I was dream-guided to start on Christmas Eve 1983, held a memorial service for one of our elder members who just died and another honoring ceremony for a loved elder battling severe heart disease. Through these gatherings, along with shamanically based men's groups, women's groups, couples groups, and monthly support groups, people are able to share the sacred narrative of their lives, be witnessed and affirmed. We help each other through hard times and celebrate the good. It's soul work—living like sane people are meant to live.

The last few years I've used my Huichol medicine teachings in developing workshops and training that help people strengthen their emotional, psychological, spiritual, and physical resilience to stress—what scientists refer to as "the hardiness factor"—with which to successfully face the increasing adversity and stress of modernity.

I've also developed a program that models a new relationship to aging using Guadalupe and other older Huichol as exemplars. I have witnessed how they hold a valued role in their community that deepens with passing years. As ceremonial leaders, as counselors, as transmitters of traditional ways through the oral tradition of storytelling, Huichol elders contribute to the welfare of their social group in ways that maintain self-esteem through a sense of meaning and purpose. "A New Vision of Aging" takes participants through five developmental tasks to empower conscious aging by meeting the challenges and opportunities that come with longevity in a skillful manner.

I am very grateful for the fullness of my life. A few years ago while lying in my sleeping bag at Guadalupe's rancho, it struck me in the middle of the night that when her sister Manuela dies, I will be one of the oldest ones left of the extended family who began working together in 1983 when I first met Guadalupe. Three of the shamans I have worked with have now crossed over, as well as other elders. When I was doing my closing prayers in the ceremonial hut before departing, two Huichol women in their early twenties came in and stood next to me seeking to be included in my prayer. Touched by their presence, I did a blessing ceremony for each of them. I teared up when I saw their appreciation. Having known them for almost all their lives, I realized that now I am one of their surviving elders—someone they know, trust, and care about. I felt deep gratitude for how the path of their ancestors had helped me find my life, while seeing as well the support I owe the next generation for their lives to go in a good way.

I give thanks to the Great Mystery for bringing me together with these special people that have taken me so warmly into their lives. I pray that I am able to give back a commensurate measure of what I have been so fortunate to be gifted.

The medicine teachings of the Huichol illuminate the importance of creating a healthy and sustainable living Mother Earth for future generations through the re-sacralization of daily life. A fellow explorer of perennial wisdom, Meister Eckhardt, recognized the same truth centuries ago when he stated, "It's not about doing holy things. It's about making holy what you do." May it be so for you and me and all our relations.

Note to the Reader

I'd rather learn from one bird how to sing than teach
10,000 stars how not to dance.

E.E. CUMMINGS

Nature seems to love certain shapes and forms and so she repeats them over and over in both the micro and macro levels of the universe. Thus we see the circle and the spiral in the cosmos of interstellar space, as well as in the world of subatomic physics. Both are the signature of the evolutionary cycles of life, death, and rebirth in the ongoing process of creation. Around and around, up and down. Even in apparent chaos there is an orderly sequence, which scientists are beginning to notice as their vision expands through the increasing sophistication of technological measuring instruments. The mysterious weaving of "reality" involves a multidimensional interpenetrating cosmic web, which is continuously circling and spiraling back into itself, renewing and birthing, releasing and dying. It is not a straight line.

So too this book circles and spirals back in on itself. There is movement through time—past, present, and future, as well as among different realities of form, substance, and space. It dips in for a view here, then spurts years away, dimensions away, to dip into the waters of mystery there, then back again, forward, up, down, backward, sideways—then back to where it started. But where did it start? *Quien sabe?* Who knows? It is a sacred mystery. Try and catch it in the limited container of the rational mind, and you quickly lose the sense of mystery, which is the deepest reality of all. It is the animating force for the rest of the dance.

So welcome to mystery. Welcome to the spiraling circle. The cosmic orchestra is already playing. Put on your dancing shoes. The party is going on full tilt boogie. Don't miss it. *Arriba. Vamonos.* Get up. It's time to go!

:~~~:

Introduction

The desert sun was scorching hot. It pierced my skin like the sharp spines of the cactus that pricked me whenever I inadvertently brushed against a protruding arm. The tiny needles embedded themselves in barely visible clusters, and when I tried to pull them out by hand, I only pushed them in deeper. Rub your knife gently against your skin and it will push out the spines, we'd been told. I tried it. It worked.

I warned myself to be more careful in what I was doing. And just what *was* I doing, suffering in a vast and remote desert, five thousand feet up in the mountains of central Mexico, with a group of Huichol Indians and assorted gringos? Under the guidance of a Huichol *mara'akame*, a shaman, I and twenty-three others—Huichol men and women, boys and girls, infants, grandparents, and medicine elders, plus ten *Norte Americanos*—were all out hunting for the sacred plant that is the basis of the Huichol religion.

The plant, *Lophophora williamsii*, is a cactus that grows in only one area of the world, from the deserts of southern Texas down into the high desert area of San Luis Potosi in Mexico. The cactus, more commonly known as *peyote*, has been a mainstay of ancient Mesoamerican spirituality for thousands of years. For the Huichol, it is a gift from the gods, a sacrament.

In the Huichol creation story, it was long ago before time as we know it that the gods and goddesses first appeared on this earthen realm. The world was in total darkness and the gods were guided to journey together to find the light in the center of this "middle world." Many amazing

1

Photo by Trout Black

Mara'akame (Huichol shaman)

events took place on this pilgrimage, and when the gods finally arrived, they witnessed the sun rising from a deep tunnel in a mountain to illuminate the world for the very first time. Kauyumari, the deer spirit, was the last of the gods to arrive. With the newly emerged light from the sun, the gods could see that Kauyumari left round, green, disk-like tracks all over the desert. The fire god, Tatewari, who led the pilgrimage and was the first shaman, instructed the rest of the gods to eat Kauyumari's tracks, for they were sacred food.

But first, they made elaborate offerings, *ofrendas,* and conducted a ceremony of singing and dancing and thanking Kauyumari for its gift. Then Tatewari blessed each god and fed it some of the "tracks." Upon ingestion, the gods were able to hear the songs that Tatewari and Kauyumari had been singing during the entire pilgrimage, songs that described their adventure from the very beginning. They understood now why Kauyumari had come last—to leave these important tracks for those who would come later, to help them find their way back to the "first times of the ancestors" so they could remember from whence they came and understand who they really are.

So it was then, and so it is today for those who have the eyes to see. The sacred tracks enable the devout pilgrim to hear the wisdom songs and follow the traditions laid down by the gods. As devout Muslims must journey to Mecca at least once in their life as part of their sacred path, so too must devout Huichol journey to the holy land of Wiricuta, where the sacred medicine grows, in order to find their lives. For those who are called to the shamanic path, those who wish to complete themselves, there will be many pilgrimages to Wiricuta. And for those who aspire to reach a state of mastery, they will continue on this sacred path of the ancestors all their lives.

Today the earth of Mexico has been chopped up into pieces of private property crisscrossed with highways, cities, barbed wire, and dirt roads through the desert. Yet, the Huichol still go on their pilgrimage, following

Photo by John Catalin

Pilgrimage to Wiricuta

the steps of their ancestors. There in the holy land of Wiricuta, in an all-night ceremony around the fire, the shaman leads modern-day pilgrims in the ritual ingestion of their sacrament, and in the songs, prayers, and dancing that carry them through the night in joyful communion with the numinous.

For the ceremony to commence, the pilgrims must first find the peyote. This is not an easy chore, at least it wasn't for me. We scattered out over the desert floor, each of us, children included, carrying a brightly colored woven Huichol *bolsa,* or bag. Our job was to fill each bag to the brim with peyote but not to eat any of it. The first bite would be given to each of us by the shaman after an elaborate ceremony where all the offerings we had made—prayer arrows, beautifully decorated votive bowls, small paintings of yarn inlaid into beeswax melted on pieces of wood, and many other items of personal meaning to each pilgrim—would first be "given" to Kauyumari and the spirits of this powerful holy land.

Now Kauyumari is also a trickster figure for the Huichol and so it's not surprising that the peyote is difficult to find, hidden as it is so well in the desert floor. Its top is flat and even with the earth itself, blending in perfectly with the colors of dirt and rock. It grows right next to another kind of cactus—the one with the jumping spines—so just as you reach for one, you can get stabbed by the other, a challenging arrangement that cautions you to pay attention to your every move.

Enthusiastically, I set out, scanning the ground to find the elusive quarry. I peered carefully under well-armed protectors, got down on my hands and knees, walked slowly, eyes on the ground, sweating profusely. Ouch! Pulled painful *espinas* from my hands, forearms, and clothes, from the soles of my shoes. I walked in expanding concentric circles, searching relentlessly. My initial excitement started to turn to frustration, for try as I might, I could not find one single plant. The excited cries of successful hunters all around me made me feel like a failure.

Whenever someone would find the plant, we'd all run over to examine the catch. Reinspired, I'd set off once again, only to end up sweaty, frustrated, bitten by *espinas.* Hours went by and I was still empty handed. Frustration turned to despair. Then I remembered the Huichol story about

Photo by Joe Burrell

*Huichol bolsa with image of the
deer spirit, Kauyumari*

the origin of the medicine and the importance of connecting with its spirit
before hunting its body. In the initial excitement of my first hunt, I had
completely forgotten all the shaman's instructions about how to proceed.

Since the *hicouri* (peyote) is believed to be Kauyumari's footprints, we
were instructed to first call in Kauyumari and then watch it run through
the desert. "Watch where its feet touch the ground, and that is where you
will find the *hicouri*," said the shaman. Through previous ceremonies
with the Huichol during the days leading up to our arrival at the holy
land, I had made contact with Kauyumari and so felt comfortable with
the notion of calling it in. Slowly and carefully, I sat down on the desert
floor. I closed my eyes and drew my attention inside to my heart. The
peyote is considered heart medicine by the Huichol and I wanted it to
know what was in my heart. After quieting my mind, I very softly began
to sing a Huichol deer song. I used the words of the song to focus on

telepathically transmitting my desire to find the medicine and my motivation for coming on this pilgrimage.

I come to find my life, the purpose for which you have given me my birth, Great Spirit. I open myself to your presence and give thanks for Kauyumari, the deer spirit, for the Huichol, for the hicouri, and for you. If I am meant to walk the path of a mara'akame, help me to find this sacred medicine and listen to its teachings. If this is not meant to be for my greatest good, help me to accept this with grace and open to what is. May it be so.

I finished my prayer and sat motionless, eyes closed, in deep silence, listening. After a few moments, I saw Kauyumari, the magical deer! My spirit soared. I thanked it for coming to me, then watched it bound gracefully through the desert. Watching with my inner eye, I carefully observed where its feet hit the ground. I was tempted to open my eyes and see if there really was a deer out there, but I knew to wait until the deer finished its dance. Finally, the deer disappeared into the brush. I waited a few moments to see if it would reappear, and when it didn't, I opened my eyes. I looked down on the ground and saw peyote all around me. I could reach out and touch it without even moving. Apparently it had been there all along, but in order to visually perceive it, I first had to achieve the right attunement within myself. I was then able to see what had been there from the beginning. I marveled at the workings of the trickster deer spirit helping me find the elusive treasure right where it had been all along.

I went on to find many *hicouri* plants that day and on subsequent pilgrimages. However, I didn't know that the peyote plant flowered until several years later on a pilgrimage when I noticed a plant four inches in diameter, a *grande*. As I approached, I saw a flower peeking out from its center. I stood transfixed by the soft, fragile beauty in the harshness of the heat and parched earth. Upon closer inspection, I saw that the pink and white petals formed a small circle around the minute, golden tendrils, which themselves formed yet another circle, and inside that was a very tiny bouquet of five petite white flowers rising up from a yellow bed. I was touched by the plant's delicacy, this *poca de gracia,* and my first impulse was to take it home with me so I could cherish it always. But I remembered that not only would the flower soon fade, but that U.S. Customs would

Photo by Trout Black

Harvested hicouri, or peyote, the sacramental plant of the Huichol

not take kindly to this sacred plant, which their laws had declared illegal to have in one's possession. I decided instead to take it into my "inner home" by reverently eating it. First I made an offering of purified tobacco to the spirit of the plant. Then I prayed. *Thank you, Kauyumari, for bringing me to this special medicine. Thank you, hicouri, for your beautiful gift. Thank you, Great Spirit, for bringing me here to Wiricuta with the Huichol. May they and their people survive and carry on the ancient medicine ways of respect and love. Help me to use this medicine in a good way, opening up to your presence and knowing you, loving you, and serving you.*

Upon finishing my prayer, I cut into the earth four or five inches and severed the root, being careful to leave enough root-stock there to regenerate a new plant. Gently, I then lifted up my prize and held it to my heart feeling as if it melted into my body. Then I placed the flowering *hicouri* carefully in my bag so it wouldn't be bruised and went on with my hunting.

Later that night, with the shaman's blessing, I spoke to the flower and told it of my plan: *I will take you into my body. I will eat you as the blessed sacrament that you are and I will take you right down into the center of my heart. In that way I will truly take you home and carry you with me always.* Then I slowly cut out the flower along with a piece of the flesh of the peyote. Reverently, I placed them in my mouth. I felt a gentle vibration flow down into my body. Later that night, after ingesting more *hicouri,* I felt the full impact of what had been set in motion.

When the medicine first started coming on, I saw *hicouri* plants floating through the air all around me. First it was just a few, then more, until finally they filled up the space around me and started entering my body. They headed straight into my heart and I watched in amazement as they collected there. Suddenly, during the digestion process, a small peyote flower, a *tutu,* appeared right in the center of my heart, exactly like the flower I had eaten earlier in the day. Then another flower appeared in my heart. Then another, and another, and another. Soon my heart was completely filled with flowers with no room left for even one more. But still they kept coming, overflowing from my heart into my chest cavity. The *tutus* kept blossoming. Soon my chest was filled, so the flowers began to move into the rest of my body. In a few moments, I was filled with the beautiful flowers from head to toe. Slowly and rhythmically, they circulated through me, like water through an empty container. Their beauty and fragrance was overwhelming. I entered a state of ecstasy, my spirit floating with the flowers. Deep down inside, I heard a voice speak softly but with authority: *This is what it is like when you open your heart to the love that is within you. This is the true blossoming of the flowers. We are giving you this experience so you will know with all your senses what this beauty is like. Now it is up to you to do the gardening work that will enable your own* tutus *to blossom. Always remember, no matter what kind of situation you are presented with, there is always a way to create a response to it that will help the flowers to blossom.*

I am writing this book now to help me remember. It is too important to forget. It is my life.

I write *The Shamanic Wisdom of the Huichol* also for all those who seek to make their own flowers blossom; for those who wish to find their lives, their heart paths; for those who seek the courage and strength to walk their path, tending the garden of their souls, their families, their communities, and of Mother Earth herself, with tenderness, respect, and love.

Many years ago, the Lakota holy man Black Elk said, "The Sacred Hoop has been broken." Our awareness of our interconnectedness with the circle of life has been lost. To heal the Sacred Hoop, we must do all we can to restore an awareness of respectful, right relationship. Only then will the garden blossom anew.

It is my firm belief that in order to go forward in this gardening work of healing our shattered relationships within ourselves, with others, and with the environment, we need to first go backward to the nature-based shamanic heritage that underlies all the world's religions and is humanity's oldest relationship to spirit. In this time of cultural crisis, we desperately need to rediscover what we have forgotten: our ancestors' sacred relationship with the awesome powers of creation. Within the past's rich storehouse, which is still intact today among tribal people such as the Huichol and other living shamanic peoples, there is important knowledge. We must not imitate the past, nor turn our backs on technology, nor play at being Indians, nor retreat into a romanticized fantasy of Rousseau's "noble savage" living in the pristine jungle. Instead, we must rediscover the working tools of an intuitive wisdom that knows the universe is alive, intelligent, and always transmitting information—to those who still remember how to listen—about how to live in harmony and balance with its constantly changing rhythms. In order to go forward in a way that ensures a future worth living in for the generations yet to come, we must first remember these old medicine ways and explore their relevance for today.

I vividly remember another Huichol pilgrimage in 1990 that helped me realize the importance of this notion of going backward in order to go forward. I am hurtling down a dark corridor known as the "Barranca of Death," a narrow section of two-lane country road twisting through the steep mountains and canyons between Tepic and Guadalajara, deep in the belly of Mexico. At 2 a.m., there is not much on the road other than an occasional donkey, cow, or coyote. Occasionally, a huge semi comes barreling down the middle of the road, its high beams blinding me as tons of steel careen around *curvas peligrosa,* pushing my little rental car to the very edge of the narrow road. The rusting wreckage of the semis that didn't make it lie along the roadside like beached whales. I have rented a car at the Puerto Vallarta airport and am hurrying to catch up with my fellow pilgrims who set off the day before, headed south, then east, then north up

Paola and José on the pilgrimage trail
with their family

toward Zacatecas. I'm a day late due to work responsibilities I had back in the States. My car is crammed full—José and Paola, a Huichol couple, their nursing son, Chulo, seventeen-year-old Guiliermo, eight-year-old Roselva, and all the camping equipment, food, ceremonial gear, and other odds and ends a group like ours needs to be on the Huichol Road for ten days.

I picked up José and his family in the dusty little pueblo of Santa Maria del Oro. The scene was right out of Castenada. I didn't know them, they didn't know me. They had been instructed to wait for *gringo Tomás* at the central plaza from 6 p.m. onward. I got there late, almost three in the morning. I'd gotten lost and was halfway to Guadalajara before realizing I was heading in the wrong direction. Then I faced a major decision. I had been asked by the organizers of the pilgrimage to stop by the plaza because there *might* be some Huichol there needing a ride, but it isn't a sure thing, I'd been warned. Now I wondered if they were there or not. I was not overjoyed at the prospect of retracing my path up the dangerous stretch of road that I'd just safely navigated, thereby losing what I'd already gained. Hell, I'd just seen two big semis that had gone off the road. I was tired and tense and wanted to get past Guadalajara and camp for the night. *There's probably nobody there and it's just a waste of my time to go back,* said one seductive voice in my head. *Yeah, but what if there* are *people waiting there for me?* said another voice. *If you don't show up, they won't get to go on the pilgrimage they have been aiming toward for at least a year, and maybe more than that.* I paced around the parking lot of the truck stop where I'd pulled over to get directions. The attendant confirmed my worst fear—Santa Maria del Oro was way back in the opposite direction. My bones ached with exhaustion. The pull to keep going was strong. Yet I knew I couldn't live with myself if I kept going and found out later that the folks had been waiting for me after all. I got back in my car and headed north.

An hour later, I drove down a bumpy dirt road into the little pueblo of Santa Maria del Oro. No other cars moving, no sounds, no movement. Just the quiet stillness of an old Mexican village bedded down for the night. In the shadows, I could see a couple holding hands in the doorway of a rickety hacienda. A few teenagers stood by the side of the road. I pulled over and asked, *"Donde esta el plaza centro, por favor?"* They waved me on down the street. A few minutes later, I was "downtown." I pulled up beside a bench and parked my car. I saw a few shadowy figures on the far side of the plaza, but since I didn't know exactly what I was looking for, I got out of the car and stood there quietly. It was a soft night, the stars were shining, and I sank down exhaustedly on the car's fender, searching the darkness. Several minutes passed, and then two figures stepped out of the shadows and walked toward me. I felt them before I could see them clearly. José and his son Guiliermo walked up to me, regal in their colorful, embroidered Huichol ceremonial clothing—white cotton pants and shirts covered with the sparkling designs of their deities. *"Buenas noches,"* I greeted them. *"Me yamo Tomás."* We shook hands, and with my limited comprehension of Spanish I understood that there were more Huichol waiting in a hacienda down the block. We drove there, loaded up the now-groaning car, and took off.

Heading back down the road again over territory I've already covered, I reflect on what just happened. I am glad for the company of my new travel companions and I feel good about my decision to go back and get them. It would have ruined the trip for me if I'd gone on without them and joined up with the others only to find out they were back there waiting for a ride that never came. But now we are together and I know the trip has really begun. Paola is in the back with nursing baby and sleeping young people, José up front with me, each of us trying to understand the other as best he can with my limited Spanish and Huichol. I note how my decision to go back has short-circuited my usual obsession with time, scheduling, and getting ahead. To make my decision, I had to go deeper than these programmed concerns, to get in touch with feelings more significant than my own desire for form, comfort, and getting my own way, the easy way. I realize that this is an experience of going backward in order to go forward in a good way, with a clear conscience and a happy heart.

I feel peaceful. I begin to see the whole pilgrimage in a context of going backward in terms of Western culture, to be with a people who still follow the spiritual path of their ancestors, backward to when time is measured only in relationship to the cyclic ebb and flow rhythms of nature—night and day, hot and cold, life and death, without the intrusion of the clock. Going backward for me is coming home to the primal experience of sacred "now time," being fully present with the heartbeat of the moment. *Perhaps*, I think, *this whole experience is a sign, a reminder, an alert to the importance in my own life of what the purpose of the pilgrimage is all about—slowing down, retracing steps inward to ancient ways of listening and seeking deeper vision, all of which are prerequisite to going forward down the road of life in a good way.* I look over at José and smile. He smiles back and we both settle into a comfortable silence. *Relax into it,* I hear a quiet voice say. *You're right on time.* Road hypnosis takes over and my mind begins to drift. *It's amazing,* I think. *Here I am, a homeboy from the Bronx, a middle-aged gringo on a peyote pilgrimage with Indians in the mountains of Mexico. How did I get here?*

1

Moving Backward into the Future

Shamanism is a disciplined way of getting knowledge and help, which is based on the premise that we do not have to restrict ourselves to working in one reality, one dimension, when we need assistance.

MICHAEL HARNER

In January of 1945, the world was at war. A raging snowstorm blanketed the East Coast in sleet and ice. My mother, Ruth, was in labor with me, and my father, Fred, a vet from the Spanish Civil War who'd fought against the fascism of Franco in Spain with the Abraham Lincoln Battalion, and who was touched by Spanish culture in many ways, decided to give my mother a gift of a figurine of a porcelain bull. Little did anyone know at the time that this clay bull was a harbinger of a real live bull, El Toro, who was to play a prominent role in my life almost half a century later. Sadly, my father died three years and ten months later of heart disease brought on originally by rheumatic fever as a boy and aggravated by his time in Spain during the war.

My memories of my dad are few, but they are warm and loving. I was fortunate to get so much love from him before he departed, for I believe it helped to save my life in the dark times that were to follow. Looking back, I see how his death, just before my fourth birthday, was the start of a painful initiation that led eventually to the path of the shamanism.

For the shaman is a person who has been wounded and who, through this wounding, is plunged into a cataclysmic confrontation with death, dying, loss, pain, and suffering. The confrontation with darkness is part of a rite of passage into deeper being, moving beyond the material world of conventional reality and physical appearance. In shamanic initiation, old beliefs about what is real, about who one is, must die, or else rebirth into a new identity cannot take place.

Not everyone survives the plunge into chaos. Some stay imprisoned within its dark dungeons for the course of their lifetime. Others die during the impact of the loss itself. It takes a certain amount of "soul strength" to survive, to emerge from the pits of darkness with your soul not only intact but stronger and wiser as a result of the journey. And it takes a great deal of help from "the other side," from the invisible reality of spiritual presence, to which the wounding can provide opening. You don't make it on your own.

For me, it was a very close call. My father's death shattered my notion of security and comfort in life. I was face to face with the truth: that life is impermanent, that "shit happens," that there are forces in the universe that are much more powerful than the wants and desires of a given individual.

It took me twenty years to begin dealing with these truths in a healthy way. At the time, I had another loss: my mother was hospitalized for six weeks with a thyroid problem brought on by the stress of losing my dad. She was left with big bills and small children—my sister, Ilsa, was just a year old. During the time of my mother's hospitalization, my sister and I were shuttled around to the families of my father's seven remaining sisters. There was one more significant loss during this shuttling: a relative told me that my father had gone on an ocean voyage. I knew that this was not the truth. Looking back, I see my spirit retreat inward in pain and fear. *My God, there is no one out here for me! I can't even trust anyone to tell me the truth.* I was further devastated when, following the wisdom of the day, I wasn't allowed to attend the funeral because I had to be "protected" from such upsetting circumstances. Having no place else to go, my grief imploded inward.

It's no surprise that shortly thereafter I came down with severe asthma. I'll never forget the panicky feeling of suffocation as I'd frantically gasp for a breath of air. I also developed allergies that required painful weekly shots throughout my childhood and into my early teenage years. I learned firsthand what it is like to be sick and suffering.

When the hormones of adolescence hit, my somaticized, unresolved grief turned into anger. I acted out my hurt, sadness, pain, and anguish through alcohol-fueled delinquent behavior that included gang fights, car theft, breaking and entering, property destruction, skipping school, and numerous vengeful acts against what I deemed an unjust world. I molded myself in the macho image of the tough guy, the "rock" as it was called in my neighborhood—the sullen, rebellious bad guy, which took me further and further into a destructive lifestyle. I call this period of my life my "shadow possession time." It lasted in its external form from the age of twelve to seventeen.

During this time, I read Jack Kerouac's *On the Road* and joined two other buddies in running away from home when I was thirteen. We didn't get far but I knew I wanted something more than what conventional society was offering. At fourteen, I started doing construction work on weekends during the school year and full-time in the summer with guys named Spike, Cool Poppa, and Chevy. I was one of the few white guys on the job. I was tested out in various ways—mainly by doing all the shit work without complaining—and when I passed the tests, I was accepted as an equal into their adult male community. I felt noticed and respected as a man.

I didn't respect the values and conventions of middle-class 1950s life. I wanted something more. My early experiences with death had taught me that life could be ripped away at a moment's notice. I wanted something deeper than surface superficialities, something that felt real, something that had soul and passion and that dealt openly with the nitty-gritty of life and of death. I found some aspects of this with "the bruthas" I was working with. We ran around together, sang, talked about the mysteries of women, sex, death, life, and spirit. I loved their vibrancy, their aliveness, their realness. The down side of all this was that it made me feel even more alienated from school and "straight society," which I hated for its soul-restricting rigidity, its prejudice toward my new friends, and its emphasis on social conformity and fitting in. The result? Conventional society had less and less meaning for me.

Instead, I read Sartre and beatnik poetry. I didn't understand most of it, but something got through and I felt that I wasn't totally alone in my feelings of alienation. I skipped more and more school. Even when I was there physically, I wasn't really there. In eighth grade, I got turned on to John Lee Hooker while drinking homemade wine with my buddy Boog, another alienated soul. The blues touched my pain and the booze helped drown my sorrow and self-pity.

During the time of "shadow possession," there were many close calls that with a slight turn of the wheel could have led to true disasters. There were car crashes, fights where people went to the hospital as a result of my outbursts of released rage. I was like an animal trying to survive by destroying everything in its path. In the midst of it, I felt alive and powerful, as if my life made a difference. I think it had something to do with facing death, only this time fighting against it and coming out victorious by emerging from the adventures alive and well: *Ha! I beat you this time, you old bastard!*

Yet, it was only the protection of something larger than myself that kept me and my adversaries from being killed or that kept me from being caught and imprisoned. I was never busted for the big stuff, and being white and middle class, I had everything I needed to get out of the smaller jams.

But the demands of the gang of other alienated teenagers, which I had helped to start, were getting stronger. As one of the gang's head crazies, my self-esteem was dependent upon maintaining this identity, so I didn't have the strength to say no to what was coming up—the prospect of armed robbery. I knew that my only chance was to get out. I had to get away to a place where no one knew me and where I could start over.

On the eve of running away as a senior in high school, my mother and second father, Ray, discovered my plan. After a long night of painful deliberations, we cut a deal: if I stayed and graduated high school, they would help me out financially so I could leave the state and attend junior college in Southern California, which is where I wanted to go. My mother, sister Ilsa, and I had moved there shortly after my father's death and I loved it. When my mother remarried three years later, we moved back to the East Coast and I hated it. I liked my new dad, Ray. In fact, I urged my mother to marry him after he'd won my heart by being there as I learned to ride my two-wheeler, catch a ground ball, and awkwardly meet kids in the neighborhood where I was the new guy on the block. But I didn't like leaving Southern California, and I didn't like living in suburban Maryland, where my new dad had his business. The Los Angeles of my memory was of the days before smog, when there was still plenty of safe, open space for a kid to play in and year-round clear sunshine in which to enjoy it.

I kept my side of the deal with my parents, though. I made it through high school. It was really tough for me to stay around, especially after my driver's license was taken away after one of my wrecks and my girlfriend's parents wouldn't let her see me any more. It was all more fuel for me to feel sorry for myself, victimized by the bad guys of society. But even in the midst of my overwhelming darkness, a spark of light was still flickering within me. I think it was there because of the early infusion of love I had from my father before he died.

My plan of redemption was to attend junior college and to study hard and give it my best shot academically, thus proving to myself and others that I wasn't a loser. Since I didn't respect high school, I didn't try to learn anything there. I was closed off, shut down, and unmotivated toward academics. But in junior college in California, no one would know me. I could make a fresh start without having to maintain my old "hard guy" identity. I felt intuitively that in this new setting I would be treated as an adult. Nobody would be on my case and it would be totally up to me whether I succeeded or failed. This is precisely what I wanted. I held the hope of someday getting into a position in life where I would be able to help young people in trouble as I had been. And if I couldn't actually help them, I would at least listen to them—their feelings, their ideas, their fear and pain, their hopes and their dreams—with respect, a far cry from what I experienced

with a host of school counselors, probation officers, teachers, and other sup-
posedly "helping" adults with whom I had interacted during the time of my
shadow possession. I stuck around for my senior year and kept putting off
the pressures from the gang for more serious crime. How? By drinking even
more and through fights that got me on probation so I had an excuse to say
no to the heavier stuff. Through it all, I bided my time until I could get out
on my own. That's what I ached for. My parents did their best to support
and encourage me, but I was closed to them because they represented the
middle-class society I was so alienated from. I squeaked through my senior
year taking the easiest classes and almost failing them. But I didn't really
care. All I wanted was to get out. I passed with D's, did summer construction work for two months, got a '57 Chevy, and hit the road to California
late in the summer of 1962.

Traveling out to California in the summer of my seventeenth year, I carried with me a vision of what I had done with my life so far. In the vision,
I was at the bottom of a very deep hole that I had dug for myself through
my negativity, my cynicism, my feeling sorry for myself, and my antisocial,
acting-out behavior. In this vision, I had to face the fact of injustice in the
world and that I'd had a slice of it. But I also had to face the fact that the
way I had gone about responding to it had done nothing to change it, it had
just put me at the bottom of the big hole. I wanted out. The way out was
to create a new response to the wrongs of my life, a new way of living that
wasn't based on self-pity and negativity.

I became a hermit. I went to class, studied in the library, and worked out
in the gym every day. Pushing weights around was better than taking my
pain and aggression out on people. The weight training actually helped me
with my studies—it taught me the power of the focused mind. I won some
weight-lifting contests by using mind over matter, psyching myself up to lift
weights that my thin musculature wasn't really set up to do. Meanwhile,
I read all I could in psychology, sociology, philosophy, and social psychology, trying to understand my self-destructive behavior and how I could best
turn it around. My efforts paid off. I surprised even myself by making the
dean's list and being invited to join the school's honor society. It was quite a
change from the company I had been keeping in high school.

I stayed at the junior college two more years and while I kept up my good grades, I did start drinking again, aided in part by coming out of social isolation and joining a fraternity. I managed to stay out of trouble and even met a young coed, Andrea Danek, whom I fell in love with and eventually married.

Andrea was cut from a different cloth, too. She was born in Budapest, Hungary, and lived through the Hungarian Revolution. She and her family escaped into Vienna and lived there for a year in a refugee camp before gaining entry into the United States. Andrea was from a warm, loving family, strong in her own right with values of honesty and integrity, earthy and outspoken. She loved children and animals and gave me the support, warmth, and love that I desperately wanted. Besides, she was beautiful. We were both nineteen years old when we started dating and our relationship grew even when I transferred to San Francisco State, where I got my B.A. in sociology and was accepted to the University of California Graduate School of Social Work. Andrea and I got married that summer and moved to Berkeley in the fall of 1967.

But before that, my initial arrival in the Bay Area in 1965 to attend San Francisco State was during a time of complete cultural renaissance. As I drove my motorcycle (couldn't afford car insurance in those days) across the Bay Bridge from Oakland and entered the city for my new life, I could see in my mind's eye the closing of a chapter and a brand new chapter beginning, its pages blank. A voice within gave me counsel: *This is going to be a whole new ball game for you. Open up to it. Let it take you where it will. What you learn in your classes will be the least of what is here for you to learn. Study well.*

From my first day on campus walking across the quad to register for classes, I knew that this was a different scene from the one in my Southern California junior college days. Stewart Brand, founder of the *Whole Earth Catalog,* had organized a "happening" where people dressed in white-hooded robes were dropping out of trees and popping up from bushes, dancing and swaying, chanting sounds I had never even heard before. I followed my inner counsel and opened up to it all. I got involved with the Experimental College, where students invented their own classes and put out a booklet rating all the teachers on campus. I joined the Vietnam Day Committee to protest the war, after doing extensive research into the U.S. presence in Southeast Asia and deciding it was a fraud. I helped organize antiwar protests and teach-ins. I joined the tutorial program and worked with Latino kids and gang members of the Mission Rebels in the Mission District. Took creative writing classes, spent lunch breaks at the Poetry Center listening to poets like Michael McClure and Diane Di Prima. Went to concerts and be-ins to hear musicians like Janis Joplin, Big Brother and the Holding Company, and the Jefferson Airplane.

Throughout all this new involvement and in spite of my political radicalism, I was pretty much a straight arrow in terms of psychedelics, the backbone of the hippie revolution. Alcohol was my drug, beer mostly, which I had been drinking since I was twelve years old. I thought marijuana was for the weak minded, actually believing the high school fear movies that smoking marijuana would make you an addict. Although it was all around me, I stayed away from it; I didn't smoke, had been taking vitamins and health supplements, and had been working out for years, and I didn't want to do anything that could jeopardize my hard-won health after the allergies and asthma of my youth. I remember bawling out one of my housemates the first time I found him smoking a joint. A few weeks later, he took some LSD and freaked out and asked me to take him to the emergency room of the nearest hospital. Once there, he was treated like a criminal. I was horrified; I had brought him there for help. Instead, they strapped him into a straitjacket and hauled him away. They questioned me, threatened to call the police, and then finally let me go. I was angry with the hospital staff and upset with my house mate. I swore that something like that would never happen to me. I felt quite self-righteous that it was his grass "habit" that had gotten him into the hard stuff and it was his own damn fault. But I also felt bad that I had taken him someplace where the "help" appeared even worse than his hysterical condition.

Yet as my time in the San Francisco scene went on, I gradually began to hear of a different side to psychedelics, a responsible side, from people I respected, some of whom were my professors at school and were involved with legal research utilizing psychoactive drugs. I was particularly fascinated by reports that these drugs could unlock the power of the unconscious mind. I was curious but frightened as well. I had been interested in the workings of the mind ever since I had experienced an altered state of consciousness during a high fever as a child. It was a hallucination of the wavy lines of the wallpaper in my room undulating like waves of the ocean. As sick as I was, I still was amazed to see the images on the wall change shape and seemingly come alive.

My curiosity led me to talk with people at school who had experienced psychedelics. I asked every question I could think of and read everything I could get my hands on in the literature and latest research. Gradually, I began to realize that psychedelics were tools, powerful tools yes, but used by the right hands in a responsible way, tools that could open doors to deeper, hidden parts of the mind. After a year's preparation of continued research, reflection, and facing my worst fears, I decided I was ready to take the plunge and face whatever was inside me. I found three trusted and experienced guides and on a sunny, spring Saturday at their house in Haight-Ashbury, I took a full dose of LSD.

My guides considered LSD to be a sacred substance, "like a communion wafer," they said. "It can help you see God." I had heard and read of people having spiritual experiences with psychedelics but I dismissed them all as "deranged hallucinations." It was the unconscious I was after. The spiritual approach was not something I believed in since I was an atheist. I thought religion was pabulum for the weak, those feeble dupes of authoritarian figures who couldn't face the realities of life. But I went along with my friends' approach and didn't say anything. At first, we sat together quietly in the living room. After a while, they began to speak: "I can feel it coming on," said one. "Yeah, it feels pretty strong," said another. I felt nothing. Paranoia set in. *Maybe it's all a put-on. Or maybe my physiology is different from others and it doesn't work on me.* Just then, I noticed the curtains billowing and got up to shut the window. A chill ran down my spine when I reached out to the window and found it already closed! Now I knew something was happening and that I wasn't in control of it. I remembered the words of a Beatles song repeated as instructions by my guides: "Turn off your mind, relax, and float downstream." So I released into the river of my consciousness, turned loose, and lay down on my back to watch the show.

In many ways, my life since then has been an attempt to integrate what I saw, what I heard, and what I experienced on what turned out to be a transcendent voyage. I had a full-blown, spiritually transforming mystical experience. For the second time in my life, my whole reality base was turned upside down and inside out. First had been my father's death, the initiation into impermanence, and the journey through physical illness and shadow possession darkness. Through it all, I was using my rational mind and my logical thinking processes to try and sort things out. Other than normal waking state, dream state, and the alcohol-induced state, this was all I really knew. My one other experience of an altered state had been through fever, and it had been shuttled off into my unconscious long ago.

But here was a new channel, one that I didn't even know was on the set! It was a channel of Gnostic, numinous knowledge, containing what psychologist Charles Tart of the University of California–Davis calls "state specific information." Tart postulates different channels of awareness, each containing different frequencies of energy available experientially only by tuning into the specific wavelength carrying the desired information.

My experience came to me in the form of three visions, perhaps emanating from what British botanist Rupert Sheldrake would call "morphogenetic fields," energy fields of information that exist in time and space, but like gravity, are invisible to the naked eye. The first began to appear on the white stucco ceiling. I remember thinking as the colors started to merge into shapes, *I wonder if there are microscopic specks of color in the stucco that you can't ordinarily see and now are being magnified and distorted by the drug.* It was my last rational thought for some time. As I watched in fascination, the forms on the ceiling turned into an undulating bas relief mosaic as seen in Mesoamerican stone-carved art. Then the entire ceiling came beautifully alive, portraying a complete life cycle of a group of ancient Mesoamericans living and dying, making love, babies being born and nursed, parents working in the fields, children growing up, becoming adults, having children of their own, growing old, dying, new life coming through in the next generation and so on. Mesmerized, I experienced déjà vu, a memory of being a part of this very cycle that I was now watching. I knew I was watching myself in a previous lifetime! I also heard an internal voice: *Not only did you live during this time, you will be returning to it in this lifetime as well. But it is not something to seek out or try and find. Go on with your life. It will come to you when the time is right.*

Speechless, I lay very still, not wanting to miss one particle of what was happening. After an indeterminate period of time, the undulating Mesoamerican life cycle vision merged into a new field of information. *Whoa, now what?* I wondered. *Breathe out. Release. Here it comes.* I reminded myself, *You're not in charge.* The vision took me into a vortex of time. I began to see the line of my ancestral heritage going back to the very beginning. I witnessed how each successive generation instilled its experience into the new generation all the way up to my parents doing it to me. From a historical perspective, I watched the evolution of experience, values, and concerns each generation had, and how it moved forward in time to culminate in me, shaping my very beliefs, values, and personality, my raison d'être. Simultaneously, I saw that the essence of my being was something far beyond the conditioning of my ancestral roots. It was an energy force of light that was connected with an infinite cosmic light. I saw my soul and for the first time I understood the saying in the bible that we are made in God's image. Having rejected the existence of God and religion, I'd also rejected the notion that I was made in the anthropomorphic image of an old man with a beard on a throne atop a cloud looking down and judging us all. Yet here I was, "grokking" infinity (science fiction writer Robert Heinlein's term for total and complete comprehension). In my vision, I was grokking the deepest part of "I," the part that was transcendent of ego identity, of persona, of physical being, and was made of this same substance of infinite light.

As a child, I had often tried to comprehend infinity by looking up at the stars. I could never do it; I'd short circuit the system and give up. But now I was *in* infinity! I saw how my personality, physical body, and identification as Tom Pinkson comprised a limited, time/space container that held within it a substance of infinite potential. I also saw how I had limited myself through believing that the totality of my being consisted of the time/space container. *Wow, I can't believe this* was all I could say. Previous compartmentalization of time into past, present, and future dissolved. Being one with infinity, I realized that on the level of my essence, I was one with all that had been, all that was, and all that will be. There was no separation, no division—only blissful oneness. This was new territory for me and I released into it completely. I saw very clearly how alcohol produced the opposite effect than the one I was now experiencing, and in that moment, my relationship to alcohol changed. A beer or margarita now or then, but that was it. Who would want to take anything that dulls the magnificence of what I was now in?

As strong as the first two fields of information were, the third was the strongest of all. But I'm going to put that on hold until the next chapter because I want to complete the bridge from this journey to the Huichol Pilgrimage. Actually, the bridge didn't materialize until fifteen years later, in 1981. But I'm getting ahead of myself. When I came down from the acid trip, I was in a daze. It took me several days to come back to earth and then my burning desire was to try and understand everything that I had experienced. I also wanted to see if I could replicate the states I had been in without using LSD. My research turned in the direction of Eastern religion and philosophy. Both at school and in the smorgasbord of opportunities offered in the Bay Area in the last years of the 1960s, I tried just about all that was going on. I read the *Bhagavad Gita* and other Hindu sacred scriptures, I studied the Tao Te Ching, Taoism, Buddhism, and Zen, I went to yoga and meditation classes and began a meditative practice that I still continue today. My whole life changed. Instead of trying to change the world from without, I was now trying to change my inner world. I wore flowers in my hair, which was growing longer and longer, and clothes that reflected the colors and feelings of my visions. I became a full-fledged Haight-Ashbury hippie with a pad two blocks away from all the action. Through it all, I was seeking communion with the numinous, the deeper part of who I really was.

Throughout my spiritual explorations, I did manage to stay in school. It wasn't easy, but I earned my B.A. from San Francisco State, then went on to earn a master's degree in two years of graduate work at UC Berkeley. I fused my new-found spirituality with social activism and worked with the Black Panthers in East Oakland and with street gang workers in San Francisco. I was elected vice president of the Social Work Graduate Students Association and used my position to bring in street activists to speak at the school, since I didn't find what I was learning in class very relevant to what I was experiencing out in the street. The work with the Panthers got intense. People I worked with on one day to feed hungry children would be dead the next, killed in shoot-outs with the police.

I was devastated by the shock of these violent deaths. I stayed up late one evening with friends who also knew what was going on. All night long, we debated whether the only moral thing to do was to pick up guns ourselves and defend the lives of the people we were working with who we felt were being murdered by the racist establishment. By sun-up, I had made a decision. I realized that I didn't have the right to take someone else's life unless my own were in immediate danger. But I also knew that I didn't have the right to condemn the Panthers, who were picking up guns to defend lives that were directly on the line. I decided that I had to go forward, not with violence, but with the creative potential my vision had shown me. I had to use my creative energy to help build alternatives to a system that I saw as corrupt, destructive of human values, and caring more for profits than for people. The rest of my life, I decided, would be about creating alternatives and exploring better ways of living and meeting our needs than what I had learned from my culture.

I started out by exploring the burgeoning alternative school movement, reading all I could, checking out who was doing what, volunteering with schools and people I liked, and learning all I could about ways to educate children other than the authoritarian way I had been schooled, with its overemphasis on the intellect and little consideration of the new kinds of information I now knew were available.

In 1969, I graduated from Berkeley with a master's degree in social work. Along with Andrea, who was five months pregnant with our first child and who had been working at a bank to put me through graduate school while she studied at night for a degree in nursery school education, I took a summer job teaching at an alternative junior high school in the foothills of the Sierra. We loved the mountains and the rural setting but come fall there was no job, so we moved back to the city. I got a part-time job teaching sociology at a local junior college and took a position as director of a newly forming alternative school just across the bay in Marin County. Andrea and I moved to Marin and started a new chapter in our lives. Now that I was finally out of school and through with study-ing what other people thought I should study, I could get on with my real education. Once a year, I would take another psychedelic voyage using the substance as a sacrament as I'd been taught in my first journey. These served as "existential housecleanings" and sources of continued explora-tion of nonordinary states of consciousness.

In Marin, I met a core group of health professionals from the local junior college who were interested in starting a community-based drug treatment program. I was hired as the treatment director and for the first time since graduation actually had a full-time "straight" job for two years, working with a population of heroin addicts and speed freaks, the tragic leftovers from the "summer of love" who moved from psychedelics to hard stuff and couldn't get out. I also worked with Vietnam vets who had got-ten strung out on high-grade, low-cost heroin and had returned to the States with a habit and no access to cheap dope; they turned to crime to support their addiction, and frequently got busted, or overdosed, and were referred to the drug program I was running. I learned a lot about junkie behavior and about myself: to say no and to do what I was doing because it felt right, not because of future rewards or outcomes.

But the outcome I wanted, success in the work, just wasn't happen-ing. Despite a dedicated staff working long hours with a sincere desire to help, no one was changing for the better. After two years of frustration, I started a new program of wilderness treatment to supplement the regular groups, methadone program, individual therapy, vocational training, and detox program already in place. How I got into the wilderness work is an adventure story itself.

As a child, I had always loved being out in nature. When we moved to Maryland after my mother remarried, the area we ended up in had easy access to miles of thick woods, plenty of creeks, mud flats, and wide, open fields. I wandered in it endlessly. Going to school was like being in prison. I always tried to sit by the window and watch the wind move through the trees, wishing the clock would move faster to recess time. Between sports and playing in the woods, I spent as much time outdoors as I could. Later as a young man in college, I read about Outward Bound adventure programs but never had the money to attend. But then when I was directing the drug treatment program, I found out that Outward Bound had just started a new school a few hours away. I called and finagled an opportunity to join with forty-five of their teachers on a trip to Yosemite National Park for ten days of mountain climbing and river running. I had never done either of these activities. In fact, I had a deathly fear of heights. Looking back on it now, if I had known what I was really getting into, I might never have gone! But with adventurous heart and naïve mind, I, along with two other "ringers"—people without climbing and wilderness experience—drove down to Yosemite Valley one day in March of 1972 to join up with the others and see what this adventure was all about. The other ringers and I were there to help the Outward Bound teachers learn about group process and working with young people into drugs. All the rest of the gang were experienced climbers and river runners coming to Yosemite to push their edges and have a good time.

I can't speak for anyone else, but it wasn't a good time for me. I was petrified every day! From day one, we were up onto the cliffs and I was engaged in activities that brought me to the point of paralyzed terror. Each day I would wake up and pray for rain, an earthquake, a broken leg, anything to get me out of climbing. But when no easy excuses presented themselves, I'd end up hiking with the rest of them to the base of a perpendicular sheer granite wall, rope up, and start climbing. As I looked up, I'd think, *There's no way in the world I can climb that. Maybe these other guys can do it, they're pros. But it's totally impossible for me.* Yet despite my fears, I went on, one handhold, one foothold at a time. I learned that you don't really climb a mountain, you only climb what is right in front of you. Each day we went up, usually in rope teams of two or three. At one point on our last climb of the week, I carefully made my way around a corner of a cliff, inching slowly and deliberately. Then I made the mistake of looking down.

Unbeknownst to me, I had been climbing on an overhang and below me there was nothing but air! I panicked. My body wouldn't move. I trembled uncontrollably and dug my fingers and toes into the minute holds that were keeping me on the rock face. After a few minutes, the instructor descended to me. My fear turned to anger and I directed it right at him. "Get me the hell out of here!" I growled. "I'm stuck and I can't move." I wanted an immediate rescue, but he would have none of it. "Calm down," he said. "There are plenty of holds here. Just find them. Another twenty feet above is a big ledge and you can relax there. But you'll have to climb there yourself." Then he took off and was soon up the rock and out of sight. I don't know if I ever hated anyone as much as I hated him in that instant. But hate didn't move me up the rock, so finally I started looking around and actually found a few holds just above me. I reached up and stuck my fingers into a crack, grabbed hold, and pulled myself up. Then I found another hold, and another, and in a few minutes scrambled to safety and collapsed, a nervous wreck. But when my breathing finally returned to normal, a tremendous feeling of accomplishment rushed through my exhausted muscles. I felt exhilarated and after a brief rest went on to complete the rest of the climb. By the end of the day, I found myself atop a peak that at first sight in the morning I had declared was impossible for me to climb. Standing very carefully and roped in for security, I surveyed what I had accomplished. No one had pulled me up the mountain. I most certainly had done it by myself. Then it struck me: Since I succeeded at this endeavor that a part of my mind earlier said was impossible, I wonder what else I could have succeeded at that I didn't even try because I didn't think it was possible?

I saw the many ways that my mind closed down out of fear and how I didn't even try things unless I had a pretty good idea that I could do them successfully. But now the mountain climbing was showing me a way to access the infinite creativity I'd first learned about through my visionary journey years before. It was showing me that the only way I would ever know what was possible for me to accomplish was to go for it with my 100 percent best effort. It was okay to be fearful, but the trick was going ahead anyway and not letting the fear close the door in my mind to trying. I had to own my power and no longer give it away to my fears and my negative thinking. I was exhilarated at the prospect. I now had some practical new tools for my own growth process and for my work with the addicts.

The learning with Outward Bound wasn't over, however. The next day we drove to the Tuolumne River, loaded up rubber rafts, and took off for a three-day run down the Grand Canyon of the Tuolumne. This was another new experience for me but not for the Outward Bound teachers, who were all veteran rafters. Yet, it turned into an adventure for all of us because the river was running at near flood level, the weather turned bad, and all the boats flipped at one time or another. Hypothermia was an ever-present danger.

As a youngster, I'd been plagued with a recurring nightmare of being sucked into a whirlpool. On the Tuolumne River, it actually happened. Our boat went over a waterfall and into a hole. Everyone on the boat was immediately swept overboard except me. The boat and I were stuck in a vertical whirlpool of smashing waves and white water surging up and down, with the boat taking on more and more water and threatening to be sucked into the bottom of the foaming cauldron at any instant. I was afraid of my fate if I stayed with the thrashing boat, so I stood up on the bow and jumped with all my might, trying to catch the downstream current. But the pull of the whirlpool started to suck me back into it. With every ounce of adrenaline, I pushed my legs up against the raft and propelled myself like a rocket out into the current. I caught it, then was swept downstream and out of the maelstrom. I eventually made my way to shore and collapsed in relief on solid ground.

That night at the campfire, the rafting guide said that the next day would be the most demanding of all. I climbed into my sleeping bag with a feeling that I wasn't going to make it, that I was going to get out on the river and once again be sucked into a hole, only this time I wouldn't be

Photo by Eric Ahola

Over the falls on the Tuolumne River

able to get out. I shuddered at the thought of never seeing Andrea again, of never seeing my young daughter, Kimberly, grow up, of never seeing the sun rise again, of never eating an ice cream cone or a pizza or anything else I had enjoyed in this life. I reviewed my entire life and sobbed as I said goodbye to everyone I knew and loved.

I didn't realize it then, but I was undergoing another important aspect of a rite of passage—facing your own death. For hours, I lay there alone in my sleeping bag saying my thank yous and goodbyes. I'd watched the moon rise and now it was beginning to set. I knew I needed to get some sleep, but I couldn't relax enough to do it. I tried yoga, meditation, chanting. Nothing helped. I didn't see that I had any option except to face my fate. The walls of the canyon looked impassably steep. I felt stuck and that I had to get on the raft the next day and go forward into whatever awaited me. Finally, I accepted that I really might die and I decided that all I could do was give it my best shot. "If a force bigger than me tries to take my life tomorrow, I'm gonna fight my ass off, and if it wins, it will know it had a real fight on its hands. I'm not gonna go easy," I said out loud. Only then was I able to fall asleep.

I got up the next day, did my yoga, meditation, and prayers, then prepared to fight as a warrior against anything that messed with me. I was so psyched up I could have chewed up a boulder! Ironically, though, the weather took a turn for the better, the river level dropped, and the day's ride was the easiest of all! That night I thought about all I had been through on my ten days with Outward Bound. I knew I had been stretched in some very deep ways and that I'd successfully faced new challenges. My self-esteem rose. I had learned about working more effectively under pressure and about the attitudes and behaviors necessary to tap into the creativity that I had perceived during my vision of infinite potential.

After the Outward Bound adventure, I wrote a proposal for a wilderness treatment program to work with the addicts. I tested out my ideas with pilot programs led by wilderness staff who had the mountaineering expertise that I lacked. I obtained private foundation money for a year's operation and we went into business. The program was a big success, written up in a national journal, and eventually provided the basis for a research project that earned me a Ph.D. in psychology from Saybrook Institute in San Francisco. My doctoral dissertation, *A Quest for Vision*, was published by Free Person Press, in Novato, California, and the wilderness treatment program was integrated into the budget of the larger drug treatment program itself. Finally, I felt good about the work I was doing. My previous frustration turned to excitement as I witnessed the wilderness program help others turn on to their own creative potentials for transformation and responsible lifestyles. The program grew from its original base in rock climbing to include ski touring and winter camping, winter mountaineering and river running, and finally one adventure that played a key role in the formation of the bridge that would eventually bring me to the Huichol.

As part of the Wilderness Treatment Program, the staff and I developed a week-long adventure that included backpacking into the High Sierra, climbing a major peak, and then spending a day and night alone in the wilderness to reflect on all that had transpired. As with everything else in the program, before asking one of our clients to do something, I would do it first. By now, I had spent considerable time in the mountains, but I had never spent the night out alone. When the time came to do so, I was afraid. We had seen a pretty good-size bear around base camp the night before, and I was nervous. Would it show up again when I was out by myself? The next morning, my staff dropped me off at the spot I had chosen, wished me well, and departed. They would come back the next morning to pick me up.

The day was quite hot even though we were at an altitude just below ten thousand feet. I took off all my clothes and wandered barefoot through the woods, thoroughly enjoying myself and feeling quite at home. In fact, I felt like I was experiencing memories from a million years of ancient lifetimes doing this very same thing. I picked up a stick and carried it like a club. I was caveman, a natural being in the natural world. Joyously, I ambled through my territory. Feeling so free, so in tune with nature, I could see how the life I was living at the time was very out of touch with nature and that I was paying a price for it. Forcing my natural rhythms into artificial timetables, spending too much time in buildings engaged in activities that didn't feed my soul, was painful and debilitating. I resolved to make significant changes when I came down, but for now I just wanted to enjoy the scenic wonder of High Sierra forest and mountains.

Later in the afternoon, I chose a spot to sleep in. I carefully laid out my ground sheet and sleeping bag and as the sun began to set, got into my warm clothes and shivered nonetheless. My nervousness about the bear was returning. Just then, I noticed an odd-shaped little piece of wood. I picked it up and felt an immediate connection with it, as though it had supernatural power. I laughed at myself. Was this just my imagination? I didn't know, but I decided to hang the wood on a piece of cord, leaving it dangling directly over my head. "If I'm still alive in the morning, then I'll know you really did have some power," I said to the stick.

I watched the sun go down and the light gradually disappear. Darkness descended and I got into my bag. It was a very long night. I tried to sleep, but the slightest sound in the woods gave me a jolt of adrenaline. I'd jump up with a start looking for a bear intent on devouring me. Muscles twitching, I jerked my head around, looking in all directions, readying myself for an attack. When nothing was there, I'd gradually calm down and try to fall asleep again. Twenty or thirty times, I went through this cycle of waking up in a panic state, searching frantically through the darkness for the monsters of my imagination, finding nothing, and then eventually dozing off fitfully. Finally, on one of my panic wake-ups, I noticed the predawn light starting to emerge in the east. I rejoiced. Morning was coming. Soon it would be daylight and I'd be able to see again. I had survived!

I put on all my warmest clothes and sat on my bag facing the east. I looked above me and there was my special stick. I felt a thankful kinship with it. I untied it from the rope and held it in my hand. Gazing eastward into the rising sun, I also felt kinship with all the people throughout human history who suffered through long, dark, and fearful nights, and who rejoiced in this same miraculous coming of light that brought warmth and safety from unseen dangers. I knew, as they knew, this was an event of epic proportion, literally of life-saving importance, not something to miss or take for granted. For if that sun didn't rise in the morning, there would be perpetual darkness, fear, and cold. And if it went on long enough, life itself would die. Our ancestors—and the people who still follow the ways of the ancestors, the people who still live in harmony with nature—got up before that sun rose over the horizon and waited for it. And with the first rays of a newborn day, they would offer their thanks to the powers that created this light and gave them the gift of its life-giving presence. I felt union with them all as I thanked that sun for rising and shining. I held my stick up to that sunlight and thanked it for my life. Today, I recognize that this act was the start of my ritual life.

From that day onward, I have thanked that miraculous power of the East for the gift of light. And I still have that stick in my bag of special spiritual objects, my medicine bag. I bring it with me every time I head back up into the mountains.

Shortly after sunrise, my staff came by to pick me up. I had mixed feelings when I saw them approaching: glad for their human company but knowing that I was just touching the surface of what this experience in wilderness solitude was all about. I knew then that I wanted more.

One year later, I got it.

At the time, I was very discouraged. The drug program where I worked had become a toxic place for me with the arrival of a new executive director who I felt was lacking in integrity. I desperately needed out but had no job to go to, no money in the bank, a wife, and now two children to support (Nicole, my second daughter, came along six weeks early in August of 1972). Then I remembered my experience of solitude in the mountains. I knew instinctively that I needed to go back to it. Inner guidance told me to go by myself, to climb up high, to find a place of power, and to stay there for as long as it took. Not to eat, read, or distract myself in any way. Just do my yoga, meditation, and play my harmonica to the stars at night, paying attention to everything that happened. Then, said the inner voice, *the wind and the cold, the rain and the sunlight will clean away what is not true. You don't have to work at it. Just pay attention. After the cleansing, what is left will be your truth—about yourself, your work, your marriage, and your life.*

I told several friends about what I was going to do and much to my chagrin didn't get their support. "What are you doing?" said one. "Are you punishing yourself?" Others tried to talk me out of it, citing the dangers and hardships. Despite the lack of support, I knew I had to go. I drove up to the high country, hiked into the wilderness, and climbed up a mountain to a small glacial-fed lake where I set up camp. I placed my sleeping bag right next to the lake, facing up to the summit several hundred yards above. Over the next few days, I opened myself to the forces of nature within and around me. I slowed down, softened up, paid attention.

Through cycles of day and night, I watched cosmic rhythms dance out their drama. The winds blew, the rains came, and the sun shone. At the end of that time, I had reached a state of clarity that felt crystalline pure. I knew what was true for me. I felt renewed love for myself, for Andrea, and for my life. I was filled with the power of the mountains that had been my home during my sojourn. But I still didn't know what to do about my job. That night as I readied myself for bed, I asked for help from the great powers of the universe so alive all around me and hoped for a dream, a vision, that would show me the way.

My prayers were answered through a powerful dream that shook me to my core: I was in a strange, barren landscape with a gang of thugs who were up to no good. They sensed that while I was with them physically, I was not really one of them and so I posed a threat. I knew they were plotting to get rid of me and I feared for my life. At one point, a bear appeared and chased me up a tall tree, then climbed up after me until I finally drove it away by hitting it on the snout with a soda bottle. Shortly thereafter, I climbed down from the tree and walked with the gang members down a trail that meandered through the forlorn barrenness. At one point, we came over a rise in a hill and far away, perhaps a quarter of a mile or so, I saw a long, high wall that extended in either direction as far as I could see. Right in the middle of the wall was a huge stone gate. It was just starting to close when I saw it. I knew that if I could get through that gate, I would be safe. But the door was halfway closed and there was no way I could run that far and get through safely before it closed the rest of the way. But I knew it was my only chance and it was disappearing right before my eyes. Then I heard an inner voice again. *Jump,* it said. *Let go of all messages that say it's impossible. Just go for it with total abandonment and you will be helped. But you have to do it! Right now!* So I did. I released all negative messages and jumped with all my might. The instant I lifted off the ground, a huge wind appeared. It picked me up and whisked me toward the closing gate. I shot through its massive stone slabs just before they slammed shut behind me. I was free! I was walking with my children down the quiet, rural road we lived on at the time, while simultaneously walking down a tree-shaded road I walked as a boy back in Maryland on my way to the woods. I was completely and serenely at peace.

I woke up with a start. I was alarmed and disoriented, didn't know where I was or what had just happened. Vigorously, I rubbed my eyes and peered through the darkness. I could see dim mountains around me and remembered where I was and what I was doing. Then I remembered the dream. I went back into it with awake awareness to review what had happened and see what messages it held. At first, I was worried about the "bad guys out to get me" and the bear that had threatened me. Then upon reflection, I realized the thugs were my own shadow destructive energies and the bear that I feared was in fact an ally that I wasn't yet ready to face. Its strength and power forced me up a tree, which in shamanism is the axis mundi, the sacred passageway connecting the higher realms with those of the lower. When I came to the part of my jump and being carried to safety, I saw what I was being told to do: *Step out of the security of the known, jump into the unknown and give it your best shot,* just as I had learned to do with mountain climbing. *Go for it with full effort and positive energy. Let go of all negatives. Do it with faith and you will be helped by the mysterious power of the universe. But it's not for you to know how this will happen. The door will be opened only by your going for it.*

The more I reflected on how the helping power had come to me just when I needed it, the more uplifted and buoyed I felt, just like in the dream. The dream was empowering me to leave the economic security of my position as director of the Wilderness Treatment Program and go out on my own. If I did this, offering what I had learned in my two years of wilderness work with individuals, groups, and on retreats, what I called "ecological psychology and psychological ecology," I would be helped by the Mystery in some unknown way. I stood straight up, arms reaching toward the sky, which was full of pulsating stars that seemed to dance with me in enthusiasm. "Yes, yes, I'll do it," I exclaimed.

I came down from the mountain full of confidence and faith, renewed and revitalized, my depression and confusion gone. On the drive back home, I stopped at a combination bookstore and snack shop. As I walked past the rack of books, one of them seemed to jump out and grab me. I picked it up and looked at the cover. Called *Lame Deer: Seeker of Visions,* it was about a Sioux holy man. I opened it up to the first page and started reading. To my surprise, I found a description of what I had just gone through, fasting alone in the wilderness seeking guidance from a higher power for direction in life. The author was telling of Lame Deer's retreat in solitude when he was a young man just getting ready to step into spiritual adulthood. Excitedly, I read on.

For the first time, I heard the term "vision quest." I read that the quest was a foundation stone for the Sioux people in shaping the identity of their young men and charting their future. I continued reading about how the whole tribal culture prepared the young person for the quest, usually as a rite of passage at the onset of adolescence. It was expected and honored. I was deeply touched by this. Finally, I had found understanding for the forces that had brought me to the mountains in my time of need. I had received no support from my culture, only incredulity and fear. Now I was becoming aware of a whole culture that not only understood the importance of this kind of empowering rite, it built these rites into its way of life. As I read on, I discovered that these rites were considered part and parcel of a process of birthing the sacred. They didn't just help people cope with times of transition and crisis, they took it a step beyond coping. They helped people use times of transition to actually grow stronger and healthier and to become more of who they really were. I was curious about what other life cycle transitions they dealt with in a growth-promoting manner. I sensed another door opening and knew that the next step was to find a Native American teacher who could introduce me to their ways on a firsthand basis.

I put out a psychic "call" to the universe and several months later discovered an art teacher, a Native American, at the local junior college and told him what I was seeking. He was quiet but intense with fiery eyes. His people were from the Northwest. At first, he didn't want to have anything to do with me. But gradually, after I told him of my visions up in the mountains, he began to open up.

"If you want to learn the ways of medicine," he said, "you will have to learn to penetrate the Buckskin Curtain. You will have to learn to be humble. Right now you are full of yourself. You will have to learn to listen. To be still. To open yourself to your feminine—to your intuition.

You will have to learn to really listen to nature with respect and humility. Perhaps if you do these things long enough, *perhaps,* you will someday learn to recognize a spiritual person."

I felt chastened, but I continued to stop by his office on a regular basis. He never welcomed me with warmth or enthusiasm; he tolerated me, like a pesky mosquito that you can't get rid of but learn to accept and go on with whatever you are doing. But he also never told me not to come back. Then one day, when I mentioned to him how high I had gotten on my quest, he looked at me angrily. "Don't talk to me about feeling high," he spat at me. "When you come back from a quest, you should be exhausted. When was the last time you got down on your belly and stuck your face next to Mother Earth and thanked her for all the gifts she has given you? When was the last time you thanked a tree for giving you the air you breathe? When did you last thank the Great Spirit for the gift of your life? That's what you do on a vision quest. That's what you do the whole time with all your might and all your strength!"

I was speechless, embarrassed. No where to run or hide. I felt that my beginning efforts to express thankfulness to the forces of nature were just a small drop in the bucket for all I had taken in my life and not given thanks for. I mumbled feebly in response: "I don't know. Maybe never."

I went home and thought about what he had said. I saw that a primary modus operandi in my life was based on taking or asking for more of whatever I wanted in the moment. I was learning that there was a very different way of living on this earth that was about giving, about balance, about genuine respect and the opposite of a "me first, gimme-gimme" mentality. As hurt as I felt, I also knew that everything he said was right on the mark. I also knew I was on the right track and that now, more than ever, I had to keep jumping into the unknown.

Shortly thereafter, I went back up to the mountains, this time with the intention of giving heartfelt thanks for all the precious gifts of my life—my health, my loving family, parents, sisters Ilsa and Briane (my second sister born a year after my mother's second marriage), and friends, my grandparents and ancestors. I gave thanks to all the powers of nature in each of the four directions around me, in the direction of Mother Earth below me and upward toward the heavens. Then I gave thanks to what my teacher called the "Great Mystery," the creative, generative power that is at the center of all things, from whence we come and whence we return at the time of our deaths. I gave thanks for my teacher and prayed for his life and the life of his people and all the people who still remember how to live in balance and harmony with all of creation. I did come back from this quest exhausted, but I felt good inside, moving toward something that would carry me for the rest of my life. When I went back to my teacher and told him of my experience—of the deer that came to me in a meadow as I sat there in stillness, of the energy I felt pouring out of the earth and into my body to the point where I thought there was an earthquake—he listened quietly. When I finished, there was only silence and the sound of our breathing. In the absence of words, my fears began to rise. Well, *I guess I blew it again,* I thought, getting ready for another blast of condemnation. He looked at me for a long time, carefully studying my face. Awkward and nervous, I fidgeted. Then he spoke so softly that I had to lean forward to hear.

"There is a festival taking place in a few weeks up north. It is to honor the acorn harvest. Many people from all over will be there to join in the dancing and celebration. I will take you there if you want to go." My heart pounded. I was being invited inside the Buckskin Curtain for the first time!

Several weeks later, I went through that curtain and met a medicine man, a respected elder. He took me and another Caucasian man into the woods away from the dance grounds. He looked into our hearts and souls with penetrating eyes. When he spoke, his words were similar to those of my teacher—about respect for all that lived, that white people had forgotten that everything is alive, that all of creation is equal in the eyes of the Great Spirit, and that we have lost our way and were now polluting our own nest and the nest of others. I listened intently, taking in his words and his spirit. He must have sensed something that he liked in me, because he became a teacher for me, and over the next few years I spent a good deal of time with him whenever he came to town. I also visited him and his people in the Nevada desert. It was one of the sanest times of my life.

Over the years, other teachers showed up, sometimes close to home, sometimes far away and I traveled to them. They taught me about the *inipi*—the sweat lodge, about the *chanunpa wakan*—the sacred pipe, about the medicine wheel, the Sacred Hoop of the Seven Directions, and how to interact with it all in correct relationship for healing, knowledge, and power. I tried to apply all that I was taught each time I went to the mountains on retreat. The vision quest became my new vehicle for existential housecleaning. I stopped using psychedelics and used my new teachings instead. Once a year, I returned to the same place of power that I had gone to for my first quest for vision. I took others with me, people who wanted to quest alone to seek deeper vision for their lives. After a period of preparation, we would backpack in for two days to reach a beautiful alpine lake in a forest-filled bowl surrounded on three sides by towering granite cliffs. There we would have a Giveaway Ceremony where each person offered something to the Great Spirit and the group regarding his or her purpose being on quest, then we would go off for our time alone, swallowed up in the deep forest for the turning of the wheel of night and day. Each quest brought more teachings, testings, and vision. I'll talk more about them in future chapters, but now I want to add the last few steps of the bridge to the Huichol.

In the spring and summer of 1981, people who were interested in my quest retreats kept asking me when I was going on the next one and if I would take them. Strangely, the answer that kept coming up was, "I don't know when I'm going. I don't even know *if* I'm going. Something keeps telling me to just stay right here. Something else is coming and I don't know what it is. Call me in another month and I'll see what's cooking."

In midsummer of 1981, the "something" arrived: a Caucasian Huichol shaman was going to take a small group of gringos to Mexico to take part in a Huichol pilgrimage. I had heard of the Huichol but never dreamed that one day I would be with them, retracing the steps of their ancestors on the sacred journey to their holy land of Wiricuta. Prem Das, the Anglo man who was leading the trip, had studied in India with a master there, then returned to the West and apprenticed to a Huichol shaman. He finished his apprenticeship, married into the Huichol tribe, and was now inviting a select group of others to learn about the medicine ways of a tribe considered to be most in touch with their still-alive primal spiritual heritage of all the indigenous peoples of Meso America.

I was thrilled. I contacted Prem Das's representative here in the States, liked what he had to say, and put in my application. I thought back to my vision fifteen years earlier, when I saw the whole panorama of aboriginal Mesoamerican life and heard a voice tell me I once had been a part of it and would return in this life. *Is this it,* I wondered, *the start of the return?* I wasn't sure, but it felt right to check it out. I wrote a letter explaining why I wanted to go and a few weeks later received a letter saying that I had been accepted as one of the pilgrims. The letter also provided information on what to bring, an itinerary, some Huichol vocabulary, and where and when to meet.

In October, I flew south to Puerto Vallarta. There I boarded a bus to Tepic, a four-hour road show of locals, chickens, children, babies, all sorts of exotic plants and foods being prepared and consumed, and all the sights, smells, and sounds of *la gente* on their way to and fro through the sweltering Mexican humidity. I got a room in a hotel by the central plaza where we were to meet at noon of the following day. Early the next morning, I walked out to the already crowded plaza and found a seat facing the steps of a huge church whose spires could be seen half a mile away. From my perch on the bench, I delighted in watching the citizenry pour into the hub-bub of a downtown Saturday filled with street hawkers, cars, trucks, motorcycles, pedestrians, kids, and dogs, all competing for space in the highway of activity that was the streetlife of central Tepic.

I was curious to meet my fellow pilgrims and every time I saw a gringo, I wondered if he or she were part of the party. But it wasn't until shortly before noon that a group of us gathered in front of the steps. Some of the people already knew each other and had been traveling in Mexico for a while. Others were like me, connecting up for the first time. Prem Das wasn't there yet and wouldn't arrive until the next day. He had gone to the shaman's village and couldn't get in; the rains had been particularly heavy and the river was swollen, allowing no passage, and the shaman, Don Jose Matsuwa, couldn't get out. So Prem Das went to another village

Photo by Larain Boyll

Doña Andrea with power objects,
making an offering to Grandfather Fire

where Don Jose's daughter, Doña Andrea, lived. She too was a shaman. Prem Das asked her if she would lead the pilgrimage since her father was not able to. At first she refused. To lead a pilgrimage is a tremendous responsibility requiring extensive preparation. The shaman is considered to carry the pilgrims on his or her back, conducting all the ceremonies and protecting the *peyoteros* from all harmful forces. But Prem Das was persistent. Doña Andrea went off alone to consult her allies. After a while, she came back and reported that she had received the guidance to take us to Wiricuta. We were on the road!

That's how I ended up in the desert looking for peyote with the Huichol. Not only did I find peyote in that harsh desert landscape, I found my life. From the moment I got there and started doing ceremony—singing, praying, dancing, and making the prayer arrows we were instructed to carry with us as offerings to the gods—I felt completely at ease, at home. Memories from a distant past came alive: *I remember this. Yes, this is how people were meant to live!* For the first time in my life, I felt completely sane.

2

⌇⌇⌇

Identity and Purpose

The Indian can forget neither the body nor the mind,
while the European is always forgetting the one or the
other . . . the Indian . . . not only knows his own nature,
but he knows also how much he himself is nature. The
European, on the other hand, has a science of nature and
knows astonishingly little of his own nature, the nature
within him.

CARL JUNG

Springtime 1978. New life coming up from the earth. But I am in a hospital and there is sickness and death all around me. I first heard the shrieks as I walked down the long hospital corridor. I shivered but continued walking. The screams got louder and I realized they were coming from the room I was approaching. I was there at the request of the mother of thirteen-year-old Sarah, who had painful osteosarcoma, bone cancer. I knew Sarah and her family from our mutual involvement at a program in Tiburon, California, called the Center for Attitudinal Healing. The center provides peer support groups for children and families facing life-threatening illness. I was a facilitator in the children's group and had worked there with Sarah. I'd also had several individual sessions with her, teaching her self-hypnosis skills to help control her considerable pain. Now she was hospitalized and her mother asked me to visit her.

Sarah had postponed entering the hospital for as long as she could.

One year earlier, her younger brother had come to this same hospital and had died there from aplastic anemia. For her, just being there was an awful reminder of what had happened to her brother and what could happen to her as well. I reached the doorway and paused to gather courage. I wanted to run away and pretend it wasn't happening. But the cries of anguish did not allow me this luxury. Gingerly, I opened the door and took one step into the room.

Sarah was on the bed, screaming. Her mother was beside her and her father stood against the wall facing her. Two nurses were on either side of her, trying unsuccessfully to calm her down. Nobody noticed that I had come in, and I stood paralyzed, unable to speak. I sent my breath into the floor as if I were a tree extending roots deep into the earth. I breathed down into those roots, trying to release the tension that tightened my muscles and froze me to the spot. For several minutes, all I could do was breathe in and out, trying to center myself in the midst of the storm. Then a voice inside me said, *You are supposed to be a professional who knows what to do in situations like this. They need help and called you. Step forward and help them now.* I felt guilty, not believing that I had anything adequate in my "tool bag." I still hadn't said a word, nor had anyone spoken to me or acknowledged my presence. I hadn't even moved since my first step into the room. I felt desperate to do something to help—but what? A hypnotic intervention using visualization to help reduce Sarah's anxiety? But would the nurses think I was some kind of quack and throw me out? I was stuck in my own fear.

Meanwhile, the drama in the room continued unabated. Sarah was on pain medication but it wasn't touching her fear about being in the same hospital where her brother died. I could hear it in her cries. But I still felt powerless. Time stopped. Again, I breathed in and out. Then, like a bubble rising slowly up to the surface of a pond, I heard the inner voice: *You say that you believe the Great Spirit is present always, that its love and peace is in the center of all things. Well, what about this situation?* The question broke the spell. *One way to find out,* I said to myself. *I've got to open up and see what happens.* At that point, just by saying what was true for me, the pressure I'd put on myself to come up with some kind of helping intervention disappeared. *Well, Great Spirit, you brought me here, so if there is something you want me to do, just let me know and I'll do the best I can.*

As I silently spoke these words, I realized that even though I was off the hook about knowing what to do for Sarah, I wasn't totally off the hook in terms of my responsibility to the situation. I saw that I must pay attention to everything, just as if I were on a vision quest, not knowing how the Great Spirit might reveal itself and therefore mindful of every little thing that occurs. With the burden of having to know what to do lifted from my shoulders, I felt my body release tension, and a wave of relaxation started to wash through me. Then I heard a soft voice: *Open your heart and send her love—not to her body, nor to her illness or fear. That is not who she is. Send it right into the center of her heart, to that place within her that is light, that is who she really is. And send it to her without any conditions, like making her pain go away or having her stop screaming. That is not in your hands. See her receiving it. That is all.*

Hearing the voice took me back in time to when I first learned about the presence of this deeper love that transcends romantic and personal love. It was revealed in the third morphogenetic field of information from my first visionary journey back in 1966. In this vision, I saw Christ on the cross, his body being impaled, his shudders at receiving the blow. Then my awareness went inside his body, feeling what he was feeling, and I wanted to kill the bastards who were inflicting the torture. But a voice from within Christ said, *Forgive them, Father, they know not what they do.* At that moment, I felt the presence of a kind of love that I didn't even know existed, welling up in Christ's heart and extending toward his abusers. *They are asleep. To punish them will serve naught. They are hurting themselves and do not even know it. They are like unconscious children crying out for love.* This vision was to come back to me in many forms in the ensuing years, but this was the first opening of the door.

I burst into tears for all the pain in the world, all the unconsciousness. I cried for myself, my family and friends, all of humanity, and all of life. In that instant, I realized that the rest of my life would be about doing my best to stay in connection with this love. I understood then why Christ symbolizes the healing power of love for millions of people around the world. Christ-consciousness is unconditional love, a spiritual energy force of infinite light, wisdom, and compassion. *This is the greatest treasure of all,* I affirmed.

Now, standing in the hospital ward, being reminded of this love and that my purpose in being there was to extend it unconditionally to Sarah, I recognized that it was a vehicle for my own healing as well. I focused my attention on my chest, visualized my heart opening, with the Christ light emanating from my heart into Sarah's. I had to work to get through her body and her pain, but I persevered and eventually broke through. In that precise instant, I felt total peace. No longer did I want to run from the room nor control the situation. Instead, I was relaxed, thankful for being right there in the fullness of the moment. If someone had told me beforehand that I could be peaceful with my heart open while a young girl was suffering, I would have said they were nuts.

Then a doctor came in to take Sarah downstairs for X-rays. She screamed even louder as she was transferred to a gurney. I heard my inner voice: *Go along behind them. Place your hand on her forehead. See the light pouring down from above, through your arm and into her body. Once again, just fill her up with love. And don't have the reason you're doing it be so that she calms down.* Feeling foolish, I asked the doctor and parents if I could walk behind her down the hallway. They all nodded yes.

I followed my inner instructions while we walked to the elevator, took it down several flights, and then went to the X-ray room. All this time, I kept my hand on her forehead and focused on being an open pipeline for the love to flow through me. As we approached the doorway to the room and the doctor went in to talk with the X-ray technician, I stood there silently, continuing my assignment. Gradually, Sarah calmed down and to my surprise even stopped moaning and crying. She was quiet now, her body starting to release. I was amazed at the changes. Then I asked her if she wanted to use her mind to help herself and she said yes. So I took her through a guided visualization that induced her relaxation response even more, and she entered into a peaceful state. She went into the X-ray room very serene and I knew that my work there was complete.

Great Spirit really is present always, I thought as I got into my car. I felt a rush of thankfulness toward the Native American medicine elders and spiritual teachers I'd been meeting in my travels through the Buckskin Curtain, who continually emphasized that the Great Spirit was present in all things. Their teaching had held up under pressure. Now I knew from direct experience that peace really was inside me all the time and that it never left. I could leave it, but it was still always there, waiting patiently for me to reconnect with it whenever I chose to do so by opening my heart, extending the love, and wanting nothing back in exchange. I thought about one of the principles of attitudinal healing that I heard many times before, but now understood, thanks to Sarah, in a much deeper way: giving and receiving are the same, for what we give to another, we also give to ourselves.

The Center for Attitudinal Healing, through which I had met Sarah, was started in 1975 by Gerry Jampolsky, a psychiatrist who had his own transpersonal awakening through reading the *Course of Miracles,* a book of channeled writing that, like my vision, was based on the unconditional love of Christ-consciousness. I had come to the center in a roundabout way, just a few months after it opened. Again, it was the vision quest work and the voice of inner guidance that brought me there. I was finishing my doctoral work based on the Wilderness Treatment Program. The medical director of the drug program, Dr. William Lamers, was also on my doctoral committee and knew me quite well. I asked him what kind of people he thought I should work with and his reply shocked me: "People that are dying. They are on a vision quest although they would not articulate it as such. They are seeking a deeper vision for the meaning of their lives as they prepare to face their death." I was speechless. Bill went on, "You have been taking people out on vision quests for years now. I think you would work very well with the dying." I knew intuitively that what he was saying was right, but I didn't feel capable or confident that I was up for meeting the demands that working with the dying would entail. I told him I needed to think about it.

Not long after that, on the July Fourth weekend of 1976, I was out on a quest with a group of students from an adult education class I was teaching at a local college. We were on a three-day retreat on a mountain overlooking the Pacific Ocean. It was time for me to leave for several hours, as I had told them I would be doing. My two young daughters had decorated their bikes, got all dressed up, and pleaded with me to come back from the retreat and walk with them in the big community parade celebrating the bicentennial, only an hour away in rural West Marin.

Afterward, on my return to the quest. I was driving down a curvy, country road and ran into a traffic jam. People were standing by their cars trying to see what was going on. I got out and walked the quarter of a mile to where a crowd stood in the middle of the road. I edged in to see what they were looking at. A young man had been in a motorcycle crash. He lay unconscious in the road, his boots knocked off by the force of the impact. One man was holding his head up, another was looking at his chest. I could see immediately that he was losing life-force energy through the bottom of his feet. *Someone needs to go up there and block up his feet so he stops losing that energy,* I thought, but I was reluctant to act—I looked like a bum, unshaven and dirty from being in the woods. How would people react to this shady-looking character coming up to the fallen cyclist and doing something weird like holding his feet? How would I react if he died while I was holding him?

I thought about the synchronicity of this accident with the question I was asking on my quest—I had been seeking guidance on what to do about Bill Lamers's feedback to me several weeks prior. Bill had also asked me to teach a class with him on death and dying and join with him and a small group of others who had been meeting for several years in preparation for starting the second hospice program in the United States. I was flattered but hesitant there, too. Could I handle being in such intimate contact with dying people? Now, I was faced with the possibility of someone dying right in front of me.

I realized that if I didn't do something about the motorcyclist on the ground, it wouldn't be done. *Let people think whatever they want of me.* I walked over to the prostrate figure. The two men looked at me curiously. I gestured to them to go on with the ministrations. Then I bent down and placed my hands against the motorcyclist's feet. I closed my eyes and imagined my hands were dams, completely closing off the leaks. To my surprise, I felt very calm, and I knew that even if he died while I was there, I was doing just what I needed to be doing. Shortly thereafter, an ambulance arrived. I walked back to my car and continued on my way. *Yes to Bill, to the class, and to the hospice work.*

Yet, the Mystery wasn't finished. Back at the retreat, I did a meditation taught to me by a spiritual teacher in the spring of 1974, a shaman woman who was part Mohawk, part Apache, and part Scottish. It involved raising and lowering the arms while seated on the earth, maintaining synchronized breathing, and building up an intensified energy charge. The final movement releases all the built-up energy into the center of the earth as your forehead touches the ground in an act of surrender. You remain in this position as long as you can, then sit upright and continue meditating, allowing the energy of the earth to enter your body. I had first used this meditation after this same teacher taught me about using crystals for healing. After she completed her lengthy instructions, she said with a mischievous twinkle in her eye, "Now you have to pray for a crystal. You can't buy one. It has to be given to you, either by Mother Earth herself or by someone else. Do this meditation and it will help you."

I had diligently followed her instructions. Each morning at dawn I got up with the sunrise and went outside, sat down facing the east, and did exactly what she had shown me. It was an interesting experience because it turned into a trial of self-examination. *Why do you want the crystal? To show off? To impress others? What will you do with it if you get it? What are you prepared to give of yourself in exchange for it?*

After sitting with these questions for a period of time, my response was clear. *I want the crystal to use for healing as I have been taught by my elder. I will only take it out and use it if I am guided to do so, and only to help those who need healing. I will use it with respect as I have been taught.* Then I offered a prayer. *Thank you, Mother Earth, for the food and drink you share with us, for the clothing and shelter that protect us from the elements, for your light and love, your strength, your beauty, and your teachings about harmony and balance. I pray for your health and your healing, for all those living, all those who have crossed over, and all those coming into bodies. I pray for my family, for all the children, the elders, those yet to come, and the ancestors. I pray for all those seeking light and those helping in the birthing processes of health and healing. I pray that you use me as a channel for your healing ways. And if it is meant for me to have a crystal, I open to that and welcome it in. If it is not for my greatest good to have this medicine, I surrender to you and what it is that you bring me that is for my greatest good. Ho. May it be so.*

I sent this prayer into the earth beneath my forehead every day after being told to pray for a crystal. Ten days later, I drove into town to pick up my daughter at her gymnastics class. I was early, so I sat in the waiting room with the other parents. A young man whom I had never seen before walked in. He looked dirty and bedraggled, as though he'd just come out of the earth itself. He had a nice smile and I was in a friendly mood, so I nodded to him. "How ya doing?" he asked. "Fine," I responded. Then he took off on a meandering conversation about how he came to be there. He had, in fact, just come down from Nevada where he had been working in a mine. Suddenly, he stood up and said he had something for me and would be right back. He walked outside and several minutes later was back. He held out his closed fist and said, "Here, something tells me this is for you." He opened his hand and in it was a beautiful crystal. The mine he had been working in was a crystal mine.

After receiving the crystal in such an unexpected manner, I used the meditation whenever I went on quest or whenever I needed guidance on a big decision in my life. Now, back at the quest site after my experience with the injured motorcyclist, I decided to use the meditation to help me integrate the information I had received about work with the dying. As I reached the point where I placed my forehead to the earth, a voice boomed up from the depths, *You are supposed to work with people who have cancer!* It was so loud I was shocked. I sat up and looked around. No one. I knelt back into the meditation position with my head touching the ground. The voice boomed again. I tried to ignore it. Working with cancer patients wasn't my plan for my life; I didn't know anything about the process. I hoped the voice would go away. It didn't. It only got louder and louder. Finally, I surrendered. "Okay, okay," I said aloud. "I'll do it. But you will have to show me what to do because I sure as hell don't know."

The voice stopped. I was relieved but mystified. When I got home two days later, Andrea told me someone had called from Los Angeles and wanted me to call them back as soon as I got in. "It sounded urgent," she said. I dialed the number. A woman answered and I identified myself. A chill went through me when she said, "I hear you work with cancer patients. My brother has a brain tumor and we want to come up and see you." *You sure didn't waste any time with that one, Great Spirit!* I thought to myself in amazement.

So I started working with Bill and the other volunteers who were starting the hospice and began seeing cancer patients. Remembering my quest experience, I used the following prayer to allay my anxiety and to open to guidance about what to say and do with the patients: *Thank you, Great Spirit, for bringing me here and for your presence. Help me to open myself to you and whatever it is you would have me do here. I know that I am weak and nothing without you. Use me as a channel for your light and love, flowing in loving, unattached service to thy will.*

I visited the hospice patients at home and during their hospitalizations. Through the surrendering and listening process, I received guidance that helped me. I tried to listen to them, respect them, and allow my own intuition to tell me what to do for them. I was particularly interested to notice the impact of their belief systems on the quality of their remaining days of life—and in some cases apparently the quantity as well. I noticed that those who believed in some greater power—whether it be God, nature, the cosmos—seemed to reach a state of peacefulness that the others did not. The people who lacked a belief in something larger than themselves seemed more fearful, angry, and anxious. I was fascinated by this observation and wanted to explore it in more depth, but I felt uncomfortable doing so within the strict medical model under which the hospice operated. The program was doing a wonderful job in meeting the needs of the patients, but I sensed staff members' discomfort with the spiritual issues that I often raised at staff meetings. Perhaps it was just my projection, but in any case I didn't feel that they were open to exploring this realm within that setting.

About the time of my increasing discomfort, I happened to read an article in the local paper about a young woman who had taken part in a cancer treatment program that used meditation and guided imagery to help cancer patients battle their illness. She had been through the program first as a patient, then as a trainee. Now she wanted to start a similar program herself. It sounded interesting, especially since I had found mediation, prayer, and guided imagery to be quite helpful with the people with whom I worked. I tried to reach her several times by phone, to no avail. Shortly thereafter, I left for my annual quest in the high Sierra. When I came home, surprise: she had called me, totally independent of my calls to her, which had never gotten through. I was amazed at how the Great Spirit was bringing us together. I returned her call; we met and spent the day together. It felt like old soul partners meeting each other after a long separation. We decided to work together then and there. She taught me her approach, and I shared with her what I had been learning from my visionary journeys and what the Native American elders had taught me about spirituality. It was a good match. Beyhan was almost thirty years old when I met her, thin but strong, soft but powerful. Warm and loving. She was in remission at the time, inspired and inspiring.

So it was Beyhan who brought me to the Center for Attitudinal Healing and introduced me to Gerry Jampolsky. At first, she and I worked with adults at the center, but after several months, Gerry asked me to join the center's children's group. I felt flattered but nervous. While I love kids and I love playing and goofing around with them, I felt completely inadequate to the task of being a professional who knows what to do in working with children facing life-threatening illness. Gerry tried to reassure me. "Leave your credentials at the door. Come into the group as an equal to the kids. We are all here to share openly, face our fears, and find inner peace." He reminded me that the main principle of attitudinal healing is that the essence of our being is love. "Just love the kids, Tom," he said, "That's all you have to do." I thought, *Yeah, sure, Gerry, that sounds nice, but what am I* really *supposed to do in the group?* He seemed to read my mind, because then he reminded me of another principle of attitudinal healing—we are students and teachers to each other. "Let the children be your teachers," he said. I was still nervous but decided to give it a try.

From the very first group, I found what I was looking for. I learned from watching Gerry—about using psychodrama, role play, art, puppetry, hypnosis, and visualization. I learned to talk openly with the children about death and dying and our deeper beliefs about the meaning of life and how best to live it, especially when time seemed short. What influenced me the most however was witnessing the empowerment that the attitudinal healing principles offered to those in need, both young and old. The center defined health as inner peace, healing as letting go of fear. It focused on making a conscious choice about what you want to experience in the moment—love or fear. Gerry and the kids showed me that it is possible to experience inner peace no matter what is happening in our bodies as a result of illness or invasive treatment procedures. The key is to choose peace as our only goal, then open the heart and extend unconditional love and forgiveness and want nothing back in return.

The center's philosophy emphasized that giving and receiving are the same. By letting go of the past and the future and seeing each instant as an opportunity for giving love, the giver of love also experiences it. Thus we become love givers and love finders instead of fault finders and love seekers. We can learn to love ourselves and others by forgiving rather than by judging and to perceive others as either extending love or calling for help. Attitudinal healing further affirms that we can choose to be peaceful inside regardless of what is happening outside. All of these beliefs fit quite smoothly into the framework within which I had been working for many years through my involvement with yoga, meditation, and Native American spirituality. The principles comprise a cognitive approach to behavioral change starting with the head and eventually reaching the heart. I was delighted to find its similarity to Buddhism—the belief that the cause of suffering is in the mind and that by changing how we use our mind, we can transform our experience. My ongoing quest was to learn how to tap into the enormous potential of the mind and use it for transforming our lives. The principles offered a set of conceptual tools with which to do precisely that.

I used relaxation and visualization techniques with eight-year-old

Keith to help reduce his freakouts when he went to the hospital for the painful chemotherapy treatments he needed on a regular basis. Keith would get so agitated that the nurses had to hold him down to insert the IV needle. In addition, his veins kept collapsing. I taught Keith to induce his relaxation response and visualize himself in a peaceful place. I rehearsed this procedure with him over and over until he could get into a deep state in just a few minutes. When he went to the hospital for his next treatment, I spoke to him over the phone in the waiting room and helped him elicit his relaxed state. Keith also visualized Superman inside his body holding up his veins at his command so the needle could be inserted with no problem. When Keith was ready, his mother picked up the phone and told me Keith was in a deep trance state and they were now going to enter the doctor's office. I hung up and visualized everything going well and Keith surrounded by love. I couldn't wait to hear how it went. Hours went by before his mother finally called me back.

Everything had worked perfectly. Keith was calm and relaxed. His vein came up as directed and the insertion went smoothly. Keith lay there completely at peace while the chemotherapy entered his body. Then one of the nurses walking by his bed inadvertently bumped into his IV pole and pulled out the needle! Everyone was greatly upset, especially Keith, and they had to start all over. Now if I were Keith, I would be angry at the nurse who had blown the whole carefully orchestrated scenario. Well, Keith *was* mad. But, his mother reported, Keith later saw how upset the nurse was with what she had done, so he went over to her and took her hand. In his sweet eight-year-old voice, he said, "It's okay, I forgive you. We all make mistakes sometimes and I know you didn't mean it." When I heard this story, I realized that the most important thing here was not what I had shown Keith about relaxation and visualization techniques, but what he was teaching me about the healing power of forgiveness. Instead of holding on to judgments, Keith demonstrated how to choose peace by extending love.

A few years later, this teaching reappeared through another vision-ary experience with Christ-consciousness. It took place on a Huichol pilgrimage during the all-night ceremony around the fire at the Huichol holy land of Wiricuta. Under the guidance of the *mara'akame,* the sha-man, we sang, prayed, danced, and observed silence in continual rounds throughout the evening. I was in a deep trance state gazing at Tatewari, Grandpa Fire, when suddenly I saw again the image of Christ being cruci-fied. Here I was, deep in the mountains of Mexico, with Indians follow-ing their ancient ceremonial way that predated the birth of Christ, and what was I seeing? Christ again. *And I'm not even Christian,* I thought.

I watched a vision unfold in the midst of the flames where each time I, or someone else, made a negative judgment about ourselves or someone else, another spike was driven into Christ's body and he cried out in pain. Then I saw that each time a negative judgment was not repressed, denied, or projected onto another, but caught in consciousness, then released, a spike was taken out of Christ's body and a radiant light shone forth, illuminating the desert. I watched in fascination as Christ, as real as the ground I was sitting on, smiled with thankfulness, radiating a peace that took me into ecstatic rapture. *It's true,* I thought. *That is exactly what I have been learning at the center. This is the second installment of the vision I had fifteen years earlier. It is all about forgiveness. God's love is here for us always, but the instant I make a negative judgment, my heart closes and I am cast into the darkness of separation from the healing power of that love. The healing comes from joining with this love in every possible instant!* I saw then that the love in our hearts, which, like the breath of life, was given to us by our Creator, was there for one purpose only—for giving. *And that is the essence of forgiving,* I reflected. *To let go of judgments that block aware-ness of love's healing presence, then let the love flow outward to all that cross your path.* In that instant, I realized that I had spent a great deal of my time and energy judging others, myself, and the world, fueling a great deal of misery and depression. Now, through spiritual vision, the teachings of medicine elders, and the children at the Center for Attitudinal Healing, I was being shown a whole new way to live, a whole new purpose in being.

I thought back to another vision I had on the pilgrimage, a few days before the Christ vision in Tatewari. We were camped at the site of an ancient ruin. During the day, we roamed over the hillside that housed the extensive ruins, which included a huge temple with massive stone col-

Tatewari (Grandfather Fire spirit)

umns, a pyramid, numerous ceremonial sites, and huge stone rooms built into the earth, one above the other from the bottom of the hill all the way to the top. At night, we sat around the fire as the shaman chanted and prayed. I was mesmerized by the sublime beauty of the ancient rhythms. A Huichol mother nursed her baby while warming tortillas in the fire. Moonlight softly bathed us as the fire danced and shadows moved. Suddenly, a serpent slithered out of the desert and headed toward me. I froze. The serpent approached. It was a rattlesnake, six feet long and thick in body. I didn't know what to do—or whether it was real, a figment of my imagination induced by the hypnotic chants of the shaman, a spiritual visitor bringing gifts, or a test that I needed to face. I didn't have long to contemplate what to do or what it was, for the next instant it magically entered my body. Then my body became the serpent! Just as I was getting used to this, an eagle swooped down and slammed into me with all its might. Sharp talons grabbed me and I felt myself rising upward, clutched tightly in its claws. We soared into the heavens, the earth rapidly disappearing below. The eagle flew toward a celestial light that grew brighter as we approached it until it was overwhelming. We went straight into it and were consumed. The "I" of personal identity was obliterated. There was no thing, only light everywhere. Infinite bliss.

How long did I remain in the state of oneness with the light? All I know is that eventually my awareness was drawn downward. Far below, I saw people around a fire, all sleeping except the shaman, who was still praying. Then I saw a body I recognized as my own. The next instant, I was back in that body. I shook myself to make sure I was me. Everything checked out, so I relaxed into my sleeping bag, grateful for the appearance of two new power animals, the serpent and the eagle. I thanked them for entering my life and for their help and power.

The serpent, I reflected, is symbolic of the life force, the *kundalini* awakening. The eagle grabbed the serpent from the earth and lifted it to a higher level of total immersion with celestial light. The joining of earth and sky, serpent and eagle, on solar journey into light, symbolizes the blissful union with spirit that is the goal of all spiritual practice. I radiated with the joyous aftereffects of my journey and gave heartfelt thanks for an answer to prayer. Like the Huichol, I had come on the pilgrimage to find my life. Over and over again, I had heard the *mara'akame* say that if we truly open our hearts, if our prayers are "good," we might be able to pass through the *nierica*, the doorway, into the Sacred Mystery and there receive guidance for our lives. Well, here it was. *Call in the great eagle. Use its power to raise your kundalini to join in oneness with the light of the Great Spirit.* This was the shamanic solar journey I had read about, the archetypal journey to light. Now it was real. I fell asleep in deep thankfulness for what I had experienced.

The next day, I excitedly shared my vision with one of the gringo pilgrims who knew a great deal about the history and culture of indigenous Mexico. He told me that one of the greatest mythic figures of ancient

Author's drawing of visionary experience—Quetzalcoatl

Mesoamerica was the God-like Quetzalcoatl, the feathered serpent. For the Native People, this was a figure equal in importance to Christ for the Christians. The myth related his death through treachery thousands of years ago and with his demise, the loss of the sacred. It also spoke about his eventual return, that when he came back, it would be time for the return of the sacred. The light from my journeys with the Huichol was shining bright, illuminating my path back "home."

I could see the various pieces of my life starting to fit together. The death of my father shattered illusions of security, causing me to search desperately for that which is permanent. Aided by hindsight, I recognize now how I had to first face death and destruction in order to find a new life. The old had to be vanquished before I could open to a larger, transcendent awareness. The shamanic medicine ways, the vision quests, the work with the hospice and the center all played a role in bringing me to my life work. Now, with the insight I found in Mexico, I saw my future. In fact, I saw a vision of a wide road, stretching out from where I lay on the ground by the fire going forward in a straight line and disappearing into the horizon. I knew without the slightest doubt that road was mine and I was to walk it with Spirit doing my best to honor the teachings that I was being shown. I knew I was to stay with it all the way to the end, to my own death, when I would return to the mystery from whence I came. The Huichol say that once you've "found your life," you must also find the *kupuri,* the energy and the strength by which to live according to your vision. Only then can you "complete yourself." When I saw the vision of the straight road before me, I decided then and there that this was my goal: to walk my heart path to completion.

3

Becoming Powerful

It is from understanding that power comes . . . for nothing can live well except in a manner that is suited to the way the sacred power of the world lives and moves.

BLACK ELK

When I was a sickly youth, then a stringbean young adolescent, I was obsessed with physical power. It looked to me that strength was the best bet for some kind of protection against a constantly threatening universe. I decided to do something about it when I heard that a neighborhood girl down the block could lift more weight over her head than I could. I had to do something. Some of the older guys in the neighborhood lifted weights and since they were my role models—the best athletes, the toughest bad guys that nobody would mess with—I decided to start training with weights, too. My first set of weights was a gift for my thirteenth birthday. I started eating health food supplements and following the weightlifting scene. The Olympic training center for weight lifters was not far from my home, so I went there to watch my heroes work out and try to pick up some pointers. Paul Anderson, the 1956 Olympic Gold Medal winner, acclaimed the world's strongest man, was my hero. I took my other cues from movie stars like Hopalong Cassidy and Bob Steele. A strong man was always in charge, knew what he was doing, risked his life to save others, and was *tough*. I grew up trying to emulate what I'd seen on the silver screen. Because I was involved with sports, I was even more influenced by the tough-guy ideal. Only a wimp would complain about injury. "Be tough. Shake it off. Play with pain. Stop whining. Be a man." These were some of the messages I got on the football field, the basketball court, the wrestling mat, and the baseball diamond. My tendency toward juvenile delinquency meant that I took all of this posturing to an extreme and got stuck in it: the crazier you could be, the more risky the challenge, the greater your status as a tough guy. When I left the East Coast and came to California to try to escape my delinquent identity, I was successful in distancing myself from that life. But I still carried an image of strength that was based on physical prowess.

The first crack in my conceptual armor was my vision of Christ being crucified. It showed me a different kind of strength, an inner strength with enough power to overcome the desire to return violence for violence and to instead send out love and peace. In my studies of Eastern religion, I read about the battle to overcome the ego in order to find God and about the different kind of strength that is required for this battle. I also read about Martin Luther King and Gandhi and their use of nonviolent resistance. I knew that it takes a great deal of inner strength to turn the other cheek to your attacker yet continue to resist injustice. So I had an intellectual sense of another kind of strength, different from my adolescent notion, but it was all an abstraction, not something I witnessed in my daily life. Therefore, it had no impact on me.

It wasn't until I started exploring Native American spirituality that I discovered living models for a new understanding of strength, lessons that were, interestingly enough, reinforced over and over again by my experiences at the Center for Attitudinal Healing. Power in shamanism stems from your relationship with powers that are bigger than you. The entire universe is considered to be alive, to have power. Everything is equally sacred in the eyes of the Great Spirit. It is the Great Spirit, the Great Mystery, present always in everyone, everything, everywhere and all the time, that is the source of all power. True personal power comes from your relationship to this sacred source and its various manifestations in the world of nature with all its domains, seen and unseen. For my shamanic teachers, power is not about domination and control. It is about being in proper relationship to the powers of the universe so you can live your life in a *wakan* way, a sacred manner, thereby fulfilling the purpose of the Creator who gave you this lifetime. It is about walking your heart path to completion, honoring the medicine you have been given to carry for your own good and the good of the people.

Power on the shamanic path can be hunted and it comes in many ways—through a great dream, through a vision, through visiting a place of power to pray and make offerings, through a disincarnate intelligence that appears as a power animal, such as the serpent and eagle who visited me on my first pilgrimage in Mexico, or Kauyumari, the deer spirit of the Huichol. Power can also come from objects and forces in nature. The trick is to listen and learn from these various sources of power in a respectful manner.

My experience with poison oak is a good example of this sometimes painful but effective learning process. We were living in West Marin at the time in a beautiful rural valley filled with oak trees, madrone, Douglas fir, and yes, plenty of poison oak. I had extreme sensitivity to its oil and had suffered numerous outbreaks of itchy, swollen rashes in the past, the worst of which required cortisone cream and medication. Poison oak was threatening to overrun our yard, so one day I carefully covered my entire body, then went outside and pulled up plants by the roots and cut down what I couldn't uproot. Afterward, I immediately went in and showered off with soapy lather and threw my clothes into the wash and felt thoroughly clean. That evening, I drove up north an hour and a half to visit with the medicine man I had met at the Acorn Festival years before, who was in town overnight and had invited me to see him. About sixty years old, he was hard as flint on the outside but with a big heart and a twinkle in his eye for those he liked. We talked until dawn, when I had to get back home and then to work. I watched the sun rise as I drove down the freeway singing a welcome song giving thanks for this new day and for the good sharing time with a wisdom elder. My joy was short lived, however. Right in the middle of it, I felt a sudden flush. *Oh no,* I thought, *this is the exact feeling I get when a poison oak attack is coming on. But that's impossible. I made certain not to get any oil on me.*

But alas, that's just what it was. I could feel the itching start and my body's heated response of panic and anger. I went immediately into victim state, feeling sorry for myself. I envisioned great suffering and being out of commission for the ten days it took me on previous attacks to finally get rid of it all. Then I dimly recalled what the medicine man had been talking about all night—that the Great Spirit is present in all things working for the good. *Yeah, sure, how the hell could the Great Spirit be present in this bullshit!* Then I remembered the other main point he kept making throughout the night: "You have to give back to nature. It's not okay to just take. Every life is as valuable as the other in the eyes of the Great Spirit."

Then I thought back to when I cut down the poison oak. Yes, I had done everything right to protect my physical being, but I had not been conscious on the spiritual plane. In fact, I had been totally unconscious. In my fear of the poison oak plants, I had not once thought of them with respect or thought that their lives are valuable, that they have a spirit like mine. Yet the elder had basically been saying that very thing. I saw now how I had treated the plants with no respect, given them no explanation, offered nothing, no exchange for their lives. It had been an unconscious, fear-based act of destruction. Well, damn, I knew what I had to do now: I had to make amends for what I had done. I couldn't bring the plants back to life, but I could go back and apologize to them and make an offering to their spirits.

When I got home, I walked over to the dead plants. I kneeled down before them and took some tobacco out of my leather pouch. I looked around to make sure no one could see me or hear me, embarrassed to be talking to dead poison oak plants. Yet I knew I had to do it. Assuring myself that I was alone, I apologized for what I had done and asked their forgiveness. I sprinkled tobacco over them and said a prayer for their spirits. Then I began to wonder in how many other areas of my life I also took without giving, thereby creating imbalance and disharmony. I knew now that the poison oak attack was a very important teaching, opening up greater consciousness of my everyday activities.

I resolved that every time I felt the urge to scratch, I would catch that impulse and use the energy of it to search through my behavior to find areas where I took without giving. For the first time since the initial rush of the attack, I felt my anger and fear begin to subside. From that moment on, whenever I itched, instead of scratching, I examined my relationship with family, friends, and co-workers to find places of unconscious taking—and found plenty.

To my amazement, my poison oak was completely gone in two days, whereas I'd never before gotten through an attack in less than ten days, sometimes even two weeks. As I reflected on what had happened, I saw that I had absorbed the medicine, the spiritual teaching of the attack. *Whoa,* I thought, *the elder was right. Great Spirit is right in the middle of everything, working for the greatest good. I just have to open up to see it.* Once I got the message, there was no further need for the rash to stay on. Its teaching had been delivered, received, and honored. I was deeply touched by the power of this entire experience, plus thankful to the guidance of the medicine man who had helped me discover it. To this day I hold great respect for what I call the Poison Lady. I thank her for her powerful medicine whenever I see her. She helped me learn about "right relationship," the importance of balance between giving and taking. Understanding this dynamic helps bring healing power to the person who makes it a practice, for healing is a manifestation of balance and harmony in all relationships. Knowing this, we can act with power in all that we do.

Acting with power involves recognizing the source from whence it comes and realizing that we are never alone, that we are always in relationship to a living, breathing, intelligent universe that is trying to communicate with us. For shamanic people, that universe comprises seven directions from which power flows: below, above, the four "around powers" of East and West, North and South, and the seventh power, which is the Great Mystery whose presence is everywhere yet simultaneously in the center of all. Every indigenous people has its own understanding of these powers. Their symbols, myths, and creation stories differ in content but all share the respect for sacred mystery and the need for humankind to be in right relationship of sacred reciprocity with it all. My own newfound beliefs in these powers were put to a test of faith when I left the job security of the drug program in 1974 and went out on my own. During this time, I was forced to develop a whole new relationship to strength. It was either that or collapse into a paralysis of failure and depression.

This testing was the next step on the initiatory passage of the wounded healer—the call to power.

My father's death in 1949 had been my first call. With it, I was plunged into confrontation with destructive forces, which attacked my body, mind, and spirit. I was lost in self-pity and despair. It wasn't until the first vision of Christ, with its message of the existence of unconditional love, plus the grokking of infinity and the vision of a life lived in ancient Mesoamerica, that I started to wake up from my long period of shadow possession and began to consciously commune with spirit. Before that, I hadn't known that spirit existed or that I had a soul to reclaim.

My plan upon resigning from the drug program in 1974 was to start a private practice, offer retreats and workshops on what I then called "holistic education"—learning from nature and the ways of the indigenous people—and to work with the hospice program. I was fresh and eager, full of enthusiasm for what I had to offer. I distributed flyers describing my work, rented an office, went to all the mental health and social service agencies I could think of to let them know what I was up to. I anticipated an enthusiastic response. To my shock and chagrin, I got almost nothing back. The bills mounted, our small reserves dwindled, we had to go on food stamps, we were threatened with having our power and phone cut off when I couldn't pay the bills. I was a nervous wreck worrying how I was going to pay each month's mortgage. I felt humiliated, a failure as a man, a provider, a husband, and a father. Had the vision on my quest of jumping with all my might into the unknown led me astray? Was all this belief in the Great Mystery just a bunch of bullshit, my own imagination and fantasy run amuck?

I couldn't see what else to do except try to keep going forward with faith and trust that if I continued putting out what I believed in, literally and spiritually, something would eventually come through for us. I knew it was testing time and I was afraid that I wasn't strong enough to meet the challenge. Every morning, I got up before dawn, went outside, and purified myself with the smoke of burning sage. This was how I had been taught to release negative energies and open to Spirit. After purifying, I went for a run to a nearby lake to be alone with the forces of nature. There I stopped to offer my prayers to the seven sacred directions of power just as I'd been taught. First I faced the East. I'd time my run so I would get to my spot just as the sun rose up over the trees with its first rays of the new day reaching the spot where I stood.

Ho, Father Sun, thank you for shining today, for giving away your light and your love and bringing the life force to Mother Earth. Thank you for your teaching reminder of my true nature and for your power to cut through darkness. I get stuck in my darkness so easily so help me to open to your light and love and to extend it outward to my family and all who cross my path today. Thank you, Father Sun and Golden Eagle, you who fly highest in the sky and closest to Father Sun.

I then offered purified tobacco to the East, remembering my teacher's stress on giving and not just taking. Then I faced the South, trying as hard as I could to open to its power, the power of faith and trust, the fuel I needed to keep going.

Ho, Serpent of the South. Power of faith and trust. Power of innocence. Help me please, for I am weak and nothing without you. Help me to surrender to your loving presence as the newly born infant trusts it will be taken care of by the parents. Help me to be like you, Serpent, who sheds your old skin trusting that new growth is already on its way. With my body close to Mother Earth's body feeling her heart beat. I give thanks to you and pray for strengthening of my faith.

Then I offered my tobacco to the South, opening my heart and my mind to take in that power I needed so badly. Next I turned and faced the West.

Ho, Black Bear, you who show me your power up in the mountains, power of the looks-within place. I give thanks for you and pray for your life and the life of your people Thank you for the gifts of light and love, of courage and compassion, of peace and of healing, the gifts to be found by going within. Give me the strength to overcome my weakness and to honor the medicine gifts that I have been given and to bring them out successfully in the world.

Taking some more tobacco out of the medicine bag I had carried with me on my run, I offered it to the power of the West. Then I stood and faced the North.

Ho, Old Wisdom Elders of the North, those living and those who have crossed over into the spirit world. Thank you for your being, for your wisdom guidance. Like the rainstorms that come from the north, you bring new life. Help me to open to your wisdom teaching that Great Spirit is present always in everyone, everything, everywhere, and all the time. Help me to see you working for the greatest good in all the challenges of my life. Help me to walk the Good Red Road, from the place of the South trusting your presence, to the place of the North, knowing your presence always. Knowing you, loving you, and serving you.

After offering tobacco to the North, I knelt down and placed my hands on the earth.

Ho, Mother Earth, Spirit of Turtle Island. Thank you for the gifts of your creation. You open your body and give us the food we eat, the water we drink, the clothes we wear, the shelter of our homes. You give us teachings of how to walk upon you with harmony and balance and medicine when we are out of balance. Thank you for your mysterious, healing, growth power energy and your beauty. I pray for your health and your healing, that your sacred body, waters, air, and spirit be clean and fresh and pure and strong. Help me to open my heart and feel your heartbeat so I walk a healing path in harmony and balance with all of Creation.

Hiiiiyeeeeeeeeeeeeeeeeeeeee, I chanted down into the earth as I offered tobacco in a sacred circle. Standing up in the center of the circle, I then faced the sky.

Ho, Sky Father. You who are above. Father Sun and Grandmother Moon, you with the gifts of the feminine energy, the dream power, and intuition. Star people, rainbow spirits, thank you for your light and love, your company through day time and night time. Cloud People, thank you for your gift of the rains that come to quench our Mother's thirst. Help me to open myself to your medicine teachings, to your balance of the feminine and masculine. Thank you for the gift of vision. I give thanks to you who are above and pray for your health and your healing.

I threw some tobacco up into the air as an offering for the Above Powers, then closed my eyes and went down inside, down to my own center.

Ho, Great Spirit, Great Mystery. You have been always and you will be always. You are the source of all. You birth me and receive me when my life path is over as you have done for all who have come before. You are here now in my center and the center of all. Thank you for this day and the opportunity to know you and serve you. Thank you for my family and the work you give me to do. I pray for strength, Great Spirit. Please help me. I want to do the best I can to honor what I have seen to be true. Use me as a channel for your healing ways to help the people. I give thanks to you, Great Spirit, for you, I give thanks for right now. Hiiiiyeeeeeeeeeeeeeeee! Hiiiiyeeeeeeeeeeeeeeeee! Hiiiiyeeeeeeeeeeeeeeeeeeee! Hiiiiyeeeeeeeeeeeeeeeeeeee! I chanted out my thanksgiving, offering tobacco to the center of the circle.

This prayer work was the only way I knew to try to bring in spiritual nurturance, the juice I needed to keep going when everything looked so dismal. Afterward, I ran back to the house to make a fire and have some breakfast with Andrea and the girls. I tried to carry with me the energy I felt when doing my prayers. I visualized it going out into the world and bringing me to those people and situations that would help me materialize what I had to offer. I saw it helping people, which in turn would help my family and me. It was a long, cold, and discouraging winter. I had to constantly battle against depression and despair. *Work that power of the South,* I'd repeat to myself. *Keep your faith up. Springtime will come. Find the light within and keep shining it. Keep pulling out the weeds from your mind of pessimism, fear, defeatism, and feeling sorry for yourself. Remember Great Spirit is watching you. Trust the turning of the great medicine wheel, the growth process, and its mysterious timing. See it in your mind. Give thanks.*

I learned a lot about patience that winter. Eventually spring did come and the seeds I had planted all took—my proposal to teach a class on questing was accepted as a credit course at a local four-year college. I was asked to be on the counseling staff of a nearby theological seminary; my private practice started to pick up. We got off food stamps, paid the bills, and I felt good again, that I was providing for my family and doing it in a fully conscious way. My daily prayers gained renewed vigor as I gave grateful thanks in the woods each day for the gifts of increasing prosperity.

My faith muscles had been given a good workout and had grown stronger as a result.

My new understanding of what strength is really all about continued to grow in leaps and bounds when I started to work at the Center for Attitudinal Healing. There I met people like Debra. She was a high school student when she first came into the Young Adults Group where I was a cofacilitator. Debra was born with a congenital heart disorder and had undergone a number of operations during which she had almost died on more than one occasion. Her body was shrunken and weak from her ordeals. At times she came to the center with an oxygen tank in order to breathe. I was awed by her determination. Her spiritual heart was as big as a house though she professed no belief in God. But her strength came from somewhere, as over and over again she'd bounce back from one crisis after another. Through it all, she wanted to go on with her ambitious life plans, to finish high school and to have a career. *My God,* I thought, *Debra, you are lucky if you are alive tomorrow. I can't believe you want to take on more stress. Why not stay home and just take it easy? You sure have paid your dues in my book.* But Debra finished high school. She couldn't go to graduation because she was in the hospital, but she wore her gown to the center and we gave her a graduation party there. I'll always remember how radiant she looked. "I told you I'd make it, Tom!" she said proudly.

Debra didn't stop there. She was accepted into a business school in San Francisco. She took the bus into the city and got left off at the bottom of a steep hill. The school was at the top of the hill. You or I could make it up that hill in a few puffing minutes. It took Debra almost half an hour to get up to the door of the school. But damn if she didn't do it, not once, but all the times she needed to in order to graduate and eventually get a job and her own apartment. Debra, and many other children and young adults at the center, became my new models of strength. Their courage, their ability to keep going without bitterness or self-pity taught me about real strength, soul strength, about the healing power of inner peace. They helped me see that peace was within me always. Many times, I would inadvertently leave it, focusing my attention elsewhere. I noticed that when I chose to not get up first thing in the morning to do my prayers of thanksgiving, I was unconsciously giving my power away to an ego-based identification that ran mostly on fear and reactivity. Then I was ripe for what I call the "button pushers" of my life. These button pushers could instantly trigger a reaction of negative judgment and condemnation. Of course it was I who paid the price, walking around with a tightly closed heart. I lost energy and power and set myself up as a victim. *If only those bad button pushers would get their shit together, then I could have my peace back and be all right.* The only problem with this line of thought was that the button pushers never seemed to get it together and I seemed to be in reactive negativity far more than I liked. In fact, I didn't like any of it.

One of the strongest button pushers of my life was my mother-in-law, Val. She meant well but got on my nerves. I thought she was insensitive to my feelings, bossy, arrogant, had to be in control and get her way, loud and obnoxious, and always wanting to be the center of attention. I could get uptight just thinking about her, let alone being around her. For the first ten years of our relationship, we would either be in a state of hostile silence or else get in horrible fights that upset the whole family and ruined many a holiday gathering. It was all her fault, of course. If only she would stop being such a controlling bitch and behave the way I wanted her to.

Occasionally, I'd vaguely recall words of wisdom from my medicine teachers about how everyone is a mirror, showing you something about yourself. I'd hear from Gerry or others at the center that what you judge in another, you are denying in yourself. I'd believe this was true in most cases, but not with my mother-in-law. This went on for years. I figured that Val just wasn't open to looking at herself; she was too stubborn and just wasn't going to change or grow. Then once on a quest I had a very disturbing dream in which she and I got into a horrendous fight. I recorded it in my dream journal, which I had been keeping ever since I started going out on quests. Wouldn't you know it, two weeks later we were in Los Angeles visiting Val and she and I got into a huge brouhaha. I pulled away in disgust: *I can't do this anymore. Why does this keep happening?*

I went into the bedroom and slammed the door. I took out some sage and tried to purify myself from the bad feelings that were pouring through me. Then I noticed my dream journal lying on the floor. I opened it up and there was my dream of two weeks ago showing me the very fight we'd just had! Something clicked. I had to look within myself. *What have I been unwilling to see in myself and totally projecting onto Val? How weak can I be? I totally give my power away here and get pushed into acting out by the things she does.* For the first time in my relationship with Val, I let down my defenses and picked up the tools I had been learning and applied them to myself. I didn't like what I saw, but at least I felt like I was on a better track. I began to face, then own, that all the qualities I disliked in Val were those same qualities I didn't like in myself. How much easier it was to blame her as the bad guy and see me as the good guy. The only problem with that approach was that it kept us locked in combat and we both were losing, as was the family.

I wanted to create a win-win scenario. In order to do so, I had to use my power in a different way. Calling upon the wisdom of my visions and the principles of attitudinal healing, I saw that I needed to accept the truth of what was inside me and no longer project it outward. I also needed to reframe how I saw Val, not as a villain but as a teacher who was enabling me to see inside myself, to heal myself instead of wasting my energy on denial, self-righteous judgment, and attacks. In that moment, my heart began to open to Val for the first time. I felt love coming out of my heart and going into her heart. I thanked her for being my teacher and made a vow—that whenever I felt my buttons pushed, I would silently thank her for being my healing teacher and send her love. What happened next was a real miracle: Our relationship did a 180-degree turnaround. We started getting close to each other. I discovered she was deeply spiritual and we could connect on that level, talking about God in a way that she wasn't able to do with her own family. Over the years, our relationship deepened. We got so close that years later when she got cancer, which eventually led to her death, she and I entered into telepathic communication. When she was on her deathbed, in and out of a coma state, her daughter Chris, Andrea's sister who lived in L.A. and took care of Val at her house, would ask her how she was doing and Val would reply, "I'm talking with Tommi on the phone." I would get her message and call up to say what I had received. Upon confirmation that she was getting close to the end, I flew down to see her and say good-bye.

I sat bedside with her for hours, holding her hand and feeling the love between us. I connected with peace inside myself and then sent it to her. It seemed to help her settle down. I comforted her and filled her up with love. Tears rolled down my cheeks. What a waste it had been, all those years of fighting. Compared to this love that we now shared, all else fell by the way-side. I supported her the best I could in her letting-go process, helping her talk out her fears, her regrets. We prayed together, I prayed for her. We held each other. I thought back to the principle that everyone is either extending love or giving a call for help. I understood now Val's different calls for love over the early years of our time together. I also understood, in that sacred time of helping her birth back into spirit, that people who act in a hurtful way are simply crying out for love in the only way they know how. Yes, we do need to stop their hurtful actions, but for our own healing, we must see that they are hurting. "Do what you need to do," said Ram Dass, a medita-tion teacher who once met with members of the young adults group at the center, "but don't put the other person out of your heart."

I felt tremendous thankfulness to Val for all the love she had given me, compassion for her and for the hard times we had been through. *Keep your heart open and keep sending the love, no matter what's happening on the outside,* the inner voice said. I did, she did, and we went into a state of joining where there was no separation. Val died soon after.

The night of her memorial service, I awoke to light. I thought it was morning and went over to close the blinds so we could sleep late—Andrea and I were in one bed, the girls in another, and we had been up late and were worn out with sadness and grief. But just as the windows were closed years before when I went to stop the billowing curtains, so too were these windows and curtains both closed. But it was also dark outside. It was the middle of the night! I went back to bed and lay down. The light was at the top of the ceiling now. I looked right into it and there was Val. *Goodbye Tommika,* she said. *I am fine. Take care of my girls for me. I love you.* Then the light rose up through the ceiling and was gone.

The medicine of Val's passing wasn't over yet, however. While I was driving Andrea's car back up Route 5 on my way home, it began to sputter and jerk. Unfamiliar with the gas gauge, I had let it go past empty and was running out of fuel right on the freeway. I coaxed the car down the mountain, trying to get as close as I could to the gas station I had seen from the top. A mile and a half away, the car rolled to a stop. I coasted off the road and onto the dirt. I was in the San Joaquin Valley with cars and trucks whizzing past me in endless succession. I scooted across the front seat to avoid the traffic and opened the car door but drew back in shock. Just beneath my foot was a dead golden barn owl.

I got out to look at the owl. It didn't have a mark on it and its body was still warm. I reached back into the car and got my medicine bag. I knew right away the spirit of the owl was watching me and that this was a gift for me, a new power animal. I was nervous and didn't know if I wanted it. For some tribes, the owl is a harbinger of death, for others it is associated with sorcery and is considered bad medicine. I knew that I needed to make sure the owl's spirit was treated in a good, respectful way, loved and honored, just as I had tried to honor Val during her last time on earth and during her memorial service when I had spoken about our love and prayed for her oneness with the Great Spirit. As my elders had taught me, I took out some tobacco and spread it around the owl's body. Then I purified everything with the smoke of burning sage and offered tobacco and prayers for the spirit of the owl. I thanked it for its life and prayed for its family and for its journey to the light. As I finished my prayer, a soft voice gave me directions: *Cut off one of my wings and take it with you. Do not be afraid. I hunt power at night. I will help you see through darkness. I will help you see the light and hunt the power you need to turn death into life. Bury the rest of my body with respect. I thank you for coming to me. I brought you here to help me, so I could help you. It is a sacred circle. Carry on.*

I was moved by the circumstances of running out of gas at the exact spot where the owl's body lay. I looked up into the big Central Valley sky and marveled at the mystery of it all. *Ho, Great Spirit, thank you for all the gifts of your medicine. Help me to use it in a sacred way. Help me to honor the life of Val and this owl. Help me to use it all to honor you.* I completed the ceremony as I'd been directed, then jogged on down the road to the gas station, feeling lighter and stronger then ever. But it wasn't my body muscles that were growing, it was the "muscles" of my heart and spirit. Growing stronger in the shamanic belief system involves learning how power can be acquired, stored, maintained, and enhanced. Similar to the Chinese practice of *t'ai chi*, in which the practitioner learns to follow certain physical movements aligned with breathing down to *dan t'ien*, the solar plexus, in order to gather and store the flow of *chi*, i.e., life energy, so too does the student of shamanism learn to gather and store power in the body. Daily prayer practice with the seven powers, communion work with power animals and spirit guides, and regular quests and pilgrimages to sacred places all offer opportunity to take in power and increase its potency. Concurrent with acquiring power is the process of eliminating, or at least reducing, the patterns by which power is lost or given away unconsciously. "Energy leaks"— from heart-closing judgments, from fear, from not being in the present, from reactivity to button pushers, from identification of self with ego, from not being in alignment with one's heart path and in integrity with all your relationships, including those with the natural world—all weaken personal power. Stopping the leaks is a must. It involves a lifelong process of disciplined, focused intention and mindfulness practice. Without a consistent means of working consciously with mind and spirit in a sustained manner, the ability to move forward into integrated states of empowered higher awareness will never be fully achieved. Shamanism provides many means of time-tested, psycho-spiritual technology by which to do this work.

For the Huichol, a major path to power is completing the number of pilgrimages to Wiricuta proscribed by the shaman, along with satisfaction of the associated behavioral requirements and additional assignments, plus completion of a Bull Ceremony in the shaman's village. For other tribes that follow the path of the vision quest, each successive quest can be a way to increase one's personal power and take care of "leaks" if it is done in a sacred way. A key dynamic in the empowerment process for all shamanic groups of whatever path is, paradoxically, learning to work with the act of surrendering.

Western culture gives bad press to the act of surrendering. Surrender implies losing, as on the battlefield, General Lee surrendered his sword to

General Grant to end the Civil War. It carries the judgment of quitting. It wasn't until I crossed through the Buckskin Curtain that I learned another view of this act, one that served me well in working with a dying young girl shortly thereafter. My teacher was the same medicine woman who taught me about working with crystals. Surrender, she explained, is not the same as quitting. The latter is usually accompanied by feelings of anger, despair, frustration, depression, and lowered self-esteem; after all, you weren't good enough to win. Surrender, on the other hand, is a conscious choice. You voluntarily choose to take yourself and your burden—or whatever you are working on—to that which is higher than you, that which is bigger than you, the Great Mystery. You then surrender it into the infinite "hands" of the Sacred Mystery to work for the greatest good with divine intelligence, divine order, and divine timing.

Surrender is the work of the South, believing with faith and trust that there really is a divine intelligence working for the greatest good in all situations and circumstances even though we might see no evidence of this in all the injustices of the world. The faith muscle is strengthened when we exercise it not in times of seeming good fortune but in times when everything seems to be wrong. Then we find out what we really believe in. Sometimes our physical life, not just our emotional and psychological state, can be at stake when we are called to release what no longer serves us.

This lesson was pointedly brought home to me during a scuba-diving trip with a friend off the Northern California coast in the summer of 1986. Ruck was an old friend; we had climbed mountains, done many river trips together. Our families were close. A few years older than I, he was like the big brother I never had. He was a big, strong guy, an experienced diver, and loved outdoor adventure. On this particular outing, we were standing on a desolate shore looking out at the big breakers and trying to decide if it was too dangerous to go out. Our families were back on the beach enjoying a picnic. We figured it would be a real challenge getting out past the fifty yards of churning white water, but once past them, the sea looked smoother, with the promise of good diving. We decided to go for it. We put on our wetsuits, fins, tanks, and masks, then waded in and began to swim out to the white water. Soon the waves were smashing us about like little corks. I had to pull and kick with all my might to keep going forward. I was trying my best but I couldn't get enough air in my lungs to get my muscles to cooperate with my mind. I started to panic. The waves smacked into my face and I swallowed water. My weight belt was pulling me down as I tried to stay afloat. Frantically, I reached for the tube of my buoyancy compensator to try and blow it up so I would be able to float and overcome the downward pull of the weight belt. But I just couldn't get enough air into my lungs to breath anything out. I could see my family on the beach having a great time. *I'm on the verge of drowning right in front of them and they don't even know it!*

My mind raced backward to earlier events of the day. I had just gotten a new weight belt as a present from Andrea and I was eager to try it out. I went to the local dive shop and rented a wetsuit. It felt too tight when I tried it on in the store but the dive pro at the shop checked me out and said it was fine. First mistake on my part: I didn't trust the wisdom of my body and intuition and gave my power away to the expert. Well, damn it, it turned out that I was right and he was wrong, but I was paying the price. In the exertion of having to swim so hard, the muscles of my chest, arms, and back had pumped up and had nowhere to go. The wetsuit had become a straitjacket and I was imprisoned inside. No wonder I couldn't breathe.

The thought did occur to me that if I dropped my weight belt I would be much lighter and wouldn't have to fight so hard to remain afloat. But the blood supply to my brain was inadequate, so I wasn't thinking clearly. *Damn, I can't drop the belt, it's brand new. I'll never find it again.* So I kept the belt on and almost lost my life. But thank God for my buddy Ruck. He had been ahead of me in the water and hadn't realized at first the difficulty I was in. He was busy just trying to get through the breakers himself. But when he turned back, he saw I was about to go under. He swam back to me, and got right into my face, "Give me your weight belt, right now!" His command got through to my dazed brain and I unbuckled my belt and handed it to him. Immediately, I was more buoyant. I unzipped the front of my wetsuit and released my lungs from their imprisonment. Gulping huge gasps of fresh air, I blew some into my BC vest and got it inflated enough to hold my body afloat without any effort on my part. *Whoa, I'm going to make it!*

I leaned onto my back with my head toward shore and kicked my exhausted legs as hard as I could. Soon the momentum of the waves carried me to shallow water and I crawled onto the beach and collapsed like a clump of seaweed. It was a good twenty minutes before my breathing returned to normal. I looked up gratefully at Ruck. "Thanks for being there for me. You saved my life. I couldn't breathe. I couldn't let go of my new weight belt!"

So knowing what to let go of is the first step. The second is letting go with an open heart, which allows faith and trust a chance to breathe. "Surrender is a conscious decision to turn over to the Great Spirit whatever it is that is troubling you," said the medicine woman. "You give it willingly, without strings, fear, remorse, or dread. You are not going down. You are going up—to Spirit. It's not about quitting at all. It's about surrendering to what is higher than you."

This differentiation between quitting and surrendering stood me in good stead a few days later when I was asked by the mother of a fourteen-year-old with cystic fibrosis to make a home visit. I knew Jennifer and her mother from the Center for Attitudinal Healing but had not seen them for quite a while. Jennifer's mother greeted me at the door somberly. "She's dying, Tom. I can't help her. We tried everything and it hasn't worked." She was trembling but regained her composure and said, "She's downstairs in her room. She can barely breathe, even with the oxygen. God, I've tried to keep her from this and now it's here. I can't stand it." She began to cry. I reached out to comfort her but she stopped me. "No, go see Jennifer. I think she feels that she's letting me down by dying, that she's failed. Now she needs to let go and she's stuck. See if you can help her let go." I turned to leave, but she said, "Wait, let me show you her latest paintings." I thought it strange that she wanted me to see the paintings now, but I did what she asked.

She had told me previously how much Jennifer liked to paint, but I never imagined how good she was until I saw the six different paintings, all full of bright colors, happy animals, delightful scenes. But the last two really caught my attention. One was of a big mouth filled with toys, balloons, and candy. The other was of a helium balloon with a gondola rising up into the sky filled with a child and her toys. I understood immediately that Jennifer had things inside she needed to say and that some part of her knew she was dying—there it was in the painting, the release into the sky.

I took the pictures downstairs to Jennifer's bedroom. She was tiny, fragile. Each breath was a struggle. She had been fighting so hard for so long. Her eyes opened wider as she recognized me. I sat down on the bed and took her hand in mine. "It's good to see you again, although I can see you are having a really rough time," I said. "I know it's hard for you to speak, so don't worry, I don't need any words back from you. I'm just here to give you my love." She squeezed my hand and managed a weak "Thanks." I noticed a picture of Christ above her bed, then remembered her pictures. I picked them up and showed her the last two. "It looks like you have some things inside that want to come out. You can let anything out that you want to with me. Your mother thinks that you are ready to die but are afraid to because you think you'll be letting her down." Her face grimaced into a look of even greater pain. "Do you think you've failed and now are afraid to be a quitter?" I asked. Jennifer nodded.

"You know, I just had a conversation with a Native American friend of mine a few days ago and she had some interesting things to say about this. I think maybe it would be helpful to you to hear what they are. Are you open to that?" Jennifer managed a softly whispered yes.

I explained about the difference between quitting and surrendering, then gave her support for the battle she had waged for so long and so hard. She sure wasn't a quitter by a long shot, I reassured her. "But now your body is shutting down and you no longer have to fight. You can release, you can surrender to God, to Christ's love. Look," I said, showing her the picture of the rising gondola. "I think your soul, the part of you that does these happy paintings, already knows this and was trying to communicate it through this picture."

Jennifer's face suddenly brightened. It was the most energy I'd seen in her so far. "You really don't think I've failed?" she asked.

"No, I think you have won. You've finished your work here. Remember

Drawing by Jennifer Purvis

Will?" I asked. Will was a fourteen-year-old member of the children's group who died of Wilms tumor. I visited him at home the day before he died. Teacher that he was, Will looked at me and said, "You know, I think we all have assignments in life. When we finish them, we get to graduate. We go home. Some of our assignments are longer, some are shorter. That's why we're here, to work on our assignments."

Jennifer didn't remember Will, but she liked what I said. I could see a light come into her eyes. "So you mean I've finished all my assignments and now I can graduate?" she asked.

"Yes," I replied, "all but one. Your last assignment is to surrender your spirit into God's spirit, to get on the gondola and release it up into the sky. You are going right into God's light and infinite love. You're a winner, forever!"

Jennifer looked at the picture and breathed out a big sigh. "Please go get my mother for me, Tom. I need to talk to her real bad. Thank you. I love you."

I bent forward and kissed her on the forehead. "I love you too, sweetie. Thank you for being in my life. *Vaya con Dios.*" Go with God. I wiped a tear from my eye, got up, and went back upstairs to Jennifer's mother. "She wants to see you now," I said. "I think she is going to be okay. Just go be with her and let your tears come out and whatever else needs to. Jennifer can handle it. You don't need to protect her. She knows what is happening and is ready for it." I gave her a big hug, then left. She called me the next day to let me know that Jennifer died peacefully with her family around her, and oh yes, her pictures as well.

The power of conscious surrender continues to be a living practice for me. I am reminded of its rewards regularly. Once, I was counseling a woman I had known from a vision quest retreat ten years earlier. I hadn't seen or heard from her since then until one night when I got an anxious phone call asking for help. She was in the last stage of terminal cancer and wanted help with her dying. From my quest retreats, I know that one of my assignments in this life is that of midwife, helping birth people back into spirit. I also have role assignments as garbage man, gardener, and heart path warrior, but Barbara was definitely calling me in to perform in my role as a midwife. We scheduled an appointment, and Barbara filled me in on the last ten years of her life. She was a divorced mother of two children, had lived a hard life, and now in her early forties was coming to the end of the trail. She was concerned about her children and their relationship with their father after she was gone. She had unfinished business with all of them, and finally, she wanted help with her dying process. We spent time with each area she wanted to cover and I assured her I would stay with her up to the end and do all I could to support her in addressing what she had outlined as important to deal with before she died. At the end of our session, we held hands and sat in meditation. I prayed in silence.

Thank you, Great Mystery, for your presence here now with your healing power of light and love. Help us to open our hearts and know your unconditional love and forgiveness. Help me to be a channel for your love, extending it into Barbara. Help her to find the peace she is looking for and to use it as a force for healing in all her relations. Thank you for you, thank you for right now.

After a few minutes of silence, I heard the following instructions: *Give Barbara your big crystal, your favorite one. Give it to her clean, without any strings of wanting it back. Release all attachments to it and tell her it is up to her what she does with it when she is through. She can give it away, take it to the grave with her, or whatever she decides. Teach her how to use it, to draw out pain, fear, and darkness with her right hand, then purify with sage smoke, and bring in healing light with her left hand.* The crystal I was being asked to give was large and beautiful and I treasured it. I tried to bargain.

What about one of my other crystals, the clear two-headed one, or the one from Brazil?

But the voice was insistent. *Give her the big crystal and do it with an open heart, with no attachment.*

In order to comply, I first had to release and surrender to Higher Will with faith and trust. My mind raced backward to another time I was asked to let go of something I really didn't want to release. It was on another raft trip down the Tuolumne River in Yosemite in 1973.

The Tuolumne is considered one of the most challenging white water rivers in the western United States when it is running high. On this particular run, it was running full force through the deep canyons it had cut over thousands of years. This was a river trip sponsored by the Wilderness Treatment Program I was running with the drug addicts. We had a crew of mostly experienced rafters and I felt pretty good about them. But when we got out of the boat to scout out the run into Clavey Falls, I started to get nervous. The falls were about four and a half feet high and pounding. If we set up into the chute directly above it just right and stayed in position, we would hurl down the 150-foot approach, building up enough speed to shoot us right over the falls and past the huge hole that lay right beneath it.

We wanted to avoid that big hole. I well knew what holes were like and my nightmare experience years before was still fresh in my memory.

The captain of our raft, a "river rat" with years of experience, looked at the hole, looked at me, then looked at our crew. "Well, I think we can make it if we keep our line good and really paddle hard when we first hit the water after the falls," he said. Then he added with a chuckle, "But just in case we don't make it and somebody goes into the hole, don't try to fight it. There's nothing there to grab on to. It's only air and foam. Just allow yourself to be sucked under. After a while, you'll hit bottom and then you'll catch some downstream water. If you let go into it, just let it take you, it will pull you out of the hole and into the river itself. Then come up to the surface and you can swim to shore."

It sounded simple enough, one of those clean, neat theories that you hope you never have to test out in real life. I could feel my stomach tighten as he told us the formula for getting through the hole. "Let's do it right so we don't have to find out if the theory is true or not," I said to our crew. I saw tension in every face. As we walked back upstream to our waiting raft, I prayed for safe passage, vowing to paddle like a maniac to help get us through.

We took our positions in the boat and waited for our captain's commands. "All right," he said, "let's go get 'em!" We paddled out to catch the current and were immediately swept into its roaring maw. Like a bullet, we shot toward the falls. Oh my God, we were out of position! "Straighten it out, right turn, hard right!" yelled our captain. We pulled as hard as we could, but it was too late. We hit the falls at a 45° angle instead of straight on. We roared over the abyss and slammed into the river. Our bow was past the hole but the rear of the boat didn't clear it. "Pull hard forward, *now* damnit!" came the frenzied command. The next thing I knew I was sucked out of the boat and into the hole. *Oh God, not again!* Then I remembered the formula. Down into the hole was the last place in the world I wanted to go, but I knew it was my best chance of getting out. I relaxed my body and let go, surrendering to the ferocious pull downward into the foaming depths. Down the chute I went, holding my breath and trying to stay upright. After what seemed a lifetime of watery descent, I thought, *Well, it's just about time to hit bottom and catch the downstream water.* No sooner did I finish the thought than I did hit bottom. My body was yanked out of the hole and thrust into the downstream current with tremendous force. Relieved to be out of the hole, I was still petrified because I was also still under water. My lungs were about to burst. At that point, my mind kicked in again: *Well, it's just about time I hit the surface.* No sooner was the thought finished than my head bobbed up into fresh air. *Hallelujah!* I gasped for air and kicked madly. A few minutes later, I was safely on shore, catching my breath and checking for others. We were all okay. I let out a whoop of joy. "Thank God old Ken knew what he was talking about with his formula!" I yelled.

Now, as I sat in silence with Barbara, listening to the inner voice telling me to surrender my prized crystal, the memory of the surrender experience on the Tuolumne reminded me of the wisdom of letting go. *Okay, okay, I'll give it to her,* I said to the voice. I opened my eyes, opened my heart, and gave both the crystal and my love to Barbara. She was delighted. She gave me a big hug and held the crystal over her heart. "This is going to help me do what I have to do. Thank you, Tom." She left for home and bedrest, and I left for the center to facilitate a children's group. When I arrived, there was a letter for me from the mother of an eleven-year-old boy with whom I had worked in the children's group for several years and with whom I had gotten quite close. Billy had died almost one year before. He was a very sweet boy with a gentle, loving heart. He and his family lived out in the country with horses and farm animals. His favorite horse was Apache. Whenever I visited Billy in the hospital to help him with his visualization exercises that he used to overcome the vomiting effects of his chemotherapy, he would hold tightly to a feather I had given him and think about his horse. "Close your eyes, Billy. Use the feather to imagine yourself as a great big bird. Raise your wings upward now and fly back to your farm. See yourself landing on Apache and riding through the fields, totally enjoying yourself. Tell me what you see." Billy's body would soften. He would smile and imagine an adventure that he and Apache would have together. His nausea would disappear and he was happy.

But after years of attrition, the cancer had finally eaten up Billy's body and he died just one week before coming to the next scheduled children's group at the center. I didn't know it at the time, but he had found something on his last ride with Apache that he planned to give me at that group. Now, here was a letter from his mother, one year after his death. We had talked on the phone a number of times, I had worked with her and Billy's siblings and father, helping them to deal with their grief, but no mention was ever made of this gift from Billy to me. I took the envelope into the group room and closed the door. I opened it carefully. Inside was a letter and something wrapped in tissue paper. I read the letter first. In it, Billy's mother explained how Billy had found a gift for me and was excited to give it to me. But then his death had pushed the gift out of her mind and it wasn't until a year later that she picked it up and mailed it to me. Tears came to my eyes. Slowly, I opened the tissue paper. To my astonishment, a beautiful feather fell out and glided gracefully to the floor—a golden eagle feather! In shamanism, the eagle is considered one of the holiest of creatures; it flies highest in the sky and closest to the Great Spirit. To have one of its feathers was a gift I had never even imagined. But even more touching was the timing, the connection between receiving this gift and having just been previously "told" to give up the crystal to Barbara.

Great Spirit, I said softly, *thank you for helping me hear your voice and surrender what was never really mine to begin with. Thank you for helping me see that we never really own medicine. We are just the temporary caretakers. Thank you for helping me see the sacred connection of the circle. Thank you, Billy. You sure were a good listener in life and now you are helping me from the spirit world. Thank you, little brother, thank you, Eagle Spirit. Thank you, Barbara.*

I went into group with the kids and shared what had just happened. They too were touched by the circle of giving and receiving. One youngster reminded me of a relevant principle of attitudinal healing when she commented, "When you gave the crystal to Barbara with love, you opened the door for God to give back to you, Tom. Then Billy gave his love to you through that feather. I bet he's still riding Apache!"

It was through experiences such as these that I learned that the pathway to real power lies not with taking but with giving from an open heart with no strings or attachments. As the bible says, "As ye give, so shall ye receive." The ability to give in this way is based on the act of surrender. It takes a particular kind of strength to surrender, to cut through ego grasping and desire, but it is through this surrender that one is filled with the power of spirit with its ever-present gifts of inner peace, healing love, and forgiveness.

The following short story, told by Sufi teacher Idries Shah in *Tales of the Dervishes,* speaks eloquently to the process of surrender and to its ample rewards.

A stream was working itself across the country experiencing little difficulty. It ran around the rocks and through the mountains, then arrived at a desert. Just as it had crossed every other barrier, the stream tried to cross this one, but it found that as fast as it ran into the sand, its waters disappeared. After many attempts, it became very discouraged. It appeared that there was no way it could continue the journey. Then a voice came in the wind. "If you stay the way you are you cannot cross the sands, you cannot become more than a quagmire. To go further, you will have to lose yourself."

"But if I lose myself," the stream cried, "I will never know what I'm supposed to be."

"Oh, on the contrary," said the voice, "if you lose yourself you will become more than you ever dreamed you could be."

So the stream surrendered to the dying sun. And the clouds into which it was formed were carried by the raging wind for many miles. Once it crossed the desert, the stream poured down from the skies, fresh and clean, and full of energy that comes from storms.

It is an interesting irony that my pathway to learning about the power of surrender and a new understanding of strength came from two sources: from people who were weak physically from illness and from people whose culture was weakened by five hundred years of oppression that began with the invading armies of Europe. It is, as the wisdom elders say, a Great Mystery.

4

~~~~~

Healing the Sacred Circle

The Four Laws of Ecology: There is no such thing as a
free lunch. Nature knows best. Everything is connected to
everything else. For every action there is a reaction.
BARRY COMMONER, *THE CLOSING CIRCLE*

I n Northern California, just fifty miles below the Oregon border, sits
Mt. Shasta, a huge, volcanic mountain rising up more than fourteen
thousand feet from the floor of the San Joaquin Valley to its snow-
covered summit. It is considered to be a place of spiritual power with
many mythic stories about its other-worldly inhabitants. Some speak of
huge bells within a body of hollow chambers. Others think it is a landing place for UFOs. For the indigenous Pit River people, whose ancestors have lived by the mountain for thousands of years, it is known as
Akoo Yet. They believe it was the first mountain made on this earth.
The Creator placed within Akoo Yet a little spirit, Mis Misa, with a
big responsibility—to maintain the balance between the earth and the
universe. Mis Misa does her work by singing. When visitors, or pilgrims,
come to this holy mountain with clear purpose, with respect, with open
heart, when they come to be still and listen to the song of Mis Misa, then
Mis Misa is supported in her work.

But when people come to Akoo Yet and do not listen to the song,
when they come without respect and humility, then gradually Mis Misa
stops singing. If people continue to tread upon her without listening, then
Mis Misa will leave. If she leaves, say the old people, then the delicate

balance between earth and universe will be struck asunder, causing disharmony, imbalance, chaos—which, of course, is what we have today.

When I first came to the mountain, I did not know anything about Mis Misa. I was on a car camping trip with my family. We arrived at the mountain about one o'clock in the morning. All we could see were shadows in the darkness. We drove up the road as far as we could go, parked our VW bus, which was the de rigueur means of transportation in those days, and tried to fall asleep on the floor of the bus. But I could not. I felt a huge presence looming behind me, an energy field that would not let me do anything except know its power. I couldn't wait until daybreak to see what it was all about. Finally, I dozed off, only to be awakened some time later by the sound of clanking metal. I sat up and peered out through the window of the bus. It was still dark but the sky was beginning to lighten. All I could see was grey-white landscape slowly coming to life. Peering into the rising mist, I saw the outline of two figures walking past the bus with ice axes and crampons swinging from their shoulders, heading northwest. *Ah, they're climbers,* I thought. A surge of excitement shot through me. *I've got to come back someday and climb here too. I've got to go to the source of the power.* I crawled out of my sleeping bag, put on my down coat, my boots, wool hat, and gloves, and opened the door of the bus. Stepping out into the frigid air immediately shocked away the last vestiges of sleepiness. The light of predawn was just arriving from the eastern gateway. I looked directly ahead and there it was: looming higher and higher into the sky, it looked endless. I traced its trajectory as the first rays of light illuminated its snow-covered shimmering white beauty. I fell in love.

Since that time, I have returned to this magnificent holy place on a regular basis. It has become a yearly pilgrimage that I make with a group of twelve people who have been working with me for a year in a shamanic healing and empowerment group, learning, among other things, how to empty ourselves to listen to the song of Mis Misa. We go to the mountain with the goal of climbing as high as we can as a team. But high is measured not just in physical terms; it is also measured in terms of how we stay in touch with each other—with hearts and spirits opened and

Moonrise over Mt. Shasta (Akoo Yet)

Photo by John Jackson

united, listening to Mis Misa and her teachings. Every time I have gone to the mountain, even when I first went just to climb it and didn't know it as Akoo Yet but still had tremendous respect for it, I have received a major lesson through a major adventure. Mis Misa speaks loudly to those who listen.

On my first climb, 1973, I learned about not letting desire impede judgment. We three climbing partners were exhausted as night descended and we still hadn't reached the summit. I wanted to camp where we were, thirteen thousand feet up in an exposed snowfield without a tent, because I did not want to lose the altitude we had gained. Eric, the youngest but most experienced mountaineer of our party, went on ahead to check out the route. I stopped with Ed, who was suffering from the debilitating effects of altitude sickness, to rest until Eric came back. I was dizzy and weak myself, but not as bad as Ed. I spread out an Ensolite pad on the snow and Ed quickly collapsed on it. I collapsed next to him. The extreme seductiveness of sleep began to overcome me. *Just close your eyes for a few minutes,* it said. *How wonderful it will feel. Come with me, I'll give you everything your aching body desires.* I started to release into the open, beckoning arms, drifting into sleep, when a soft voice of warning said, *No! Get up! Wake up Ed. You'll fall asleep here and freeze to death. Stand up! Walk him around. Get the circulation going. Stay awake until Eric gets back.*

I fought through my exhaustion using the freezing air to clear my head. The sun was going down. Eric was nowhere in sight. Ed was out. I reached out and shook him violently. "Get up, Ed. We're going to walk around. Come on, buddy, we've got to do it." Ed was in a stupor but I pulled him to his feet, threw his arm around my shoulder, and walked him in circles around the pad that could have been our deathbed. Despite my fears and determination to keep walking, I could feel my energy draining down to its last supply. Thank God, Eric appeared in a few moments. "Let's get over by those rocks and dig out a shelter," I said. "I'm beat and Ed can barely move. I think we'll be all right with some rest and then we can go for the summit in the morning."

Eric shook his head. "No, we're going back down to base camp. The temperature is dropping too low and we won't make it if we stay here. If a storm comes, and it just might," he said, pointing off to the west where threatening clouds were rushing toward us, "we don't stand a chance. We've got to get down to our tent as soon as we can!" I didn't like the tone of urgency in his voice. Eric was usually a very calm guy. I knew he meant business.

I glissaded back down through Avalanche Gulch, a twenty-five-hundred-foot steep sliding board of snow, ice, and boulders. I descended in fifteen minutes what had taken us two and a half hours to cover on the way up. In camp, I set up the stove and started heating hot water for tea and soup for Eric and Ed, who were somewhere behind me. The sun had now set and darkness covered the mountain. I hoped Eric would be able to find our tent up on the barren ridge where we'd set it up the night before. When he didn't show up for a long time, I started to holler his name. The echoes spun around the peaks before finally disappearing into a dark void. A few minutes later, I was greatly relieved to hear Eric's voice booming back. "I'm almost there. Come give me a hand." We got Ed into camp and with the hot drink and food, he slowly came back to life. It didn't storm that night, but the temperature dropped into the teens. We probably would have survived up at the thirteen thousand-foot plateau if we had followed my impulse, but it wouldn't have been pleasant and I was very glad that Eric was adamant about returning to base camp. The next morning on our drive home, I opened a book lying on the seat. There was a discussion of safety rules for winter mountaineering. I laughed to myself when I read the first one, "Do not let desire impede judgment."

My more recent pilgrimages to Akoo Yet brought teachings that had been sneaking up on me for quite a while but only came through with the help of Mis Misa. They had to do with my new understanding of power. Early conditioning as a male in this culture is always about pushing harder to get what you want. So I did this with weight training, with running marathons, with mountain climbing. But even though I trained hard to be in good cardiovascular condition with plenty of physical strength as well, I'd still get tired every time I went mountain climbing, tired enough to be unable to fully enjoy being there. My last two climbs of Akoo Yet changed this whole driven push pattern. Now I know I can still push when I need to and sometimes that is precisely what is needed in a given situation, but I have found a much better way to accomplish my goals both in the mountains as well as back here in the lowlands.

A climb in 1993 with members of the year-long healing group demonstrates how I discovered this new approach to climbing. The night before the climb, we gathered around the fire. We were in our base camp at 9,600 feet. The stars were sparkling like diamonds in the rarefied high mountain air. The temperature was below freezing and dropping fast. We huddled inside our parkas, leaning against each other for added warmth. I took out my drum and warmed it up over the flames. Before us loomed the gigantic shadow of the mountain we would try and climb the next day. Wake-up call would be at 3 a.m. We had to be out of camp and on our way so we could make it up through dangerous Avalanche Gulch before the sun came up. Otherwise, the sun would begin to melt the snow and ice, loosening the rocks and boulders above and turning the gulch into a bowling alley of rockfall shooting by like bullets. Most of the rocks were small, but not all of them. Some were as big as your head, some as big as your chest. Occasionally a rock as big as a car came shooting down. You could hear them coming, then have an instant to duck and hope you duck the right way. Not everybody does. People get killed up here every year or worse—smacked by a boulder and pulverized, not enough to kill you, only enough to maim you. So I made sure to get us up early enough to make it through the most dangerous part before it became a bowling alley.

As we pulled closer to the fire, I placed sage into the flames to give thanks for its gift of light dancing with the shadows of the cliffs and the starlight. I gave each person some purified tobacco and we went around the circle offering our prayers for a safe journey.

Ho, Mis Misa, Spirit of Akoo Yet. Thank you for your beauty and your power. Thank you for allowing us to come here and be with you. Help us to be with you in a good way, a sacred way. Thank you for your medicine song, the work you do for us all. Thank you for all the Native people who have been coming here for thousands of years to pray and to listen to your guidance. I pray for their protection today. I pray for your protection from the forces that do not yet see that you are a holy one. Help us all to open our hearts, Old One, to listen with respect to your wisdom song of harmony and balance so we too may learn how to walk in balance for the healing of the sacred circle of life. May it be so.

I finished my prayer, then listened to the prayers of the eleven other members of our pilgrimage. One man spoke worriedly about the dangers. "It's possible that we won't all be here together tomorrow night," he warned, looking toward the distant summit. "The powers here are very strong and we are not in control of them " He prayed for our safe passage. We all added a hearty "Ho" of affirmation. "May it be so!" When each person had spoken, I picked up my now warmed drum, its skin stretched taut by the heat of the fire. "Now is the time for us to call in our power animals. With the beat of the drum we will send them up onto the mountain to get whatever information and guidance they can that will help us with our climb." During the year, we had worked to connect to our power animals, dancing them out and sending their spirits up to the mountain. Now, we were finally here in physical form.

The beat of the drum began slowly. After a while, I felt an energy pouring into me that was playing the drum by itself, as though I were the one being drummed. I closed my eyes and called in Kauyumari, the deer spirit. *Thank you, Kauyumari, for all you do for me helping me on my path. I appreciate you and I love you. I want you to go up on the mountain and listen to Mis Misa. Ask her to tell you what is most important for me to be aware of tomorrow as we come up onto her body. Ask her for the wisdom guidance that will best help me be with her in a way that is for my greatest good and for the greatest good of our group. Ho, thank you, Kauyumari.*

I felt Kauyumari enter my body and whisk my spirit up to the heights. I expected to go to the summit. To my surprise, Kauyumari took me right into the center of the mountain. There I saw the heart of Mis Misa. My awareness went straight into her, blending and joining until there was no sense of "me." Then I heard her speak: *Listen to my heartbeat, grandson. When you climb tomorrow, go slow enough so that you can stay in touch with my beating heart with each step. Don't get ahead of me. I will give you heart. You do not have to climb the mountain by yourself. To try to do so will be a mistake. You are never alone. Your strength is puny compared to the strength of the forces that created me. Keep your heart open and connected to mine. Sing your Deer Song. Kauyumari will carry you up the mountain on its back. But only if you stay with my heartbeat.*

The next thing I knew, I was back in my body, still playing the drum. I looked up at the ridge of Akoo Yet, deep gratitude in my heart. *Ho, thank you, Old One, I will do my best. Thank you, Kauyumari. I will sing your song up to the top!* We each spoke about what we had gotten from the drum journey and then went to bed.

Three o'clock came very quickly. I woke the others, had a quick hot breakfast, and by four o'clock we were on our way with flashlights and moonlight to guide our steps. I tried my best to follow the instructions I had been given the previous evening. I used the pounding of my heart to remind me to stay open to Mis Misa's heartbeat. I sang the Huichol Deer Song silently as we snaked our way up the mountain. Eight hours later, I stood atop the summit with five others. Tears flowing, wind blasting, we hugged each other and offered our prayers up to the Great Spirit and the powers of creation. There was nothing above us but the free space of the heavens. The landscape spread out below us for hundreds of miles. We each signed the summit register, left our prayer offerings, and posed for pictures while wolfing down candy bars and drinking from our remaining water supply. I took stock of my feelings: elation, exhileration, and gratitude to all the members of our group and to all those who had come before. I felt connected to them all. In the midst of all this jubilation, I was delighted to notice that I felt no fatigue whatsoever. On other climbs, I'd also been elated to reach the summit but was exhausted as well. This time, there was no fatigue, no aching muscles. *I've got to remember this,* I thought. *I need to bring Kauyumari into all the mountains of my life. No more climbing alone. This is the way to do it—with spirit leading the way and me following. Spirit's got infinite juice, mine is drastically limited.*

The descent began uneventfully, although I reminded people to be extra alert because this is the time most accidents take place; you subconsciously think it's over because you are on your way down and so you don't pay as much attention as when you were climbing up. We were fine until we got to an icy section of a steep, narrow gully lined with sharp volcanic rocks. I demonstrated how to go slow using the ice ax as a brake, and we got down on our butts and started a slow slide through the gully. One woman lost control of her ice ax and started shooting down the chute at breakneck speed. There was only one person who could save her. At the last moment, he reached out and grabbed her just before she smashed into the rocks. I didn't see this because I was up higher in the chute helping another member of our group who was frightened by the steepness and needed some reassurance. When I reached the point where they sat collecting their breaths, I saw their ashen faces and knew something drastic had happened. As I listened to their story, my knees went weak. A split second off and we would have had a very different outcome. *Thank you, Great Spirit, thank you, Mis Misa. You are opening my heart even more than on the summit. Thank you for this gift of grace.*

We made it down safely the rest of the way, humbled by our near miss and our newly sensitized awareness of the thin thread that separates being here from not being here. Lying in my bag that night, looking up at the jewels of the night sky and thinking back to the events of the past twenty-four hours, I was overwhelmed with emotion. *We're safe, we're all well. Thank you for your protection, Great Spirit. Thank you for showing me how to honor your teachings about following you, dear Spirit, and you, Deer Spirit Kauyumari, in whatever I do. Help me to use your power, Mis Misa, to never forget how to live my life in this better way.* After my prayer, I fell into a deep sleep and didn't awaken until the new day was breaking over the horizon.

The next morning, we had breakfast, said our farewell prayers of thanksgiving, and headed back down the three-hour hike to the parking lot and our waiting cars. Turning around for a last look at the peak, my mind went back to another mountain, another climb where I had received a gift of grace in the form of a teaching about relationship to spirit, one that came exactly when I really needed it.

In the summer of 1984, I had been hired as a consultant by a Fortune 500 corporation to help them develop a motivational film for their national managers. The film would introduce a training program teaching skills to sell a new product in a new market. Mountain climbing was the metaphor to be used in selling the training program. I'd train two of their managers, flown in from around the country, in the skills of rock climbing. Then I'd lead them on a roped climb with microphones taped to our bodies and a film crew shooting our every move. I helped them develop a basic plot with dialogue for the climbing section of the film, then with the help of a climbing friend, scouted out a route to climb. It had to be one that was visually dramatic, within a few hours of the San Francisco Bay Area, and with good access so the ten-person film crew could get in with all their gear. The climbing footage would be interwoven with footage of the managers working in their office, taking part in the new training program, and then selling successfully in the new market the company was planning to enter. The basic idea was that just as I trained the managers how to successfully climb a mountain, so would the new training program teach the managers to successfully climb the mountain of a new and challenging sales market.

I met the managers on a sunny Saturday and we spent the weekend learning how to safely ascend and descend the face of a cliff. The managers were nervous but game. Both were athletic, one man and one woman, mid-thirties, personable and outgoing. We had a good time together. It was easy to see their leadership qualities and their adventurous attitude. We finished off our Sunday session in good spirits. I assured them they would enjoy tomorrow's climb and that they were capable of doing it. We set up our meeting and location time for the next day and said goodbye.

I drove home excited about working with Mike and Dee. That evening, I packed up all my gear, had dinner with Andrea, Kimberly, and Nicole, then went to bed early. I'd have to leave at three in the morning to reach the climb site by our agreed-upon time of 6 a.m. The film director estimated a ten-hour day and our location, Pinnacles National Monument, would be baking in over 100-degree heat by mid-afternoon. I hoped we'd be off the exposed face of the mountain before it got unbearable.

Despite my intentions for a good night's sleep, I couldn't relax. I tried all kinds of relaxation techniques, meditation, listening to soft music, but nothing worked. I was too wound up—scared to death, actually. I kept seeing the route of the climb. The first hundred feet or so were okay, but then there was a section that was very exposed and had only tiny, flimsy holds for my fingers and toes. It was precisely at this point when I most wanted the security of my hands and feet anchored to the rock that I'd have to take one hand off the rock, reach down to my climbing belt, and unhook a small piece of protection to fit into a crack, then snap a carabiner through it and hook it into the rope. I had to put protection in that spot specifically because there was no other place to put it for the next part of the route. Without protection, a slip could turn into a bad fall, something none of us wanted, especially me, since I was first on the rope and the most in danger. So this is where my mind kept returning as I tried to fall asleep. I had done the climb before but not when I was the lead climber. My previous climb there, I had been second on the rope, so while I had to climb over the scary point, I didn't have to worry about placing protection; it had already been placed there by the lead climber. This time, I'd have to do the whole show myself and I was scared at the prospect.

Had I gotten in over my head? Would I fall and blow the whole operation for everybody involved, thereby demonstrating my ineptness as a climber, costing the company time and money, and undermining my ego and my safety? The images in my head were of failure and disaster at the moment of truth. After hours of tossing and turning in fruitless effort to fall asleep, I finally tried a new tack. *Face your worst fears,* said my inner voice. *Stop running away from them. You're exhausting yourself and getting nowhere.* Nothing else had worked, so I had nothing to lose. I looked at my worst fears—that I would fail at the climb, that everyone would know that I was no good, an impostor, that I'd fall to the rocks below and be killed, or worse yet, fall and not be killed, just mangled and have to live the rest of my life in that condition. I certainly didn't want to create any of those outcomes. I accepted them as possibilities but resolved that I'd give it my best shot the next day to prevent them from occurring and that's all I could do. Interestingly enough, just by facing my fears, I noticed they began to lose some of their charge and soon thereafter I fell asleep.

The alarm clock blasted me out of my short slumber. I got up and staggered to the bathroom. My stomach tightened as soon as I remembered why I was getting up so early. I knew I needed help. I picked up one of the books on the window shelf. It contained spiritual passages from different traditions. I opened it up to the middle of the book and peered through groggy eyes to see what it said. It was a quote from the bible. Jesus again. "I and my Father are one." Reading the words brought me immediate relief. *Oh yeah, I'm not alone in this. Great Spirit is with me.* I marveled at how quickly my fear makes me feel totally alone. I obsessed in my place of darkness like a dog chasing its tail. Reading this one quote broke my mental set, the stuck loop I'd been in, and gave me some breathing room. A small ray of faith started to shine into my scenario of doom and gloom.

At the sink, I lathered on some shaving lotion. Grasping my razor, I stood up straight and looked into the mirror. I bent forward and put the razor up to my face. Before I could begin, a miracle occurred, a total gift of grace at 3:15 in the morning in my bathroom. A band of light appeared and circled my waist. From my waist, the light went straight up from the front of my body into the ceiling, through the roof of the house and straight up into the heavens. I was stunned. Then I heard the comforting words, *You are on belay to God. You are always on belay to God.* (*On belay* is the term climbers use to communicate to one another that the rope is secured to the climber's waist and to a secure setting on the cliff and it is being held tightly by the nonclimbing partner of the team. This safety system prevents a slip from becoming a disastrous fall.) The voice continued, *No matter what happens on the climb today, you cannot fall out of belay to God.*

I knew that what I had just heard was true. God was always present and available in infinite supply. My whole body instantaneously relaxed and I became calm. I felt renewed, healed, and filled with spirit and enthusiasm for what lay ahead. I saw myself at the crux of the climb. I stopped what I was doing, closed my eyes, and visualized the line of light secure around my waist and rising above me into the steady belay of the Holy Spirit. *I and my Father are One,* I repeated. Then I visualized my hand moving smoothly off from its hold on the rock, down to the waiting climbing nut on my belt, then effortlessly and successfully placing the protection, enjoying myself in the moment, and moving on to complete the climb. *I and my Father are One,* I affirmed over and over again as a mantra while I finished shaving, loaded up my gear, and set off down the road.

The climb itself was flawless—smooth, successful, fun. What I call the "Flow Master"—a magical being with the awareness of an accomplished *t'ai chi* master or *aikido sensi,* who knows how to "flow it, glow it, and grow it"—was leading the way. He is the one who knows in the depth of his being that "I and my Father are one." He is the one who rides on the back of the deer all the time, the one of effortless action moving in harmony with the flow of nature in the holy moment. When the "I" of my ego identity gets out of the way and surrenders to Spirit, when it grounds into Mother Earth consciously offering body-being as a pipeline to be used by Sacred Mystery without attachment to form or outcome, then the Flow Master materializes and does his dance. So it was on the mountain that day.

I used my morning mantra to help me remain open and present with my intention—to feel connected and one with spirit in everything that transpired. Meeting up with the anxious climbers, the producer, the film crew, setting up the gear, tying in to the rope, taking off on the climb, getting to, and through, the hard, scary part of the climb, getting to the top and whooping for joy, belaying Mike and Dee up the route to successfully reach the summit themselves with even louder whoops than mine, the filming all coming out well on a spectacularly beautiful day of clear blue sky and sunshine, all this and more, flowing smoothly with tremendous feelings of accomplishment, teamwork, joy, and through it all, gratitude for the presence of Great Spirit guiding the way. The belay line of God's light held secure for everyone and everything. *Pam'pa Dios, Great Spirit,* I said, which is "thank you" in Huichol, *for your teachings of right relationship and the great light that connects us with you and with all things. Help us all to see what we can do with the acts of our lives that will honor the truth that we are all related. Ho. May it be so.*

5

⸱⸜⌣⸝⸱

Befriending the Darkness

It is the wish of Wakan Tanka that the light enters the
darkness that we may see not only with our two eyes, but
the one eye which is of the heart and with which we see
and know all that is true and good.

BLACK ELK

U*h-oh, here it comes.* The awful, nauseous, churning feeling in the pit of my stomach for the past half hour was now roaring upward through my chest and windpipe and I knew there was no holding it back. I fell forward onto the ground and jammed my face into the hole I had dug earlier. No sooner did I hit the moist, cool darkness than the first tidal wave erupted with full force. My body shook with its impact as vomit spewed forth followed by gut-wrenching, hysterical sobbing. I was a four-year-old boy again, mourning his father's death. Tears of grief locked up for so long that it clogged my pipes poured forth like lava from an erupting volcano. I sobbed uncontrollably. More vomiting, then the wails of a wounded animal crying out for the loss of its beloved, a near-mortal wound to its soul. Sounds I had never heard before, that I didn't even know were in me. I had done years of grief work in counseling and on my own. I was quite familiar with the clinical dynamics of grief. But this—this was coming from a place I didn't even know existed. Tears mixed with vomit and mucus—the hole was rapidly filling

100

up. But I felt fantastic, purging old energies that had been inside me for years locked up tight, robbing me of vitality and life. Oh God, it felt so good to let it come out however it wanted to.

At long last, it was finished. The eruptions stopped. I felt like I'd been Roto Rootered and was now sparklingly clean. I rolled over onto my back gasping fresh air into my now unburdened lungs, which had held on to my unexpressed grief as a young boy and turned it into asthma attacks. Now they were free. I was free. *Thank God,* I thought, remembering the words of a black spiritual sung during demonstrations for civil rights in the 1960s. *Thank God Almighty, I'm free at last!*

I looked around me and all I could see were shadowy figures in the darkness. It was my last night of my first pilgrimage in Mexico, 1981, and I was lying by a warm lake in the mountains with my fellow Huichol pilgrims, each of us sitting or sprawled somewhere along the lakeside. I thought back to how the evening had begun. We'd all sat around Grandpa Fire doing our final ceremony of the trip. Traditionally, the pilgrimage finished up at the ocean, but for a variety of reasons we were not doing that. Instead, we had come to this lake, La Laguna del Oro de Santa Maria, wherein resided one of the power allies of our shaman, Doña Andrea. Having made our offerings to the spirit there, we then watched as a storm came in from the northwest. To my amazement, I saw a burst of energy rise from the lake and ascend to the top of a nearby mountain crest. I knew immediately that it was Doña Andrea's ally. In fascination, I saw the ally reach out and grab the approaching storm front, then pull it from the top of the peaks right down into the lake. Strong winds doused us all in gusts of pouring rain. We huddled together while trying to grab our gear, which flew madly about in the battering winds. I looked at the lake. It had become an ocean filled with big waves and crashing surf. We couldn't get to the ocean, so the shaman had brought the ocean to us! After a few moments filled with mysterious power, the ally retreated into the lake and the storm passed on. An eerie peace fell over our camp. No one spoke. The winds had blown all our words away.

The shaman beckoned to me from across the fire. She saw that I was troubled. While thankful for all the gifts I had received on this life-changing adventure, I still had some painful areas that had not been touched by any of my experiences so far. The shaman nodded to the basket next to her filled with peyote gathered in Wiricuta for the people of her village. "Take one of those Grandfather Peyotes down by the lake and face the mountains on the other side," she said. "Watch for Metserli, Grandmother Moon, to rise up between the two peaks. Then take the medicine and open your heart to its teachings. It will show you what you need to see. It will show you the truth."

Eligio holding harvested peyote in Wiricuta

Photo by Max Poppers

Fear crept up my back. I believed that what she said was right and that if I did as I was told, I would see the truth about whatever was bothering me. My fear was about facing it without the delusionary comfort of my defense mechanisms. I also didn't know if it was right for me to take medicine again. I acknowledged that Doña Andrea knew a lot more about these things than I did and that she had a lot more "mojo" going for her than I did, but it still didn't feel right to give my power away to her. "*Muchas gracias,* Doña Andrea, I will go off and think about what you have said," was my reply.

I left the fire and went off into the darkness alone. Sitting down on my sleeping bag, I leaned against a tree and wondered, *What are my worst fears?* I plunged down into my depths seeking answers. At the bottom, I found them. *Something happening to my family and something happening to me, turning me into a helpless, dependent, paralyzed cripple.* In facing my fears, I had to accept that these outcomes I so desperately wanted to avoid were all possibilities that could in fact happen. *But,* I affirmed, *while they are possibilities, I do not want to do anything to bring them to me by my thoughts and worry. I face them and I release them. If they do come at some time in the future, I will deal with them then, if I must. But they are not here now, so I release them into the Great Mystery and instead give thanks for the gifts of loving family and good health.*

After finishing this process of working with my worst fears, I realized that I did feel right about following Doña Andrea's guidance. I went back to the container and picked out *el grande,* a large peyote. I went and sat down by the lake facing the mountains as the shaman had suggested. I purified the peyote with sage from my medicine bag. Then I remembered an admonition from my first Native teacher: "Give back to the Source before you take for yourself." So I dug a hole in the ground next to me and carefully placed within it an offering of the first bite of the peyote. Then I held the sacred cactus up to my heart and prayed.

Ho Hicouri, Spirit of Hicouri and Mother Earth, thank you for the gift of this medicine. Help me to take it inside and open myself to however you would speak to me. I am seeking the deepest healing that I am capable of right now. I thank you, Great Spirit, for the gifts of this pilgrimage and I pray for the life of the Huichol people and for all the indigenous people of the world. May they survive and their wisdom ways be seen and appreciated by the rest of us so that we can find our way back to a life of respect and harmony with you and all of Creation. Pam'pa Dios.

Finishing my prayer, I carefully cut away the outer bark of the root of the peyote, placed it reverently in the hole I had dug, and slowly ate *la medicina*. After my bout of cleansing and relief, I was happy. I welcomed the feeling of relief, but it did not last for more than a few precious minutes. Then the medicine came up and grabbed me again and took me down into the depths for another look at what I needed to see that was blocking my pipes. This time I saw a vision of myself at twenty. I was with Andrea and we were spending the night together for the first time. We were staying at a friend's house whose parents were out of town. To my horror, I saw a moment when Andrea, so beautiful and innocent, was kneeling by the bedside to say her evening prayers. This was before I had experienced my spiritual opening, so I was a cynical atheist who believed religion was the "opiate of the masses," only for the weak who could not deal with reality. I saw myself ridicule her and how she recoiled at the impact, how I wounded her right at the time of her greatest opening and vulnerability. She contracted and withdrew and it had been a wound in our relationship ever since and I didn't even know it was there. Coming to the pilgrimage, I had been concerned about a spiritual rift between Andrea and me that had been there ever since my initial opening with LSD. I felt distance and resistance from her toward my new-found interest in spirituality and practice of shamanic ways and I didn't really understand it. I just knew that I was hurt by it and wished it were different. Now, as I saw the vision of how I had hurt her many years ago, I understood how the rift had begun. I broke into sobs of remorse and despair at the pain and suffering I had caused. *What an insensitive, arrogant asshole. What can I ever do to make up for it?*

The response came back from the depths of the hole that I was once again lying over, face down, to pour out my misery: *Face what you did. Accept that you can be an insensitive, arrogant asshole. Apologize to her. Accept her hurt and whatever other feelings she has about what happened.*

But then, the guidance went on, *forgive yourself. Remember the teachings of Christ on the cross about judgments closing your heart. Open your heart to yourself as you face your own darkness. Don't cut yourself off from Great Spirit's love. The love is for giving. Give it to yourself, for that is the first step on the pathway of healing your relationship with Andrea. Do it now.* And so I did. Wiping the spittle from my face, I sat upright and gulped in breaths of the fresh night air. I dipped my cupped hand into the soft waters of the lake before me, bringing up a handful of water to splash on my face. How good it felt! Then I opened my heart to the waters of the Christ consciousness guiding me to the love in my heart placed there by the Great Spirit. I released my self-condemnation and another floodgate opened. The waters of loving forgiveness washed through my soul.

The work in Mexico of facing my worst fears and repressed feelings was one important step on a long path of facing my inner darkness. Confronting darkness is a basic task in shamanism, and it is part and parcel of all initiatory rites. It is the "work of the West." The West is where the sun sets, plunging the world into the darkness of night. Taupa, Father Sun, drops into its "looks-within place," the place of introspection. Like the great bear entering its den for winter hibernation, the work of the West requires initiates to go within and face their fears, their shadow monsters, and most significantly, the inevitability of their own death. This is the gateway to finding the gifts that live in the depths beneath fear and within shadow—the gift of wisdom from "the place that knows what you don't know," the gift of inner peace, of light and unconditional love, of soul healing, power, courage, creativity, and ecstatic joy. There are no ways around, under, above the gates of the West guarding these treasures. Resistance is natural. Most of us are much more comfortable dropping our shit into convenient receptacles that take it out of sight, out of mind.

I remember when I first started doing quests in the mountains. It was 1972. My teacher emphasized the importance of paying attention to my dreams. I started keeping dream journals at that time and have kept them ever since. Shortly after I began, I had a dream that was particularly disturbing to my self-image at the time. In the morning, as I recorded the dream, I suddenly caught myself halfway through changing it around so I wouldn't look like the scoundrel I had been in the drama of the dream. I was shocked to discover how my unconscious was running the show while I thought I was fully conscious! I laughed out loud. *Who are you fooling, Tom? No one else reads your journals. You're fooling yourself, you fool, and you don't even know it.*

That moment with my journal was a significant turning point for me. I realized then that precisely what I was trying to hide from by changing my dream around to make me look good was what I needed to face. I decided to write down in my journal a list of everything I didn't like about myself. It took quite a few pages to record all my negative judgments, but it opened the door to a whole new approach to dealing with my dark side, which I'd previously repressed, run away from, or projected onto someone else—my mother-in-law, or Andrea.

Years later, leading a group of gringos interested in shamanism, I faced the dark side in the Andes Mountains of Peru where the possibility of physical death was not just symbolic but real and present. It started in the city of Cuzco, at a *brujo,* or sorcerer's, stand in the crowded marketplace at the center of town. I had gone there with Hannes, an Austrian man who had been living in Peru for years. Hannes was an apprentice of the shaman who was guiding our journey. The *brujo* stand consisted of a wooden bench with two sides extending up to a roof composed of a few boards from which all kinds of strange objects, forms, and figures were either hanging, nailed, or housed in various containers of wood, glass, animal skins, or dried-out entrails. And that was just the containers. I could smell the pungent aroma of this strange concoction of exotic substances before I saw the stand itself. When the stand was finally visible, its ominous, dark energy was strong enough to stop you in your tracks and make you think about a new direction to walk. A young woman from our group who was with us, an adventurous flight attendant from New York, swooned onto the dusty ground of the *mercado.* Before she even hit the ground, several Quechua women from nearby stalls were at her side, rubbing who knows what onto her face, arms, and neck. She came to after a few minutes and the women vanished back into the marketplace before we could thank them for their assistance.

While the flight attendant rested a safe distance away, trying to regain her senses, Hannes showed me some of the *brujo* stand's mysterious wares. There were charms for hexing, charms for fighting off a hex, strengthening a hex, protecting against a hex. Hannes bought me some small, hard, red seeds with a black spot on them, a glass vial filled with what looked like the contents of the bottom of the pot used by the witches in *Macbeth,* and some Peruvian incense used for purification. He told me they were for protection and that I "just might need them." I sensed a malevolent presence about the place that grew stronger the longer we were there. I wanted out.

Later that night, our group drove up into the mountains outside of Cuzco. Our destination was an ancient Incan initiation site, the Cave of Darkness and the Cave of Light. Leaving the cars, we hiked by flashlight down a trail to a flat area at the base of some cliffs. There the shaman carefully set up his *mesa,* an altar of sacred power objects. On one side of the altar were the "tools of light," on the other side were the "tools of darkness." In the middle were the tools that gave him access to whatever side he wanted to work on. He said a few words of explanation about all this, translated by Hannes, then stated, "Be very careful in this place. There are many sorcerers around here who might try to harm you. Stay close by my mesa and you will be safe. Do not wander off. You may not be able to return." He went on to say that we would be doing a very important ceremony here, as people had been doing for thousands of years. Each of us would be spending some time alone in each of the caves. For now, he said, "Think about your intention and why you came here. Soon you will enter the Cave of Darkness and if you pass the first test, then you will be able to go into the Cave of Light. But now quiet your mind and be still."

He lit some candles and began chanting, then whistling, all the while shaking his rattle to the four directions. He had many bottles filled with potions he had mixed. Some he gave us to drink, some he poured up our noses. Some he spit onto our faces and some he blew into the air. The potions, the chants, the power of the place, and the extreme altitude all combined to take me into a state of heightened awareness. I looked up at the cliffs in front of us that housed the caves. "Whew, I wonder how this is going to go," I whispered nervously to the person sitting next to me. Then the shaman motioned me up to the front of his mesa. Hannes was translating and I was very glad for his presence. I trusted Hannes. He felt like a spiritual brother, following his own shamanic path to knowledge and power. We had gotten close on the trip.

The shaman handed me a large, sharp sword that had been sitting on his mesa. He told me that I would lead each person up to the Cave of Darkness and leave him or her there for a period of time. I was to assign one of our group to stand guard outside the cave while the other person was in it. The guard wasn't to enter and the person inside was not to come out until I came back for him or her. When I did, he instructed, I was to then lead that person on a path through the mountains up to a big cleft in a massive cliff that separated the two caves, where he or she would be met by someone and asked a question. If the answer was correct, I was to lead the person the several hundred yards further to the Cave of Light. *"Comprende?"* he asked. *"Si, si. Yo comprendo,"* I answered knowing full well that I didn't really know what I was actually taking on. Hannes then led me up into the dark cliffs away from the light and warmth of human company. He showed me the routes to the caves and then brought me back to where the others were sitting before the shaman's mesa. The ceremony intensified, with the shaman singing and rattling over each participant. Then he signaled me to take the first person up to the Cave of Darkness. I picked one person to be a guardian of each cave and Hannes led them away. Then I took the hand of the first initiate. He stood up and followed me away from the group. I led the way, holding tightly to the sword I had been given to cut through any obstacles that we might encounter.

All went well as we wound our way up to the cliffs and the opening in the massive bulk of rock that was the entrance to the cave. A candle burned at the entrance, but beyond that there was only darkness. The cave retreated far back into the mountain with many side chambers leading off from the main passageway. At the entrance, huge pictographs were carved into the walls, of serpents and elephants and other indecipherable figures dating back to the ancient Incan empire. People had been coming here for a long time. Now it was our turn.

Photo by Mark Montgomery

Meditation in sacred cave

I left the first initiate and walked to the Cave of Light. The guard was standing there, ready to receive the first person. A candle burned at this entrance as well, but inside there were other candles illuminating the cave as far back as I could see. Satisfied that all was well, I completed the loop back to the shaman walking alone through the rock field and very glad to make human contact when I emerged from the darkness. I sat down and joined the others and the ceremony, which was still going on. My body was hypersensitive to the energy around me and it didn't all feel good. After a while, the shaman motioned me to take the next person up. I went over and took her hand and led her up to the first cave. Leaving her at the entrance, I went in to get the one who had been waiting. As I brought him out, I sent her in. Then I took him to meet the questioner. I stood back away from them where I could not hear what was being said. After it was over, I came forward and took him over to the Cave of Light, then returned once again to the safety of the shaman's mesa.

As I sat down with the others, I noticed that one of our group, Misha, seemed to be in an agitated state. Wouldn't you know it, the shaman indicated she was the next person I was to lead up to the cave. I went over to her and took her hand. Gently, I pulled her arm to indicate it was time to go. She pulled back with great force, sending a jolt of violent energy into my body. I looked into her eyes. Her pupils looked like saucers. She seemed possessed by some evil force. A chill went up my spine. The shaman was right. There was a terrible presence here and it had struck our group. Misha tried to pull me to the ground. I felt she was trying to pull me into the depths of hell. I fought back, feeling that if I allowed her to pull me down, I'd be sucked into the same force that had captured her. I yanked back on her arm as hard as I could and pulled her into a standing position. She fought back like a wildcat. While shorter than me by several inches, she outweighed me by twenty pounds at least. She was stocky and strong and now she was fighting with the power of a mad woman.

We wrestled back and forth as I tried to pull her toward the cave and she tried to pull me down into what seemed to me the depths of darkness. I was frantic. The only thing I was clear on was that I had to protect myself and that the only way I was going to get her to the cave was to knock her out and then drag her there. I was furious at her for causing all this ruckus and I was furious at the shaman for allowing it to go on. Why didn't he step in, this was his show, why the hell was he just sitting there not doing anything? I felt trapped. Just as I was reaching back to punch out the hysterical woman, the shaman finally spoke: "Let her go. Take the next person." With tremendous relief, I dropped her arm and she slumped to the ground. Glad to be done with her, I went over to escort the next person to the cave. Upon completing my shuttling responsibilities, I sat down amidst the huge boulders that lay at the foot of the cliff. I needed some time alone to compose myself and come to terms with what I had just experienced. Possession, sorcery, evil. What had I gotten myself into? Little did I know it was just a harbinger of what lay ahead.

No sooner had I returned to the circle than one of the women in the group rushed up to me, shaking with emotion. "Misha tried to kill me," she gasped. "She grabbed me by the neck and tried to strangle me. I had to fight for my life. I almost passed out, she's so strong. But finally I got her off me."

"Did anyone try to help you?" I asked.

"No," she replied. "Nobody did anything. She's crazy, she's flipped out. I had to fight for my life."

I looked over at the shaman. He was still sitting there by his mesa, chanting away. I looked around the circle for Misha. At first I didn't see her. *Great,* I thought, *she must have run off into the night and I'm going to have to look for her.* Scanning the darkness, I finally saw her passed out behind the shaman. I walked over to her with dread. Her breathing was okay so I let her lie there. At least she wasn't causing any problems that way. The shaman motioned me to take the next person up to the cave and so in a moment I was off on my rounds again.

Shaken but resolute, I returned to the group after each cycle of shuttling people, wondering fearfully what had taken place while I was gone. Fortunately, there were no further disturbances from Misha or anyone. I started to relax. But my anxiety returned on my last cycle when I glimpsed two shadowy figures ducking behind a rock. *Great, just as it's getting to be my turn up here and with no one to stand guard for me, I'm going to have to deal with whatever those shadows are about.* I didn't look forward to finding out.

After I delivered the last person back to the circle, the shaman told me to go up to the Cave of Darkness alone, but to make sure I took his sword as protection. "Stay there until you know you have finished what you came to do. Then walk over to the Cave of Light and stay there until you feel complete. Then blow out the candles and come back here. *Buena suerte,*" he said. Good luck.

I walked slowly off into the darkness, feeling completely on my own. I clutched the sword tightly and hoped for the best. As I approached the Cave of Darkness, I saw the shadows again, two of them just to the right of the entrance to the cave. *Something is out there and it's stalking me.* I recalled the terror I felt when I looked into Misha's eyes. I trembled. *I don't know if it's* banditos *planning to rob me or evil projections of sorcerers or both. What should I do?* Retreating didn't seem like an option. Scared as I was, I knew that I hadn't come this far just to be turned back at the moment of truth. Fate had brought me to these Andes mountains and I wanted to find out why. *What's the worst that could happen to me?* I reasoned. *Jumped and killed* was the prompt reply, *by men or demons.* I gripped the sword tighter, thrusting it into the dark night to feel its power and bolster my shaky confidence. It was razor sharp and had been in the shaman's family for generations. *Mucho kupuri,* as the Huichol would say—strong energy. Bolstered by its formidable presence, I called up my inner warrior and moved forward. *If I get jumped by real people or evil spirits, I'm going to fight like a mad dog and it's going to be a hell of a battle. If I win, great, but if I lose and I die, either way, I'm going to be right there with it up to my last breath. I'm going to squeeze all the growth and awareness out of it that I can because this may be my last dance.* Surprised by my own burst of bravado, I noticed that I was no longer frightened. My whole energy state had shifted and I was clear as a bell. I felt ready, strong, determined, and at peace with whatever lay ahead. I was delighted to see that my strongest feeling was curiosity—I wanted to see what would happen.

When I reached the mouth of the cave, I stopped and looked around. I couldn't see anyone or anything that looked out of place, but now I was about to enter the cave and in there I would be at the mercy of whatever entered after me or already lurked inside just waiting for my arrival. I called up protection energy and sent it into the cave. *Don't fuck with me,* it said, *or you'll pay dues!* Having announced my presence, I strode forcefully into the cave. Fear tried to take over but I refused to give it power. Inside the cave, I used the light of the one candle by the entrance to get my bearings. The ceiling was about eight feet high and the width about ten to twelve feet. The passageway went forward into the belly of the mountain, getting narrower and darker as it went.

I walked slowly forward, my sword at ready. Each step seemed to take an eternity, every nerve ending at full alert and ready for action. Making my way deeper into the darkening tunnel, I saw there were several side passages that led off from the main chamber. I felt called to enter one of the larger ones. I walked ten feet in and stopped. One voice in my mind said to stand and face the entrance because that way I could see if anything or anyone came in after me. But another voice said, *No, stand with your back to the entrance. Face your vulnerability. Face your fears. Surrender into it. Honor the work you are given to do here.* I didn't like this guidance, but I followed it anyway. I knew that any other way would just reinforce fear.

I walked to the middle of the side chamber and stood with my back to the entrance. I felt totally vulnerable. *Surrender to God's presence,* I whispered. *Stand here and stand tall, take it all in. Stay open. Breathe. Keep your* kupuri *up and flowing. Don't rush to get this over, be here fully.* But every little sound from "back there" sent shivers down my spine. The urge to turn around and see what was there was enormous. *No, don't turn around. Stay here holding your ground!* I knew I was being tested and the implications of how I did would bear fruit in my future. Calling on every fiber of my being, I disciplined myself to overrule the tremendous urges to turn around. Steadfastly, I maintained my position of vulnerability and held my ground. I have no idea of how long I stood there, but I didn't want to leave until I had reached a state of relaxation. That would be my victory. I stayed with it until I got there and then I knew it was okay to turn around. I had passed my test. I turned very slowly, wondering if some attacking force was just waiting for me to see it before it pounced. To my great relief, I was alone.

I walked back into the main chamber and stood, peering into the depths of the cave. Suddenly, I pulled back with a start. Something was there. The hair rose up on the back of my neck. I didn't have a chance to prepare myself because in the next instant whatever it was came roaring out from the back of the cave and slammed into me like an electric current that sent me spinning. It's hard to describe or even know what happened next. Energy raced through my body. I felt like a twig in a tornado. As my body spun around and around, I heard the force speak: *This is the Dance of Darkness. Do it if you ever want to call me forth from the back of the cave.* Want it, hell no. This was from hell! It was evil personified. I wanted nothing to do with its awesome power.

Then in a flash, it left my body and raced back into the dark recess of the cave like a tidal wave returning to its source, leaving me shaken to my core. There were forces here in the mountains of Peru that I had never encountered before. Yet as shaken as I was, I was also thankful. I had been given a special gift—to see the face of evil and not be harmed by it. "I'm definitely ready for some light after that," I said out loud as I hurriedly made my way out of the Darkness Cave, blowing out each candle as I'd been instructed. It was a great relief to get out into fresh air again. I filled up my lungs and released my tension with a loud breath, *whoosh,* and then went straight into prayer: *Thank you, Great Spirit. Thank you for your protection. Thank you for my life!*

Nierica (cosmic doorway)

Photo by Jeff Anderson

I walked carefully but as quickly as I could through the boulder field to the entrance of the Cave of Light. Peering inside, I welcomed the illumination of many candles. I thanked the power of light and eagerly entered its domain. I followed the well-lit main passageway all the way to its end. Then I sat down, closed my eyes, and dropped into silence. Even with my eyes closed, I was aware of light. It was the light of love and it was coming from the wisdom elders of the North; I could see them clearly. They were the ancient ones who had completed themselves in their lifetime and had transcended into spirit. They were in their own ethereal cave, many of them, white-haired grandmothers and grandfathers. They were very happy that I had come and they were pouring their love into me. *Pick up your drum,* they said, *play for us and we will come closer.* My drum—I had forgotten all about it! I had strapped it on my back and with all the adventures I'd been going through, I had forgotten it was there. I began to beat it quite softly at first. Its reverberations bounced off the walls of the cave, picking up energy, returning amplified tenfold. The more I played, the greater the opening between the ethereal Cave of the Elders and the physical Cave of Light. The light intensified with each beat of the drum until I was bathed in it. It felt wonderful. I played harder. Every cell of my body, then my entire atomic structure and the spaces in between, were infused with ethereal light flowing from the Cave of the Elders into the Cave of Light. I played on blissfully.

Ho dear grandmothers and grandfathers, wisdom elders of the North, thank you for bringing me here and allowing me to be with you in this way. I open to your love. Help me, old ones, to be strong in knowing your presence always and to turn to you when I need guidance. I see you are present for all of us when we take the time to open and listen to you. Your love and wisdom are infinite. You are a channel of Great Spirit's love. Help me, old ones, to be a channel for you.

The drumming, prayers, and healing light went on for what seemed like eons. Then, very gradually, the light began to dim and I knew my time in the Cave of Light was over. I was sad to go but I knew I couldn't stay. I knew also that the elders were now traveling with me and that there was no place I could go that they would not be there for me whenever I turned to them in a respectful way. I left the Cave of Light feeling as light as a feather, my body floating and my heart filled with joy.

When I returned to the circle, I found the group sitting together in silence, the shaman softly chanting. I sat down next to him and watched him work with the sacred objects on his mesa. Sometimes he would pick up objects from the dark side, sometimes from the light. Sometimes he would pick up objects from the middle area, the objects that connected the two sides, the two energies, and go back and forth from one to the other, weaving his hands up and down in dancing spirals. After a while he stopped, looked up at the sky, then around our circle, and spoke: "Sometimes you have to call up the energy of the dark side when someone comes to you who has been attacked by an evil sorcerer. That is the only way you can heal them. You can't heal them with the light. You have to call up the darkness energy to fight off the attack and send it back to where it came from. So it's good to know how to do that. After you have finished pulling it out and sending it back to the sorcerer, then you bring in the light and send it into the person you are working with to complete the healing. So you have to work with the dark first. *Remember that.*"

I listened carefully to his words, reflecting on my experience in the Cave of Darkness. I felt thankful for the gift I'd been given there, but I hoped that I would never have to call on it. It was very strong medicine and I feared its destructive power. I had known enough darkness in my life. The path of light is definitely the path for me. A few days later, during a ritual on the Death Stone above Machu Picchu, my choice for light was strengthened even more.

First we traveled by bus, then a train ride through the lush Peruvian countryside as it followed the roaring Urubamba River. The sound of crashing waves joined with the clickety-clack of the railroad tracks to produce a wonderful Peruvian concerto. At the end of the line, we disembarked and took a rickety bus up steep switchback trails, where the wheels precipitously skirted the edge of the road. At least half a dozen times, I wondered if the bus was going to plunge over the side. The fates were with us however and we arrived safely at the holy city. But the place was jammed like Coney Island on a busy day, with people jostling and shoving to get through the gates. I was glad when evening came and the numbers dwindled. The shaman bribed a guard to let us in after hours and we had the place to ourselves. Us and the spirits. Walking silently without the hordes, I felt an ancient power radiate from each carefully placed stone.

The shaman led us up a steep path to a site above the ruins. He stopped by a large boulder twelve feet long and close to six feet wide. It was shaped like a boat with a broad flat section right in the middle. He taught us a chant and then we sat in a circle around the rock. His apprentice went to the front of the "boat" to help pull it. He told me to go to the back and at his signal to start drumming. Each person in turn would come forward to lie spread-eagled on his or her back on the flat section of the rock. The shaman sat next to the person and called in the spirit of the black panther of the West. The chanting and drumming provided the boat's "lift-off," and with the help of the panther, each person was taken to his or her "death." This was necessary so that we could die into our true selves—children of the sun, which is what the ancient Inca believed themselves to be. For this to happen, we first had to bring our false self of ego identity to the altar of death and surrender it. Thus, we could be reborn in fullness with our essence, the light of spirit.

I watched each person come up to take a turn. They lay absolutely still on the stone for twenty minutes or so. During this time, the shaman waved his hands over their bodies, stopping here, twisting there, doing a kind of psychic surgery—opening certain areas, closing others, moving energy from one place to another. I was caught up in the ebb and flow of the drumming and chanting. Images of barges on the Nile carrying passengers into the death realm floated by. Finally, it was my turn, again last. I handed my drum to Hannes, who came from his position in the front of the boat to the back to drum for me. He instructed someone else to take up his position in the front and to pull as hard as possible when the chant picked up speed.

I got into position on the rock, lay down, and closed my eyes. *Open up to it, Tomás,* I thought. *Die into it.* I flashed back to a time on Mt. Shasta when three mountaineering friends of mine and I were hunkered down with all our gear in a three-man tent during a vicious winter storm.

*Author's drawing of an image
of death that came to him on
a visionary journey*

We were in a very vulnerable position, perched on a platform we had cut
out of the ice-crusted cliff with our ice axes on a steep ridge overlooking Avalanche Gulch. We were hoping the storm would blow by, but it
had been thirty hours and the winds were just as fierce as when they had
started. The tent was taking a terrible beating and we didn't know how
long it would hold up. All we could do was lie in our sleeping bags and try
not to smash our elbows and feet into each other's faces. If the eighty-mile

per-hour winds that were battering the tent had their way, they would pick it up from its fragile moorings and hurl it down the cliff with all of us wrapped in our sleeping bags like stuffed sausage.

We huddled inside, hoping and praying the tent would not let us down. The monotony of the forced idleness, the cramped conditions prohibiting movement, and the drone of the wind took me into a trance state—half awake, half asleep. My mind shifted into reverie. I saw myself and the others atop a very high peak whose cliffs plunged straight down from alarming heights. On one side was the sea, sending thunderous tidal waves up the side of the cliff. Each successive wave rushed closer and closer upward to our precarious perch. I knew it was only a matter of time until the roaring waves reached the summit and swept us to our deaths. Then it occurred to me. Why wait there passively and terrified? Why not take matters into our own hands and go forward into our fate as warriors? I turned to the others. "Let's wrap ourselves in this blanket and roll down the mountain right into the waves. Why sit here waiting?" The others all agreed, so we wrapped ourselves tightly in a blanket and pitched ourselves over the cliff.

It was dark as ink inside the blanket but I remember the feeling of tumbling down the mountain in free fall, racing toward the abyss. I braced my body for the impact of the waves and wondered what it would be like to be torn to bits by the force of a tidal wave. It seemed like an eternity that we fell and fell. Each instant, I expected to be hit, but it didn't happen. Finally we were still. I opened the blanket and looked around. We were on a beach. It was a warm, sunny day and the ocean before us was calm. We stood up and walked down the beach, marveling at the surprising outcome to our decision to go into our deaths. Awakening from my reverie, I shared my vision with my tent mates. Perhaps due to our crowded quarters they didn't appreciate it much. Shortly thereafter the storm picked up force and we decided the tent couldn't hold out much longer so we came down to a Sierra Club hut in the woods below to wait out the storm.

The impact of my vision on Mt. Shasta reinforced my growing belief in the process of facing whatever was there in front of me. *Go right into it and stay present with all your awareness to get as much growth out of it as you can.* Recalling this formula helped me surrender into the shaman's hands on the Death Stone of Machu Picchu. The drumming and chanting picked up intensity as soon as I closed my eyes. The rock itself seemed to start moving. I was busy tracking the movement of the shaman's hands above my body when out of the west came a ferocious black panther. It charged straight at me. Ten feet away, it went airborne with a mighty leap and crashed right into my chest. Razor-sharp teeth ripped through skin, bone, and muscle, tearing out my heart with one mighty swipe of its massive jaws. I plunged into darkness. For the first few moments, all was stark, empty, dark. But then I became aware of stone steps beneath my feet. I started to ascend a very steep and narrow stone staircase that wound upward as far as the eye could see. I was not in my body. I had no body. I was only awareness ascending. After what seemed like a long period of climbing an endless flight of stairs, the "I" of my awareness suddenly burst out from the enclosed stairwell, rose upward at warp speed into the heavens, and finally merged into the searing light of the sun. Now there was only brilliant light, nothing else. There was no separation, no body, no personality, no physicality—just the blazing light. It was beatific, peaceful, total oneness with infinite radiance.

How long I remained in this ecstatic state I do not know. At one point, I saw a body far down below me lying on a big rock. The next instant, I was back in the body listening to the sounds of the chant, the beat of the drum, and the grunts of the shaman. When he finished, there was only silence. Slowly I opened my eyes to see what was out there. Night had come to Machu Picchu, but all I saw was light, vibrating in everything and in everyone. I saw my "reborn" body as vibrations of light as well. *So this is what the Incas were into,* I thought. I felt a new sense of connectedness with them, understanding how the journey on the Death Stone purifies you before you enter the holy city. I felt ready to enter it myself now. For I too was a reborn child of the light.

I thought about my given birth name, Soloway. *How amazing, Sol-o-way, Way of the Sun, the Wisdom Way of King Solomon, it was there from the very beginning.* I felt deep gratitude to the shaman, to my father, and to this new ally who took me into my death—the black panther of the West.

I also saw that this solar journey was similar to the one on my Huichol pilgrimage in 1981 with the eagle and the serpent, and each experience required some form of death and dissolution in order to reach light. The conditioned response of my youth—running away from fear, insecurity, or intrapsychic conflict of any kind through alcohol, denial, and macho posturing, just didn't cut it any more. The challenge was to face them fully with awareness and an open heart. The teachings of the medicine path were unequivocally clear: Everything was a potential *nierica,* or doorway, into Sacred Mystery. Find the right key to unlock their portals, and like entering the worm hole of theoretical physicists, I gained entry into different realms of reality and the knowledge contained therein.

My choice to honor the path of light took me into one of the hardest battles I have ever fought, one that I barely survived. It was with that same force of evil I had encountered in the Cave of Darkness in Peru. This time, the battle was in the remote desert of Mexico in the Huichol holy land of Wiricuta, the same place where I had received so many beautiful visions in the past. It was on the 1992 pilgrimage, the one on which I arrived several days later than the rest and had to go backward in order to go forward.

Once I did catch up with the others, things went smoothly. We covered the long miles between the holy places of initiation safely and in good time. The ceremonies went well, we found good places to camp along the way, there were no major setbacks or problems. I didn't get hit until three or four o'clock in the morning of our all-night ceremony. Most people were huddled in their sleeping bags trying to find some warmth against the freezing temperatures of the cold desert night. Tacho, the shaman, was sitting up by Grandpa Fire, staring into the flickering flames, softly singing the Huichol prayer songs that the sacred fire was telling him to sing. After a period of singing and prayers, with other Huichol doing a singsong harmony backup, they all sank into silence and the reverie of their visions. Then there was only the song of the fire and the winds that spiraled down from the surrounding mountains and raced across the desert, raising dust tails in their wake. Occasional grunts, snores, a baby whimpering, a parent or grandparent whispering words of comfort to a child. Other than that, primordial stillness.

Earlier in the evening, I had a wonderful vision in which I saw what appeared to me as the origins of the Huichol people. First, I saw the spirit of the peyote growing deep within the body of the earth. I saw this spirit rise from Mother Earth and form itself into the roots of the cactus plant

Photo by Max Poppers

Tacho praying with deer antlers and his muvieri, a spiritual tool
(akin to a wand but with special feathers) used by Huichol shamans

just below the surface of the ground. In a visual sequence similar to time-lapse photography, I saw the plant itself grow up from the roots to very gently break the surface and appear in this middle world. I watched in wonder as the evolutionary process continued: the plant opened at its center and a flower appeared. Then the petals of the flower unfurled and from its center emerged the Huichol people. Upon "hatching," they first appeared very small. But the energy pouring up from the ground and through the cactus went into their bodies and in a few seconds, they rose up to their full height as adults. They were dressed in their colorful, ceremonial costumes, which, I could see quite clearly, came directly from the colors and forms flowing into them from the spirit of the plants. These designs are a nonverbal language "spoken" by the peyote as it shares its wisdom teachings on how to live in harmony and balance with the forces of nature in the specific neighborhood of its homeland. As I opened my eyes, I saw before me in physical manifestation the exact vision I had seen with my eyes closed. Right in front of me and all around were Huichol people dressed in their ceremonial clothes. Through their open mouths came words and songs that were the same in terms of energy rate, vibration, pulse, color, and image as the spirit of the *hicouri* rising up from the subterranean depths. They were all one, an energy flow in harmony and communion throughout its various manifestations.

Illuminated by this vision, I saw in my mind's eye that the original language of the people indigenous to a specific area on Mother Earth's body grows directly out of the land itself. The vibratory essence of the natural forces in a given area grow upward from the bowels of the land and surrounding elements to form the plant life and vegetation of that area. The indigenous people live, eat, and breathe these natural elements. They die back into them and new generations birth back out again in the passage of generations. The land literally teaches them how to live in harmony with it through this ingestion process. They take it into their bodies. It "speaks" to them. Then it comes out of their mouths as their language. They speak the vibrations of that land. Their language and creation myths are embodied vehicles for the wisdom of that place. I could now understand why maintaining the original language of indigenous people is important not just to their survival but to all of humanity. Original languages contain within their vibratory structure the operating rules for how to live in their home territory in a harmonious manner. The indigenous language is a *nierica* by which to access the intelligence of place. Lose the language and you lose its vital instructions about right relationship.

My mind was abuzz with thoughts when slowly an extreme weariness began to fill my body. I could barely stand up. I went back to my sleeping bag and curled up inside. I didn't want to sleep, only to rest a while, then come back to Tatewari, the fire, to get whatever other teachings it held for me. As I was lying in my bag, I suddenly felt the presence of evil nearby. I jerked upright. My body went rigid. I couldn't see anything; all was peaceful around the campsite. I peered into the shadowy darkness. Nothing.

Then, out of the corner of my eye, I saw a shadowy figure wearing a black hat, black cape, and black pants. When it first appeared, it was several hundred feet away out in the desert. I could see it was hunting something. The figure glided closer but darted behind clumps of brush and cacti whenever it saw me watching it. It was surreptitiously working its way in toward our campsite. I looked around at the others. Almost all of them were lying down all covered up in their bags, only a few hardy souls were still up and they were all engrossed with the fire. No one else appeared to notice what I was seeing. My voice froze in my throat. I turned back to the figure of darkness. As frightened as I was, I determined not to let fear activate my pattern of shutting down, contraction, and avoidance. *What if this creature is bringing something important for me to see and learn about?* I reasoned. *If I close off to it out of reactive fear, I would never get what it was trying to bring me.* I decided to let it get close so I could carefully observe it and see what it was about and what it wanted. All my years on quest guarding food from marauding bears when questers were out by themselves, facing my fears and trying to stay connected with God's presence and peace while another part of me was freaking out, bore fruit for me now as I waited for the menacing figure to enter the circle of our camp. I was simultaneously frightened yet curious. The creature moved closer and I could feel the presence of evil growing stronger. Suddenly it was right at the edge of our circle! In a flash, I knew that it was hunting me! It wanted to invade my body and take over. *Under no circumstance let that beast into your body! You may lose your life. Fight it off!* came the call of alarm from within.

I instantly got the message. So did the figure of darkness. It charged across the campsite with the speed of light. I slammed my "doors" shut just before it made impact. Its power hit me like a tornado, knocking me backward onto the ground. It felt like a giant buzz saw trying to rip its way into me. *No fucking way!*

I fought back with all my might. It wasn't a physical battle, it was a psychic and spiritual one. I was fighting for my soul. We wrestled and smashed at each other, kicking and biting, scratching and clawing. I fought with every ounce of strength I had. I knew of people on the shamanic path who had gone crazy, who had flipped out and never come back, others who had been "taken over" by the force of darkness and used their shamanic knowledge and power to hurt others for personal gain. I knew the path of darkness was not the one I wanted, but here it was trying to pull me over to its side.

Looking back at it now, I see a cosmic battle between good and evil, an archetypal struggle for the bounty of my soul. It was touch and go for a while, but then in the middle of our violent thrashing, a renewed burst of power came shooting through my body and I picked up the wicked one and hurled it far out into the desert from which it had come. I shook with fear and the result of my exertions. I was soaking wet with perspiration, relieved it was gone, but also completely alert should it try and attack again. Exhausted and spent, I peered out into the night but could detect no sign of the evil one's presence. Relieved, I sank back in my bag and collapsed.

Sleep was out of the question. I was a nervous wreck the rest of the night. I couldn't wait for daylight. When the eastern doorway finally offered up its first signs of illumination, I jumped out of my bag to give thanks before its first ray hit the ground. I bathed myself in the purifying smoke of sage and cedar, then faced the rising sun and thanked it with great enthusiasm for its life-saving arrival. I filled myself up with light, making sure to breathe it into my entire body. I didn't want to miss a single spot.

Later, I spoke with the Tacho and he too reported a rough night. He said he had to fight for his life and almost didn't make it. A great relief poured over me as I heard his words, erasing my fear that I had done something wrong or was at fault in some way. It was comforting to know that even my seniors on the path still had to deal with the darkness force and its power to take over if we are not vigilant and clear in our choice for the light. I thought about a relevant quote I had heard somewhere: "We are given challenges to test who we are. If we don't choose the path that reveals the most of who we are, we fall back." This was definitely a case where I didn't want to fall back. I knew I had faced a serious challenge and that something of major significance had shifted within me. I wondered how it would show up in the future. I worried whether some of the darkness might have somehow slipped into me while we were wrestling, a contamination of sorts, which left me feeling uneasy.

I didn't have to wait long to get my answers. Two days after my return from Mexico, I was getting into my car outside my house when my body froze up and started shaking. My limbs were out of control. I barely made it down the steps and into the house. Andrea, Kimberly, and Nicole were sitting at the kitchen table. I couldn't speak. I trembled like someone doing St. Vitus' dance. At first, they thought I was just kidding around. But then they saw the expression on my face and knew something terrible was happening. Andrea felt my forehead. "You're burning up!" she shouted in alarm. She thrust a thermometer in my mouth. I could barely keep it in, I was shaking so hard. When she took it out, the temperature was over 105 degrees. She called our doctor, who told her to get me to the emergency room as quickly as possible and he would meet us there. They loaded me into the car and off we went.

My body was in involuntary seizure the whole way there. It was hard to get a breath in because of the violent shaking. Part of my mind was freaked out, not knowing what was happening and whether I was going to die. Strangely, another part of my mind, the witness, was totally peaceful, hovering several feet above my head, comfortably watching the whole show, interested but removed. By the time we got to the hospital and they rushed me into emergency, the peaceful part of my awareness had dropped down into my body. While my temperature was still soaring and my body still twitching, I was now very calm. Lying on the gurney while the nurse drew blood, I became concerned for Andrea, Kimberly, and Nicole. To bolster their spirits, I started to sing a song I thought would calm them down. "Ohhh, Great Spirit, I'm calling to you," I sang as loud as I could manage. Unfortunately, they misheard the words and were even more frightened, thinking I was singing, "Ohhh, Great Spirit, I'm coming to you" and that I was dying. Much later, we were able to get a good laugh out of this, but not there at the hospital.

I was kept in the emergency room for several hours. The attending doctor came back after a while and said my white counts were astronomically high, showing that my body was trying to fight off some kind of attacking force; they didn't know what type. Despite the lack of information about what was actually going on, they gave me broad-based antibiotics and after a while my temperature dropped to 101 degrees, the seizures subsided, and the doctor sent me home. Since they didn't know what they were treating, they said to come back the next day for more tests.

We drove home and I collapsed into bed. I went through several days of cyclic bouts of freezing and shaking, then burning up with heat and sweating profusely until I was soaking wet from head to toe. The test results showed nothing; the doctors were puzzled. They didn't know what to do. I couldn't sleep, couldn't rest, couldn't read, couldn't watch TV, couldn't even listen to music. I didn't know if I would get better or worse, if I would live or die. In the midst of it all, I did notice that my suffering served a very interesting role.

I was forced to confront myself and my practice deeply. I had been doing yoga and meditation along with some weight work and a run and prayers to the seven directions for over twenty years on a daily basis. It was how I centered myself and planted the pole of my intention each day. But now I could do none of this. Frustrated and deprived, I asked myself, *What is the bare essence of my practice? What am I doing with my awareness underneath all the activity?* The answer was swift and sure: *Loving*

God in the moment. At that point, I realized that I could still do my basic practice, I could still love God. Nothing was stopping me from that. So I chose a mantra and resolved to use it with every breath in and every breath out. *God loves now,* I said to myself as I took in the fresh gift of life, *or else now would not be happening. God is present now in the midst of this suffering. God hasn't gone anywhere, it's only me who has left God.* Repeating this to myself began to open my awareness to God's in-the-moment presence. I began to visualize healing flowing into me with each breath. *Thank you, Great Spirit, for the healing that is already on its way to me. I do not know if whatever is going on within my body will take my life or will let me be, but whatever the outcome, I open to you and the healing you are sending to me now no matter what happens in the next moment.*

I saw that my faith muscles were getting a good workout and that I was being tested about what I really believed in. *I believe in you, Great Spirit, in your infinite love and healing light and your presence here now pouring into me whenever I open to you. Since you are love, I know you will not force your way into me. You wait closer than my next breath for the moment I open to your presence and then you fill me up with your gifts of healing peace and love. Thank you for being here for me.*

Between the prayers, meditative breathing, and the alternating fever and chills, I was in an altered state of consciousness that lasted for days. During this time of testing, I had two clear perceptions: one, that some of the darkness energy had indeed gotten into me during the battle in the desert and it was trying to gain control in my mind through a contracted state of despair, fear, depression, and self-pity. Conscious choice about what I wanted to experience was my only salvation: *I choose to experience the peace of God's loving presence now,* I repeated to myself over and over again with each breath in and each breath out. I used this phrase as a mantra to strengthen my faith muscles. I felt that I was in a cosmic gym exercising the muscles of my mind and my soul. In the midst of the suffering, I also saw the beauty and perfection of it all. Through the work necessitated by the illness, I was burning away the vestiges of the darkness energy with the help of a purifying fever.

The second phenomena I saw clearly but understood less. I realized that the illness was a vehicle by which information from my past visions transforming my beliefs about the nature of reality was now integrating into my body. I saw that a rearrangement of the energetic structure of my physical-psychic being was necessary to hold and ground all that I had been learning. It wasn't enough that the teachings were in my *cabeza,* my head, they also had to be incorporated in my *cuerpo,* my body. I could actually witness it happening inside. My "assemblage point," how one assembles one's understanding of what constitutes reality, was undergoing drastic changes within me. I sensed this was not only to ground what had already taken place but to prepare me for work I would do in the future. Somehow, through the shamanic work, I had reached a critical mass that activated a process of accelerated evolution of who and what I had been. I realized that while I couldn't control the process, I could work with it most effectively by surrendering all attempts to understand it rationally and instead just let it do me. Another mantra proved immeasurably helpful in surrendering with faith and trust: *Love is the key, let the medicine do me.*

It took me about ten days to get through my shape-shifting rite of passage. The doctors never did find out what was wrong with me. It didn't really matter. I knew what it was, and while I would never wish it on anyone, I was actually grateful for its testings and its teachings. Another benefit of the ordeal was that it deepened my awareness of what people with life-threatening illness go through. I thought of the seventeen men in an AIDS group I had facilitated at the Center for Attitudinal Healing for three years. They had all suffered greatly in the years leading to their deaths. They had shown such courage, such dignity under incredible onslaughts. My heart went out to them and their families. *It's so strange,* I mused, *how suffering can open our hearts to the importance of love and to whatever internal work we have to do on ourselves to realize its presence.*

A few days after recuperating, the Center for Attitudinal Healing asked me to make a home visit to Jen, a sixty-two-year-old woman bedridden as a quadriplegic. She was quite depressed and talked about losing her will to live. Before visiting Jen, I started to send love to her when I did my morning prayers. This way I would connect with her spirit so the relationship was already going before we met in person. This is what I always do with new people and its importance was strengthened by the ordeal that I had just gone through. As I left my home for the drive to her house, I decided to take a back road for a shortcut. I was a little bit late, so I was driving faster than I should have been. A voice within said, *Hey, slow down. So you'll be a few minutes late. That's better then hitting a child who darts out from a parked car.* I immediately slowed down. The very next curve I went around led me right into the path of a little doe standing in the middle of the road. Because I was going so slow, I had no problem stopping in plenty of time. The doe stood absolutely still and looked at me with great innocence. I was touched by its vulnerability. All at once I had an inner knowing that the little doe was somehow connected with Jen. I gave thanks for the little deer spirit and prayed for its safety. Then I carefully drove past it and continued on my way to Jen's house. When I got there, she was propped up in bed and hooked up to various machines that helped her signal and have some degree of limited mobility. Each breath was a struggle for her and talking was even harder. She told me her story of how a cancerous tumor had cut her low just as she was pursuing her goal of a degree in psychology. She had been stuck in this body that didn't work ever since and she was frustrated, angry, and sad. She too had questions about the purpose of suffering and injustice.

I let her talk. She was a beautiful woman and I could see deep within a shining spirit still struggling for life. After she was through telling me all about herself, I told her about my encounter with the little doe. "I don't understand it," I said, "but I know that somehow that deer was connected with you." She immediately burst into tears. "That's good," I said, "let the waters come. The flowers within you need to get that nourishment in order to bloom." A door had opened and we both walked through. Jen told me that she had been criticized as a child for being a dreamer and as a result had introjected negative judgments about her natural ability to release from the physical and travel in the dreamtime. Her ability to dream had been very dear to her up until she ran into the harsh judgments of others.

At that moment, I was very thankful to my Native American friends out in West Marin, Pomo-Miwok people who had included me in some of their family ceremonies over the years. In some of those ceremonies, I had met the matriarch of the family, who was close to eighty years old, had borne sixteen children, spoke only her native tongue, and was the spiritual elder of their reservation up north. She was what her people called a *dreamer*. She was always in contact with the Great Spirit and channeled healing energy and guidance to her people from that sacred place. This was a greatly valued service within the tribe and "Grandma" was greatly respected and utilized by her people in times of need. She had done a healing with me the first time she had seen me and given me some *weya,* spirit power to help me in my work. I was grateful for it at the time and appreciated it again when Jen said that she was criticized for being a dreamer. I told her of the valued position of the dreamer within shamanic culture and offered to bring my drum to our next session. I explained how drumming could help her to leave her body and travel to wherever her spirit wanted to go. Jen felt locked up inside her crippled body because she had limited her definition of herself to her physical being. She felt her body was useless and therefore so was she.

I told Jen that traveling into the dreamtime was a medicine gift and with the drum she could go out into the world and send her love wherever it was needed. Jen was excited at this prospect. Her whole energy field changed from dark to sparkling light pouring out of her now fully opened eyes. On my next visit I brought some sage and my drum. I purified her room, did a prayer thanking Great Spirit for bringing us together and then asked for guidance for Jen to receive whatever messages were for her greatest good at this time in her life. Then I went into the drumming.

I saw the little deer spirit come to her and blend into her body. I saw that Jen needed to nurture her spirit and grow it up from a little one to an adult and that she would be helped in this process by an old wisdom grandmother. I also saw that Jen was a healer and that people would be coming to her in the future for the healing she would be able to bring them through the gifts that came from her dreaming. After the drumming, Jen was radiant. "That's the most I've been able to relax in I don't know how long. The spasms in my back are gone. I feel just great. I left my body. I was free! I traveled to see my children and I filled them up with love. And I saw this very old Native American woman. She was very kind and she had what seemed like the wisdom of the ages. She was watching over me. I think she was there to help me. Let's do this some more. I love it!" *The Great Mystery works in strange ways,* I thought. *The deer spirit is alive and well.*

Experiences such as the one with Jen helped me recognize that all who cross my path are sacred messengers from the Great Mystery, teachers to respect and listen to as best I can. They serve as "earth-plane" teachers for the lessons I am being shown on the other side.

Sharon, who was also referred to me by the Center for Attitudinal Healing, and was battling terminal cancer, is a case in point. Sharon was a bright, witty woman in her mid-thirties who was full of bitterness, fear, anger, and sarcasm. Artistic by nature, I encouraged her to express herself through drawing. She responded with enthusiasm and made huge figures on butcher paper using colored chalk as her medium. She did some amazing drawings during the course of our work together. One dramatic figure portrayed her inner forces of darkness that tormented her so. Drawing it out helped her work through these forces to gain a sense of inner peace, but she reached it only by facing the full might of her demons. She brought them into the light of our figurative campfire and allowed them a voice. She let them express themselves however they needed to. They howled and they cried, they wept and they wailed. But eventually they released the hold on her that had been so debilitating to her spirit. She developed a conscious relationship with them through a give-and-take dialogue that resulted in a negotiated peace. She also made contact with what she called her "high self." She drew another larger than life-sized picture of her high self and used it as a reference point from then on to return to a state of peace. This freed her up to work on healing relationships with her family and to begin facing her own approaching death with courage, grace, and equanimity.

Sharon's sister called me from the hospital to come see her just before she died. She was in a coma and had been so for several days. I had been out of town and went to see her as soon as I got the message.

Sharon's Darkness figure   *Sharon's "High Self"*
                                         drawing

I sat down beside her and held her hand. I thanked her for all the gifts she had given me, for the inspiration she had been for facing darkness. I told her how much I appreciated our time together and spoke fondly of memories of her that I would carry with me. I sent her prayers for her release into spirit and encouraged her to stay open to the helping presence of her higher self when it came time to go. After my words were finished, I sat in the silence, sending her my love. When it was time for me to go, I stood up and bent over to kiss her goodbye on the forehead. I whispered softly in Spanish, a language in which Sharon was conversant, *"Vaya con Dios."* Go with God. To my amazement, Sharon, who had not made any signals or communications with others since entering the coma, gently squeezed my hand. She died shortly thereafter. I carry the memory of her soft touch with me to this day. When I look back to what helped Sharon face her shadow monsters, I see that it started when I shared with her what I had learned from my indigenous teachers about facing unwanted parts of myself.

My medicine teachers introduced me to a whole new way of relating to life. Previously, I had aimed for the model of perfection presented by the life of Christ—always loving, always good, always selflessly serving others with an open heart. With this as an ideal, it is no wonder that I was constantly frustrated. Try as I might, I could never make it to the end of the day without some major failures in attitude and behavior. As a consequence, I always felt I wasn't good enough, that I was too weak, too neurotic, too whatever to ever get it right. What I found with indigenous people was a radically different perspective. Instead of a drive toward perfection, they were concerned with balance and with harmony. *To walk in balance* was a phrase that I heard over and over again. As I discovered, the ability to walk in balance is dependent upon having a solid relationship with what I call "all the legs of the chair." You can't balance a chair comfortably without having all four legs doing their job. Take one of the legs away, and the task of balancing yourself becomes much more difficult, especially if you try to do it over the course of a lifetime and you want some relaxation as well. People too cannot walk in balance without knowing all the "legs," or aspects, of their being—the shadow as well as the light, the darker, negative, destructive, and uncomfortable aspects of themselves as well as those attributes that they value. Everything must be brought into the light of consciousness, to be faced with acceptance and awareness, for they all have power, intelligence, and information. Our creative task is to free them from the imprisonment of repression, denial, and projection and create conscious, cooperative relationship with them.

By seeking our shadow energies who live out there in the symbolic darkness and bringing what we find there into the warmth and light by the metaphorical fire of awareness, we can begin to see what these forces are, how they operate, and what they want. Then we can enter into an "I/thou" dialogue, exploring the possibility of negotiating toward a win-win outcome wherein lies balance. For example, as I face and own my ability to lash out at others, I get in touch with a beast-like shadow

Author's shadow monster

monster. By owning it and carefully observing its behavior, I can begin to discover where it lives, where it came from, what triggers its appearance, and most important, what is the wound and fear that lies within its domain and what it needs for healing. My own wounds and fears resulting from my father's death, the suffering, sorrow, and repressed grief, had a tight hold on my body and my feelings and poisoned all my relations until I was finally able to face them head on and open the gates to healing. Today, I notice that my beast only comes out when the little boy in me is frightened or feeling unloved. Now, instead of attacking others, I can let the beast release feelings through deep breathing, through chanting, or through an anger dance when appropriate, all of which free me up from a state of constriction. In other words, I clean my pipes of old, reactive energy, which allows me to attend to my fearful inner child.

We all have our individual versions of the wounded inner child because it is true, shit does happen, whether we want it to or not. Our challenge is to create a response that transforms it into fertilizer. Judgments about it simply close the door to learning from it and using its energy for our healthy growth process. The wisdom elders taught me to face my shit and learn how to use it in a good way. "What you choose to be unconscious of—that is what runs you," said one. "It robs you of your power. You've got to see all the parts of yourself and your life. How else can you bring yourself into balance except when you bring all the players to the table? If you leave some out, they will sabotage the rest." With support such as this, I took on the task of facing and owning all that I previously had run away from or denied. People who pushed my buttons, situations that brought up fear and anxiety, behavior and dreams with shadow content—all became vehicles for learning, growth, healing, and exploration. Nothing was taboo now. Whatever came up in the moment was grist for the mill.

One of my strongest teachings about being in the moment came as I sat bedside with Sarah, the same thirteen-year-old girl who taught me the power of inner peace when I visited her in the hospital where her brother had died. For nine months after that, Sarah had fought bravely against her cancer, but eventually it spread throughout her body and her parents brought her home to die. I went to visit her weekly. Sarah's parents wanted me to talk to her about death. They could see it coming and wanted me to help her deal with it. I tried to bring it up, but she just wanted to watch TV and read her comics. So I sat there with her watching TV and reading her comics. This went on for two weeks. I thought, *I'm not helping, I'm incompetent, I'm failing the parents and failing Sarah.* Then I'd get angry at her for being so resistant and uncooperative. At the end of each visit, I'd ask her if she wanted me to come back. Part of me hoped she'd let me off the hook and say no. But she never did. Instead, she'd say, "It's okay if you come back." So come back I would. It took me a while, but I finally began to see what was actually happening beneath the surface. Sarah was teaching me how to be with her without preconceived notions of what to do or how to do it. She had her own agenda, not her parents' one. I gradually recognized that she was testing me to see if I would stay with it, stay with her, and not run my agendas on her. She was also helping me to face my own fears and judgments, to release them, and to come back to open heart space, sending out love to her without any demands or requirements. I came to see my time with Sarah as an opportunity for deep meditation and healing for me. I questioned if she was getting anything out of it, but continued sending her love without wanting anything back, trying to trust that in some way she was being helped.

One day, Sarah looked up at me from her bed, which faced the ocean and the afternoon setting sun. Without any fanfare or small talk, she looked me right in the eye and said, "I want you to help me to die." Through all the TV watching and comic book reading, she had been waiting for her time. In that precise instant, a ray of light poured in through her window and came right up to her bed. It was so bright that she had to shut her eyes. The sound of the surf and the beating of my heart were the only sounds I heard. Then words came out of me: "It's like what just happened, Sarah. Just when you asked me for help, in came the light. Now listen to the waves. They rise up from the sea and they return to the sea. Each wave dances out its unique movement and then it descends back to where it came from. That's just the way it is with us, too. And if you notice the wave, while the top of its reach rises upward from its source, the bottom of the wave is always connected to the ocean below it. It never loses that connection. And that too is the way it is with us. When it comes time for our last breaths, we are like the wave returning to our home, the sea of infinite being from which we came and which at the deepest level of our beings we have never been separate from. It's just that we have forgotten our connection. Death is a time to remember this connection." I paused and looked at Sarah. Her eyes were closed and she was very still. "Keep going," she said. "I like what you are saying." So I did. I knew that something bigger than me was using me as a pipeline to help Sarah. I let it flow.

"Feel that warm light on your face," I said. "Allow yourself to gently take it in. That light will help you in dying just as it is helping you now by giving you something positive to focus on. As the wave of life gets weaker and weaker, when you are getting ready to leave your body, you will float gently into that light. Just allow your spirit to leave with the breath and flow into the light. It is the light of love, the love that never dies and that unites all that has been, all that is, and all that will be. Release into it. Merge with it. You are that light. It is you." Sarah was sleeping. I kissed her goodbye and quietly left, thankful to the Great Spirit for what had been given. I told her parents what had happened and they seem relieved. We went into her room and she was still sleeping. I left shortly thereafter.

A few days later, her father called and asked me to come out to the house as soon as possible. I canceled my next appointment and drove the forty-five minutes to the beachside town where they lived, sending my love to the family all the while. When I got there, her father brought me right into her room. Sarah had slipped into a near coma state and was breathing with the help of an oxygen tank. We both sat down facing her. We didn't say a word, just watched her struggle to breathe. Sarah was getting close to her last wave. My heart was breaking for her, for her family, for myself, for all deaths of the young and the innocent. But I also knew that we had some important work to do. Sarah had called us together to help birth her back into spirit. I took her dad's hand and motioned for him to place his other hand on Sarah's leg, then I took Sarah's hand so that the three of us were joined together. Paul, her father, and I extended our love to Sarah to support her in leaving her body as peacefully as she could. We sat in silence for a long time, watching Sarah's valiant efforts to breathe. Each breath got smaller—a crest, a pause, then an ebb back into stillness. With each exhalation, we wondered if another breath would follow. After a while, all our breaths were synchronized. I realized that Sarah was once again being a teacher. Was it my imagination or did I actually hear her say in silent words, *Pay attention, Tom. Just as you don't know if the next breath will be my last, so too do you not know if your next breath will be your last. So don't miss this one. Catch it as it enters, ride it down all the way into your belly. Feel it bringing in the life force. Don't ever take it for granted. Respect it. Enjoy it. And when it leaves your body, just as you taught me, release into the stillness and just be. This is my last gift for you. This is my meditation on life. May you carry it well.*

As our breaths joined, the boundaries separating Sarah, her father, and myself dissolved. Peace permeated the room, spreading out like waves. Sarah died shortly thereafter. She followed one of those beams of sunlight out the window and back to the source. She's with me still, when I watch the waves of my breath and the waves of the ocean.

While Sarah's death was peaceful, it nevertheless raised anew a question from my youth that I'd heard many times over the years, from parents who had lost a child, from people suffering from grief of all kinds—loss of limbs, loss of functions that most of us take for granted, such as seeing, hearing, walking, going to the bathroom, talking—from people who had suffered physical and sexual abuse, including the horrors of ritual abuse, from victims of war, racial prejudice, and discrimination, from victims of natural disaster and human violence. The question is *why? Why suffering?* What role does it play? What possible good can come out of injustice against the innocent?

Over the years, I have watched this question take me and others who have asked it into the depths of despair, depression, anger, bitterness, guilt, confusion, and loss of faith. It forces us to face the truth of truths, that death and decay spare no person, and that injustice can strike anyone at any time, even the richest, most protected, and most powerful. There are forces in this mysterious universe that we do not have the power to stop. Shit happens.

So what is the purpose of suffering? In truth, I cannot say for sure. It is a Great Mystery, like the elders say. Why one person walks away from a wreck and another dies, *quien sabe?* Who knows? Possibly the Mystery knows. But I do know this. How and what kind of response we create to the shit of our lives—the injustices, the wounds, deprivations, and sufferings—determines to a significant degree what kind of life we will have. Ultimately, they are all *niericas,* doorways, opportunities to travel inward to examine our deepest beliefs as we witness what holds up against the assaults of the universe and what doesn't. Suffering, like all loss and all deaths, confronts us with the temporality of life in our bodies and pushes us to make conscious decisions about what we really value as important and what is worth basing a life on. Wounds tear us open, they take us to the core of our being. *Who are you?* they scream out. *What are you made of? What is your life all about? Why are you here? What do you really believe in? What can you depend on when the shit hits the fan? Is it all delusion, a game of chance with no purpose and no meaning? Is selfishness and materialism the ultimate way to go?*

To live authentically, everyone must face and answer these questions themselves. Until this happens, you are not fully living out who you really are, what philosopher Jacob Needleman calls a "first-hand sense of identity." You are merely living out other people's answers and definitions of who you are and how you should be. Being wounded and suffering knocks you to your knees and it is here that you can touch your deepest resources—for forgiveness, for compassion, and for empathy with the suffering of others. It seems we have to be laid low before we can make a decision to stand up and really live from our souls. This opportunity is only available in the *now*. If we are not fully present in the moment, if we are stuck in fear, judgment, ego-based identity, living out other people's answers to life, we are cut off from the power to make a conscious choice about how we want to focus our attention. And it is this choice that determines what we experience in the moment. Do we use the shit of our lives as fertilizer to help our flowers grow, or do we suffocate in our reactive responses that keep us stuck in darkness? Great Spirit is waiting patiently for us to remember the ancient knowledge that we are all related. But to get there we have to face, own, and transform our personal darkness. When we do this successfully, we return, as T. S. Eliot said, to the place from which we began and know it for the first time. Then we see what Benjamin Disraeli, Prime Minister of England under Queen Victoria, said almost a hundred years ago: "We are all born for love; it is the principle of existence and its only end."

This effort to face and transform our relationship to darkness, shadow monsters, injustice, our narcissism and selfishness, button-pushing petty and major tyrants, to loss and to sorrow, and to the inevitability of our own death and the death of everyone we know and love, is a major task of our lives. It is, as poet e. e. cummings said, "the hardest battle which any human being can fight, and never stop fighting." In a world that is doing its best, night and day, as cummings says, to make you "everybody else," "to be nobody but yourself" means that "we can never be born enough. We are human beings, for whom birth is a supremely welcome mystery, the mystery of growing: the mystery that happens only and whenever we are faithful to ourselves."

It is vitally important to remember that being faithful to ourselves doesn't necessarily make things easier. Sometimes it makes the battle even tougher. As one of the elders once told me, "When you make a decision to honor that you are a child of the sun, a force of light, that decision itself can trigger the forces of darkness to push even harder trying to maintain their hold on you. They don't want to lose you. Be careful. And always remember that the light will always win out. This is the teaching of the East. It happens every morning at dawn. Father Sun comes up and that's it for the night. *Adios* while Father Sun is up there doing its job. But for you and me, in order for the light to win out in our lives, we have to choose it. Then we have to bring it to all the dark places. It's not an easy way to go. But it is the way of the heart. It is what will bring us home in a good way so we can return to our Creator feeling good about the life we have lived."

Prayer to the East: *Ho, Taupa, Tatata, Tao, Father Sun, Golden Eagle of the East, power of illumination. Thank you for shining today, thank you for your light and your love, for giving away of your light bringing the life force to our Mother Earth, for your teaching reminder of our true nature— illumination. Help me to open my spiritual eye and see your light in all that cross my path today. May it be so.*

Dancing in the light, Grand Canyon rim

6

Responsible Ecstasy

Ecstasy is a real human need . . . a state of consciousness beyond concept. . . . And if it does not come through . . . in positive ways . . . it's going to come out in violence.

ELIZABETH COGBURN

The Huichol shamans say we are *perdido,* lost. They say we are bringing doom and destruction to Yurianaka, Mother Earth, and that Taupa, Father Sun, is coming closer to the earth to purify it. They are concerned for the future and for the life of their children. They are holding great ceremonies calling in shamans from many areas to try and "hold up the sun." But they know they cannot do it themselves, for they are not the ones soiling the collective nest. We are. We are the ones who have to wake up, who have to find our lives.

For the Huichol, this is the purpose of their sacred pilgrimage to the holy land of Wiricuta—to find their lives. This is what all their ceremonies involving the ritual use of the peyote help them to accomplish. Their technology of the sacred enables them to change channels and access "state specific information" available only on the wavelengths of specific channels. For shamanic peoples such as the Huichol, the purpose in changing channels is not for escapism, to get lost in imaginary hallucinations that have no basis in reality. Their purpose is to get a more accurate reading of the nature of reality. They seek entrance through the *nierica* into the numinous universe underlying the limited, material world of the sensory—the "mysterious, ubiquitous, concentrated form of non-material energy . . . loose about the world and contained in a more or less condensed degree by all objects," says Bob Calahan in his introduction to Jaimie de Angulo's *Coyote Man and Old Doctor Loon.* Why? To obtain information, healing, and power, which they can use here on this plane of existence to better their lives and the lives of their people.

Entering into the depths of the mystery is not something to take lightly, for the mystery is all about power and power can manifest itself in many ways. Out of respect, the Wisdom Elders observe, listen, and commune with this power in all its manifestations. From this base of phenomenological data of mind in nature, nature in mind, they came to learn the order and structure of life's connectedness and that all things are dependent upon each other and thus related. Recognizing this, the norm of reciprocity in all interactions is raised to the status of sacred. Balanced reciprocity with all of creation is observed at all costs, for without this practice, the fragile web of life is irreversibly damaged, a fate that faces us today. The eminent theologian Thomas Berry addresses this fate: "The earth asks us to accept greater responsibility. We must exchange mindlessness for mindfulness." It's an initiation process, says Berry. Humanity is "moving from a state of childhood into its adult stage of life and human community must now assume adult responsibilities."

Respect, humility, clarity of intention, right relationship with the appropriate psychospiritual technology, and sustained, focused mindfulness are all key components of successful channel-changing to access state specific information. The shaman is the state shifter, the channel-changer par excellence, for the shaman is the master technician of ecstasy.

"Open your heart. Speak to the spirit of the *hicouri.* Tell it the truth of what it is that you seek. It sees into you and is a great teacher. If you open to it with humility, if your prayers are good, it will help you find your life. It is good medicine. You are under the *mara'akame's* protection. Eat well, *mi amigo,* it is for your life, for your family, for your people." These words were from Presciliano, a young Huichol man who, along with his wife and four children, were on the 1983 pilgrimage journey to Wiricuta. We had been on the pilgrimage road for a week now, stopping at

Presciliano, young Huichol father with son

various holy places along the way to make offerings and to pray. We were eating minimally of tortillas and *fruta,* fasting at times, abstaining from washing, from salt, sex, alcohol, and drugs, spending long hours driving and short hours sleeping, awakening and bedding down with prayers and purification around Tatewari, sleeping out in the desert and mountains as we made our way over the three-hundred-mile passage to the holy land, learning all the while about the dynamics of responsible ecstasy.

Each place of power along the way required a different ceremony, which in turn took us deeper into relationship with the morphogenetic field of the Huichol path. Before we left the village, there was a ceremony

Photo by John Catalin

With Grandpa Fire in Wiricuta

into the early hours of the morning where each pilgrim received a Huichol name from the shaman. Huichol unable to go on the pilgrimage joined in with their prayers and blessings and the following morning with their goodbyes upon our departure. Several days later, we were taken through a ceremony at *Jaikitenieh,* the gateway. Here each *peyotero,* or first-timer, was blindfolded because we were now getting so close to Wiricuta that its intense spiritual light could blind us. We got back in the rented vans and continued on the long and bumpy ride to the next holy site, the Springs of Our Grandmothers, Tateimatinieri, with the blindfolds on. At Tateimatinieri, our blindfolds would be lifted and we would be blessed with the sacred waters; a bowl of it would be poured onto our heads and a drink poured into our mouths, further purifying us and preparing us for the final trek into the desert to Wiricuta.

All during this time, the dynamics of right relationship with the medicine were being articulated on many levels, for the usage of peyote does not exist in a vacuum. It is embedded in a cultural complex that determines attitudes and interactional usage patterns far richer and more elaborate than the mere ingestion of a psychoactive agent. The role of peyote within this web of relationship is best understood by listening to the Huichol creation story, as told by Prem Das, the Anglo *mara'akame* who led the first pilgrimage I went on in 1981. The story tells why peyote is revered as a gift from the gods, a sacrament, and why it is a respected teacher of the sacred, an elder who provides access to power and wisdom for one who is properly motivated and prepared. It can take you to ecstatic realms, but with this power comes great responsibility.

The story begins in the sky or celestial realm, which is the age-less home of the Huichol gods and goddesses. The sun, as central deity, became discontent with the instability and chaos of life in the sky world. Nothing here was permanent and the gods, like wisps of smoke, were in constant flux. The sun began dreaming of a great swirling tunnel of brilliant color, a *nierica,* leading to a new world that was much more stable. Here, forms maintained their appearance for a longer time and the sun, who could project his vision into the future, saw its desirable possibilities.

The sun asked Kauyumari, the deer spirit, to find the great, swirling whirlpool of a tunnel he had envisioned in his dream. Kauyumari agreed to help. He searched unsuccessfully in each of the four sacred directions but did not locate the *nierica* until he looked in the exact center of the sky world. The sun asked Kauyumari to lead many of the gods and goddesses into this tunnel, which would hurl them into the new world his vision foresaw. "You will completely forget," he said, "your friends and former life here in the sky realm. You may be frightened, but at night when you sleep we'll still be able to communicate through dreams."

Kauyumari was hesitant at first to leave the world he knew so well but finally agreed when the sun impressed upon him the beauty of this new land. So Kauyumari gathered the other travel-ers together and guided them to the edge of the swirling abyss. Grandpa Fire, Tatewari, led the way with Kauyumari, a notorious trickster, saying that he would be responsible for bringing up the rear. Carrying prayer arrows for a safe journey and singing as they

Author's drawing of Deer Spirit going through a nierica

went, they leapt into the *nierica* and found themselves hurled through a spiraling passageway. They emerged at Washadeayway, a large rock off the coast by San Blas. Each god who birthed out of the tunnel into the new world offered prayers and burned a candle to assure that the others would arrive safely as well.

Finally, they all arrived. However, they had forgotten who they were and where they were. But as the sun promised, through their dreams they gradually remembered the forgotten knowledge. They also received instructions from the sun that they were to proceed to the very center of this new realm, a journey of great danger that required a number of austerities. Such restrictions were unknown for these spirits, who had always been free to do whatever came to mind. They were told not to have sex with their spouses nor to eat until they arrived at the point of their destination—the center of the new world. They were to move in a single line and not to stop nor bathe in springs or pools, no matter how beautiful, that might appear along the way.

As they ascended the mountains eastward and camped as needed, they noticed that some of the hundreds of gods and goddesses who came through the *nierica* were now missing. Grandfather Fire, who was leading the way for he was the only luminosity in this dark world with no light of its own, dreamed to find out what happened. Through his dreaming, he discovered that the missing parties violated the rules that the sun laid down. As soon as they did this, by having sex, bathing, or whatever violation took place, they lost their free, fluid ephemeral form. They began to slow down, undergoing a strange metamorphism to become crystallized and immobile. At the exact spot where they had broken the laws, they transformed into the natural monuments of pinnacles and peaks, waterfalls, and other prominent forms that mark the land to this day. The spirits of the gods and goddesses did not die or cease to exist; they merely took embodied form as the features of the earth. Their consciousness is still very much alive and can be contacted by the *mara'akame* in dreams and visions.

Tatewari explained, "This is a very dangerous journey and if you break the laws, this is what happens." The remaining gods accepted this, traveling higher into the mountains until finally they reached the center of this middle world, Wiricuta. Climbing to the top of its central peak, they found a deep tunnel descending into the darkness below. Tatewari then received instructions from the sun that a number of the gods were to proceed out to each of the four sacred directions in order to know the full measure of the new world. For five days, those who remained waited atop the mountain. When the explorers returned, their numbers were smaller. They explained that the others broke the rules and disappeared. They were sad but there was nothing they could do. That night, Father Sun told them the time had come to prepare for a great ceremony to occur five days hence, once they completed the prayer arrows and other offerings they were instructed to make.

The gods did not know why they were to do this or what was going to happen. They gathered together materials to make the drums and rattles and the beautiful, colorful costumes they saw in their dreams. On the final night, the sun told Tatewari to sing about everything that had happened from the point when they left the sky realm, to the journey through the *nierica,* to the arrival at Washadeayway, and every subsequent step and event along the way, thereby recounting the whole history in song to all of the gods and goddesses, who are now at the central point.

So he began to sing. And Kauyumari sang after him, repeating the last few phrases to emphasize the important points. They sang all night long. Just as Tatewari reached the point where the gods have gone to the four directions, the whole earth shook! Tatewari urged them to chant louder and faster. He saw a vision of a dance and told the others to dance around the tunnel at the top of the mountain in a counterclockwise circle. Five times they danced around the tunnel and then sat down. Just then a light began to appear at the bottom of the tunnel. Tatewari told everybody to chant even stronger, and as they did the light got brighter and brighter. Then a great sphere of light lifted out of the tunnel and began to ascend into the sky. It was the sun come to join them!

For the first time, they were able to see the beauty of the world around them and they were in tears. The sky lit up and turned blue, and they saw the plains and the mesas and the valleys. They were in ecstasy seeing the sun rising and illuminating the land. They began to swoon and could not go on.

The sun stopped right at the mid-heaven, then began to descend out of the sky toward the west. "Is this beautiful thing— is that it? Is it all over? Is the sun leaving us?"

They were very frightened and began to cry. The sun went down over the horizon and vanished. It was dark again. "What happened? What did we do wrong?" they asked Tatewari, who explained that someone had to be sacrificed if they wanted Taupa to come back. He told them the sun had descended into a tunnel out in the middle of the Pacific Ocean and was now in the underworld being attacked by serpents trying to eat him up. In Tatewari's dreams, the sun told him that the ceremony they had done was not complete, for no sacrifice had been made. The sun said that he wanted someone to jump into the tunnel.

No one wanted to do this because they remembered their last journey. Once is enough. Plus this was a black pit, nothing like the original *nierica,* which was a radiant sphere of light. Suddenly a little girl goddess jumped up and said she would go. So the gods started the ceremony again. Just at the peak of their chanting, the little girl jumped into the tunnel. Everyone stopped. The girl vanished into the darkness. They did not know what to do. Then suddenly they felt the earth quake again. They looked into the tunnel, expecting the sun to appear as it had before. But nothing. Only more shaking of the earth.

Tatewari went to sleep trying to find the sun in dreaming but was unsuccessful. Then suddenly he was awakened by light beginning to fill the sky. But it wasn't coming from the tunnel this time. It was rising in the east. Everyone began to chant and sing and dance in ecstatic delight. But they were also mystified. How is he coming from over there? Tatewari saw with his vision that the sun was rising out of a tunnel similar to the one it had descended into in the west. The little girl who jumped into the tunnel had reached the sun and merged with it.

The sun ascended to the mid-heaven again and everyone was ecstatic. But then it descended, explaining, "I will descend again into the western ocean because I have to go back home. They are doing a great ceremony back there too, in the sky realm. They miss me also. But I will come back tomorrow and every day if you keep doing your ceremonies. They are so beautiful. Your chanting is wonderful. That is why I have come. And that is the reason I must return to the sky realm. There are many of us still there."

What we see in this Huichol account of creation is that the sun will return each day if, and only if, the gods and goddesses continue to do their ceremonies on a regular basis joined by human beings they enlist to help them in their efforts. Here we have a beautiful explanation of the sacredness of reciprocity: it is not enough to just take. You must also give back in a balanced interchange. To fail to do this will result in disturbing the balance of cosmic forces and in disaster—the sun will not return. In recognition of the importance of doing the ceremonies and doing them with *mucho kupuri,* strong energy and enthusiasm, the gods and goddesses created people as their principal ally. A primary purpose of humankind is thus to help the deities maintain cosmic balance by joining with them in giving back through prayer and ceremony. Sacred reciprocity through recognizing humankind's responsibility to maintain balance with the forces of nature is precisely what Huichol religion is all about. They remember who they are and what they are about. Now let us return to the creation story, for it brings us to the remembering process and ties together responsibility and ecstasy in right relationship.

After the gods and goddesses received their instructions from the sun, they set about to explore all around the newly illuminated world. They went out in all directions. As they did so, they noticed that the tracks of Kauyumari were fuzzy, green disks lying on the desert floor. Tatewari told them that the tracks were very special and that they should do a special ceremony. They prepared offerings and then gathered around the mysterious tracks. Tatewari blessed the tracks and told them that it was food and that they should eat it. When they picked the tracks, they found out that they were alive, and that they were full of *kupuri* from the sun. Tatewari touched their cheeks with the sacred plants, which were peyote plants, then fed each god and goddess the first piece. Thereafter, they were to eat as much as they wanted.

After a while, ingestion of the plants enabled the gods and goddesses to understand the songs that Tatewari had been singing all along, the songs and chants that recounted how this world had been created in these "first times," including all they had been through since first exiting from the great *nierica* at San Blas. In ecstasy, they now understood that the path of Kauyumari, he who had gone last on the entire pilgrimage procession, was to help those who came later to find their way.

To follow in Kauyumari's footsteps, the path of peyote, would help those who came afterward to remember where they had come from and understand their purpose: to find their life.

Carl Jung speaks beautifully to this purpose of finding meaningful life in *Memories, Dreams and Reflections:* "Only if we know that the only thing that truly matters is the infinite, can we avoid fixing our attention on futilities and upon all kinds of goals which are not of real importance . . . if we understand and feel that here in this life we already have a link with the infinite, desires and attitudes change. In the final analysis, we count for something only because of the essential we embody, and if we do not embody that, life is wasted."

For the Huichol, peyote is considered a sacrament that helps them find the *essential* only if it is harvested in the respectful, ceremonial manner of the pilgrimage. Each successive pilgrimage led by the *mara'akame,* who represents Tatewari leading the *peyoteros* as they retrace the path of the gods to the holy land of Wiricuta, hunts the *hicouri* in the same way. They gather a supply to take back to the villages to last them through the year of seasonal ceremonies. The Huichol know the truth that philosopher Huston Smith addresses when he says that "reality holds as much in the ways of worth beyond what we are able to see with our ordinary experience, as it holds in quantity and size beyond what our naked senses can fathom." As a vehicle for communion with the gods and goddesses, the peyote medicine enables the properly prepared user to leave the *ordinary experience* and enter into ecstatic states with an ethos of grounded responsibility. In the time-tested tradition of shamanism, the Huichol elicit altered states of reality to gain wisdom, guidance, and healing for their lives, their families, and their people. They enter with the clear intention of finding and bringing something back to this ordinary plane that will be of practical use in bettering their lives. Their cosmology, symbols, values, and usage patterns all work synergistically to build social cohesion and maintain continuity with their ancestral past. While undergoing tremendous pressure from encroaching Western society, the elders still carry out the ceremonies and the pilgrimages, and younger Huichol and families are still listening to the old ways. They have much to teach us in how to create responsible, healthy, and productive relationships with the entheogenic plant teachers, who are true elders of the earth. Entheogenic refers to plants that "contain" God within them, i.e., those that contain psychoactive properties that can induce an experience of the divine.

Paramount for the encounter with the peyote medicine for the Huichol is preparation, which I call "strengthening the container" work. The container is the body-mind-spirit field. When entering an altered state, the journeyer is not in charge of what is going to be released, appear, or be transmitted. The energy will be on a higher "voltage" than the level of ordinary reality. If the container is not strengthened beforehand, the higher level of current could cause a short circuit and burn out the system. Strengthening the container involves exercising the muscles of concentration and endurance through meditative mindfulness, as well as cultivating the faculty of the unattached observing witness. The journeyer must be able to maintain focused, alert concentration for hours on end in order to stay present with the unfolding information. It is also important to be sincerely humble and yet also courageous, with a willingness to surrender into the Mystery while maintaining awareness of all that happens in order to bring back the fruits of the journey for integration into everyday life. Rainer Maria Rilke speaks with great eloquence to how far we have come from this attitude of respectful right relationship with mystery: "That is at bottom the only courage that is demanded of us, to have the courage for the most strange, the most singular and the most inexplicable that we can encounter. That mankind has in this sense been cowardly has done life endless harm; the experiences that are called 'visions,' the whole so called 'spirit world,' death, all those things that are so closely akin to us, have by daily parrying been so crowded out of life that the senses with which we could have grasped them are atrophied."

The Huichol, with the help of the peyote, do not have atrophied senses. They say the spirit of the *hicouri* knows what you are thinking; it knows what is in your heart from the moment you think about going on the pilgrimage. It is not to play around with or take lightly. The medicine will show you truth about your life and if you are not prepared to face this, then the medicine path is not for you. It likes a "clean home," so if there are places within your life that you are not facing or owning, the medicine will take you there. Then you must work to clean up your home, as happened with me during the purging by La Laguna del Oro de Santa Maria. My Huichol compadre, Presciliano, spoke with deep conviction as he told me about these things.

"The *hicouri* watches how you live, how you treat the earth and her plant people, and how you treat all people. It knows you better than you know yourself. It seeks out your sincerity, how much you want to know and why—your motivation. Is it to help others, or is it to gain powers for your own advancement at the expense of others? This is what the medicine is examining when it listens to your prayers. The relationship doesn't start when you take it into your body. It starts way before."

The plants themselves have taught me that all of creation is in communication with its constituent parts. Thus there is no place to hide when doing sincere medicine work. You must be willing to face your death, your shadow, your worst fears, your wounds, your narcissism, your projections, i.e., the full contents of your ego dances and the contents of your personal unconscious, as well as the tremendous forces of the collective unconscious. The inner pipes must be cleaned out before the higher energies will come through on a consistent basis.

The medicine will show you what you need to face and do. You have to be present for it. In this regard, my work with yoga and meditation over the years developed the function of the observing witness, so that I was able to get what was being presented to me through the visionary journeys. The skills of working with energy in and through the body, of blending with it, no matter how scary or threatening or upsetting, of getting its message, then moving it or allowing it to move instead of clamping down out of fear, all are skills that can and need to be cultivated in order to best work with the teachings of sacred plants. The plants are not indulgent teachers; they hold you to your best. They show you your evolutionary potential and give you a psychic kick in the butt to work to realize it.

It is not easy. On the pilgrimage, there is massive sleep deprivation. You stay up late at night, sometimes all night, making sure to feed Tatewari continuously. Do you tell it the deepest truth of your life and what you are seeking? Do you honor it each evening and morning in a ceremony of thanksgiving? Do you show it your offerings of prayer arrows and other sacred objects that you have prepared and brought with you to leave at the various sacred sites, gifts of thanksgiving and prayers for your life, your family, and your people? Each car carries a "spirit bag" and each person is responsible for saving up all the first bites of food during the day to give to Tatewari at night. It is a very good exercise in self-discipline and remembering.

At various times during my work with Huichol shamans, I have been assigned different objects to make and carry with me to Wiricuta. One year, the shaman Tacho told me to make a cross with flat pieces of wood to symbolize the four directions. Where the pieces met in the center was the fifth power, the Great Spirit, El Dios. I melted beeswax onto the wood and then covered the entire surface of the cross with Mexican coins with *wierica* and *ku,* the eagle and the serpent, facing up. Every day, I was to greet Taupa Father Sun, holding this cross up to its light and give thanks for my life and offer thanksgiving prayers to the sacred fire Tatewari, the *hicouri,* and Wiricuta. The shaman said he would be checking up on me to make sure I did this and the results would bear good fruit on the next pilgrimage—but only if I did it each morning. Otherwise, it would show the gods and the goddesses that I was not really serious in my work, and things would not go well for me when I returned.

Another assignment was to make a *quadro,* a small yarn painting. Since Tacho saw that part of my medicine had to do with the eagle and the sun, my homework was to use colored yarn inlaid into melted wax on a flat piece of wood to make a pair of two-headed eagles facing the sun. I had to take it with me wherever I went and feed it with prayers and offerings of tobacco and chocolate. Again, I would be watched to see how I held up. During the time of my apprenticeship, I felt I was always being watched. There was no place for me to hide, no thoughts that were not being noticed, no actions that were not being scrutinized by unseen forces watching me and testing me. I was also watched in another way. Since I was married, I was not to sleep with any other woman except my wife until the time of completion. If I broke these vows, I would have to start all over again. I also had to honor the wisdom guidance of what I had been given in my medicine teachings—things such as staying aligned with the sun during the day, and the fire at night.

During the last three years of my eleven-year apprenticeship, my assignment was to light a candle each morning and connect with its light, which represented both the light of the sun and the light of Tatewari. Whatever came up during the day, I had to do my best to stay with that light, to let it guide me, and to be a healing channel for it to others. I had to keep my heart open to everyone and to El Dios and never stand between someone else and the light. Instead, I was to help them see, find, and work with their own light and the light of spirit. I had to do regular ceremonies thanking Mother Earth. I had to stay in daily communion with Kauyumari and the elders. If not, it would be known, and I would be showing the spirits that I was not fit to receive their continued gifts and teachings. The daily work of heart prayers gave *kupuri* back to the gods and goddesses and earned their favor, which would be bestowed on future pilgrimages, through the dreamtime, and through *niericas* that opened up in the course of my daily life if I stayed on the heart path.

Thus I created a respectful relationship with the medicine over the years that did indeed bear fruit during the actual times of ingestion, as well as in between. The gifts given had to be honored, integrated into my life, and used for my healing, the healing of my family and community, and for all those whom the Great Mystery sent my way or brought me to in order to be a channel for its healing love. If the gifts were not honored, the powers would be taken away and there would be no more gifts given. In fact, there could be illness, despair, and suffering from having fallen off the path.

I remember one vision in Wiricuta that came on my second pilgrimage in 1983 that gave me encouragement to keep going. In this vision, many elders came out of the darkness, stood next to me by the fire, and each one gave me a gift. Then, as I mentioned in the beginning of this book, I saw a wide road appear at my feet, continuing straight on until it disappeared over the horizon and into infinity. I knew immediately that it was my life path, a straight road that I was to walk all the days of my life bridging the shamanic world of spirit with the materialistic world of Western civilization. I was filled with awe when I saw the *sendero direcho,* the direct path, that was my future. I looked at the fire and I saw its flames, as the Huichol said, its flowers, rise up and become rainbow-colored spirit figures dancing, singing, and celebrating the beautiful mystery of life. They told me they were the Singing Rainbow Grandmothers. Then they showed me how to "sing them in" whenever I needed their help with healing or transformation work. Tears poured down my cheeks as I took in their beauty and the medicine they were giving me. *You are becoming who you are,* they said. *Go forward in a good way. Remember you are a child of the light and to honor it in all that you do. We are always with you. Enjoy your life. Sing. Dance. Pray. Help others. We will send them to you and then we will help you to help them. You are a channel we will work through. Go forward on your straight path. It will lead you toward your completion.*

As human beings, we have many different channels of awareness available to us, perhaps an infinite amount, and each one holds its own state specific information and capabilities. Like a TV set or a radio, each channel has a different program. If you want news, push the button for the news channel. If you want sports, or music, or cooking, push the button for the appropriate channel, and *voilà.* To obtain the desired information, you have to know there is a channel that has what you are seeking, which one it is, and how to access it. If any of these three components are missing, presto, you miss out on the information. Western culture provides knowledge of a very limited number of channels and very little input on how to shift them in a productive manner. In short, we've been issued a great set of equipment but no user's manual.

We are hypnotized into a consensual trance. We believe that the main

Photo by Joe Burrell

Yarn painting by Guadalupe depicting one of the author's visions.
Kauyumari, Tatewari, and Hicouri are in the center with dancing rainbow
feathers on the outside of the nierica.

channel is the one we access through our sensory modalities, the one that brings us information about the material world. We interpret this information through the cognitive processes of our ego-based identity, functioning on the wavelength of rational-logical, sequential, linear thinking. Anything else, we are taught, is not to be trusted.

My experience growing up was that the only channels available were those of the normal waking consciousness, dream consciousness, and, when I started drinking at thirteen, the altered state induced by inebriation. The only crack in that belief system was the hallucination induced by the high fever I had as a child. Since I had no context with which to understand that experience, it soon drifted off into the recesses of my unconscious.

It wasn't until my first psychedelic experience in 1966 that I realized there were other channels on my operating set. Through this window-opening experience, I learned firsthand about Charles Tart's concept of "state specific information" referred to in chapter 1. In accessing the channel for mystical experience, I remembered Albert Einstein's statement that "I did not arrive at my understanding of the fundamental laws of the universe through my rational mind." My solar journeys of transcendent fusion into light, one in Mexico with the Huichol, the other in Peru on the Death Stone at Machu Picchu, introduced me to a state of ecstatic rapture, a state that transpersonal psychologist Ken Wilber calls "unity consciousness," in which there is total union with all of creation and with all of time, no separation between people, place, or thing, only the ecstatic presence of love joining all. As the Huichol say, *"todos unidos,"* all united. To experience this state is to experience the true wisdom of ecstatic enthusiasm, *en* meaning "in," *theo* meaning "God," i.e., "filled with God."

We in the West live in a monophasic culture. We derive our world-view from a single cognitive mode—normal waking state, which we sanction as the only valid state of consciousness. We suffer from concentrism, a narrow, limited view of what constitutes reality, because we are tuned in to only one channel. Ours is a might-makes-right, patriarchal, fear-based control paradigm, and we are well defended against other channels that might bring information that threatens our notion of how things are and ought to be. With our emphasis on individualism and the accumulation of material goods, we become well versed in the destructive use of power based on the control of others but are babes in the woods when it comes to the forces of Eros. The popular saying of the 1960s "Make love, not war" was an apt reaction to a society that teaches and glorifies violence but offers little on how to create loving relationships with ourselves or with others. Many decades later, we are still feeding the violence. It is ironic to see the popularity of violent acts on TV during "family hours" and the uproar that arises at the proposition of lovemaking portrayed during these same shows.

Polyphasic cultures, on the other hand, construct their reality

Photo by Mark Montgomery

Harmonious blending—nature with nature

models from multiple states of consciousness. They do not suffer from concentrism. They draw on an expanded array of channels, each bringing in different wavelengths of information regarding the nature of the universe. Shamanic peoples are prime examples of polyphasic culture. What appears paradoxical and/or contradictory on the rational, linear, sequential channel, with its conceptual models based on dualistic perception of separation, does not appear in the same manner on channels whose perceptual-cognitive modes are based on different states of consciousness, such as the intuitive, the visionary, or the dreamtime. Different channels not only have different information, they have different ways in which the information is coded and communicated. Polyphasic cultures, open to a wider attunement with the forces of nature and the cosmos, learn on a firsthand basis that the universe is erotic, i.e., constantly making love to itself to produce the physical world. They recognize that without this cosmic lovemaking, there would be no world and there would be no creation, for both are offspring of the acts of Eros. In recognition of this, shamanic cultures include within their cultural milieu socially approved ways of inducing states of union with Eros. They teach their members how to join ecstasy with responsibility and that the pursuit of pleasure is not only healthy but an inherent part of human nature.

Language itself is an abstraction; it is not reality. Numerous studies of linguistics show that language itself shapes how and what we perceive of the various energy dances from the universe within and around us. It conditions us to perceive certain patterns of vibration and not to notice other ones. The benefits of spoken language are obvious in the evolutionary advancement of humanity. But as with everything, there is its shadow side as well. As a shaman from Brazil told me once, "You can't have the light without also having the shade."

The shadow side of language is that it can limit our perceptions of reality because it serves as a lens that we don't know we are using. For the wavelength it is set up to perceive, it sharpens the range and clarity of awareness. But given that we do not know we are wearing it due to a culturally induced blind spot, we miss out on a great deal of other information dancing all around us. Change the perceptual lens, the channel, and presto, like using a microscope, we see the world of the micro. Change to another lens, that of a telescope, and boom, we see the universe of the macro. The lenses do not create information; the information has been there all along. We just didn't have the requisite attunement to pick it up. By limiting our conception of reality to perceptions of physical matter observed through the lens of language-based ordinary consciousness, we create an illusionary world based on the notion of separation. Then we conduct our interactions predicated on the pathological notion that what we do to others and the environment is separate, unrelated, and disconnected with our own lives. As a result of the faulty information obtained from our culturally conditioned monophasic channel, we are fouling our own nests and the collective nest of our planet. We are in dire need then, of a channel shift to those that provide information based on reliable truths of how the universe actually works—as an interpenetrating unity, which is, as the Huichol say, *todos unidos,* all united.

To know this unity is to know ecstasy. Shamanism is based on the experiential knowing of this ecstatic unity. With this awareness as the bedrock of their existential metaphysics, shamans know that what you give or do to another, you give or do to yourself. Shamans work with an array of lenses and channels which enable them to access information from wavelengths usually unseen, i.e., you won't see what you don't believe exists.

As the Huichol tradition makes plain, psychoactive plant usage is one means to shift channels to perceive the unity of life. But as their tradition also makes quite clear, this numinous knowledge brings even greater responsibility—that of living in respectful interaction of sacred reciprocity with all of creation. To put it mildly, this goes against the grain of a materialist society based on capital accumulation. It is no small wonder that we in the West have the irrational and hypocritical biases against psychedelics that we do. As Terence McKenna, author and investigator of shamanic cultures and shamanic states, says, "The use of psychedelics is a call to authenticity which is threatening to our culture since its whole structure is to keep you away from what is real. *Psychedelics are repressed because they are deconditioning agents, they dissolve boundaries based on ego identity of separation and they dissolve linguistic structures that we use to build 'reality' so the person can die to the old and be born anew*" (italics mine).

To be born anew requires recognizing that the problems we face today begin in our own distorted mind-sets. We must learn how to use our minds, our consciousness, in a more skillful, compassionate, and loving manner, i.e., an expanded consciousness from the constricted one that imprisons us like the greedy monkey with his hand stuck in the bottle because he doesn't see that he needs to release the food in his grasp in order to gain his liberation. But let me be quite clear that I am not advocating psychoactive plants as the salvation or panacea for all our cultural crisis.

Spirit dancer

Photo by Mark Montgomery

Quedado! Be careful! Beware. Be aware. The use of psychoactive power plants is not for everyone. Similar to nuclear energy, in the wrong hands they can be agents of great destruction. They are not to be played with or tampered with by the uninitiated or the untrained. They open doors and the user is not in charge of what will come through those doors. Right relationship entails knowing how to work effectively with the forces released. The temporary dissolving of defense mechanisms can free up and amplify the energies of the unconscious, potentially plunging the voyager into hell-like realms of panic, terror, and the complete disintegration of identity and reality frameworks. This in turn can trigger psychotic breaks with acting out self-destructive and/or anti-social behavior. So these substances are not toys for escapist fantasy of the immature. Handled correctly, these experiences can be *niericas* to greater health, healing, creativity, and enriched living. Handled incorrectly, they can lead to a complete breakdown of the personality, resulting in a crippled psyche and a destroyed life. Handle with care.

Make sure there is a wisdom elder you are working with whose integrity and expertise you trust. Remember, these plants are gifts from the Great Mystery, given as sacrament, to be used with respect for healing, growth, and exploration of this sacred universe of which you are an integral part. The purpose of the journey with its potential of ecstasy (from the Greek word *ekstasis,* meaning "flight of the soul from the body") is, within the shamanic model, to find something of practical worth to improve the quality of life and *bring it back* and use it for good in the world. The strength of the vision is measured by the results it produces in your actions. In the words of Meister Eckhardt, "What is taken in by contemplation, must be given out in love." And finally, remember the sacredness of reciprocity: before you take in the gift and teachings of the plant medicine, give back your heartfelt thankfulness for the gifts of your life. Give back to whatever is your sense of the source of these gifts, for gratitude, as Blake said, "is heaven itself."

7

Shamanic Pathways
to Healing and Fulfillment

You create the garden, you don't grow the flowers.
RAM DASS, GRIST FOR THE MILL

The night-long ceremony at Wiricuta was over. It was late winter of 1987, my third pilgrimage. We had already greeted the rising sun, circled the fire, and purified ourselves, and each pilgrim had placed a piece of wood into the flames to feed our Grandfather as we offered up our prayers for the day. Tortillas were cooking over hot coals, the sun's rays and the fire's heat were easing away the night's chill, and I was exhausted. It's not easy staying up all night with Grandpa Fire, struggling to override the body's desire for sleep. But staying awake as long as you can is what is called for—fall asleep and you miss the teachings of Tatewari. "Keep your heart open to Tatewari. It will teach you, it will show you the way," the Huichol elders stress. "To become a *mara'akame,* you must learn to hear its voice. Give yourself over to Tatewari, to the *hicouri,* to Kauyumari. If they accept you, they will show you how to live."

I tried to stay awake for as long as I could. Occasionally, I nodded off, but for the most part, I was able to stay up, wrapped in my serape and sleeping bag, trying to stay warm, gazing into the flames—watching, listening, and praying. I was not disappointed. At one point during the evening, I saw a rainbow-colored serpent crawling amongst the flames. It

166

stopped in front of me. I thanked it for coming to me, then asked, *Old one, what do you bring me?* The serpent replied, *Give me your beliefs, attitudes, identities, and behaviors that no longer serve you, that get in the way of your healthy growth and the blossoming of your flowers. I will take them into the heart of the Tatewari and he, the first shaman, will burn them up. I am always here, with the fire, to help you clean out your pipes—that way you will be able to stay in contact with Grandfather Fire and Kauyumari. Always respect Tatewari. Then he will help you in your life. Stay with the fire as much as you can. It is your Grandfather.*

I thanked the serpent for its medicine, then proceeded to follow its directions. I focused my mind on finding the energies that were blocking my pipes. I breathed down into them and then sent the breath into the fire, carrying my toxic energy with it. Negative judgments, guilts, thought forms of limitation—"I can'ts, I'm not good enoughs, that's impossibles," fears—all this and more I sent into the serpent's mouth during the long hours of the night. Then about four o'clock in the morning when only the shaman and I and a few others were still upright staring into Tatewari, I saw, in the middle of the flames, a huge, red, beating heart, pulsating out healing waves of love to all the pilgrims. Excitedly, I woke up my friend Alijandro, who was curled up in his sleeping bag next to me. I jabbed him in the ribs. "Look into the fire. Tell me what you see."

Groggily, he sat up, rubbed his eyes, and looked into the flames. "Do you see it?" I said again. Suddenly, Alijandro grinned. "Yeah, I see it. It's a big heart. It looks beautiful. It's taking care of us while we sleep," he replied. I was delighted. It wasn't just my imagination. Just then, from across the fire, twenty feet away and directly opposite us, Tacho said softly, "Look into the center of Tatewari, you will see its heart. This is how it is. Tatewari *is* our heart." Then he began a long series of prayers and songs that carried on into the dawn. I marveled at his stamina. "It is Tatewari that gives me my strength," he said later. "I am like a machine. It is in my stomach. I get my *kupuri* from Tatewari. Do not try to do it alone. You will only fail. But if you stay with Tatewari, he will make you strong."

My strength stayed with me pretty much right up to the time of eating those tortillas for breakfast. I gave my first piece to Tatewari in thankfulness for the gifts of the evening and to the purifying serpent for its healings and teachings. Then a wave of exhaustion began to seep through me. I was ready for sleep, but just as I started to lie back down in my sleeping bag, I noticed some dried-up peel from the outside of the peyote root lying all around me. It would be disrespectful to go to sleep with the pieces of the medicine lying around in that way. I couldn't put them in the fire either, because it was not right according to the Huichol way. No, the "bones" of the peyote had to go back out into the desert and be buried in Mother Earth. So, tired as I was, I gathered up all the leftover pieces of medicine and put them in my *bolsa,* my medicine bag. I picked up my knife, purchased in the *mercado* at Charcas, the last pueblo we had passed through on our way to Wiricuta, where we had stopped for supplies—water, tortillas, candles, chocolate, fruit, and knives that would only be used to hunt the peyote. These knives were to be purified and used only to touch the medicine.

I put my knife in my *bolsa* and stood up to get my bearings. Our circle was surrounded by a vast desert filled with all kinds of cacti, creosote bushes, and the occasional skeletal remains of a fallen scrub tree. We'd driven for miles through this dusty terrain, stopping only when the shaman said, *"aqui,"* here. I gazed over the barren landscape, which looked like a greenish-brown ocean stretching as far as the eye could see. Looking straight out, I could only see so far, but looking up and away, I could see the far-off mountains that gave a truer perspective on the immense terrain.

I strode out several hundred yards. I had to pee and wanted privacy for that as well as for putting my plant scrapings back into the earth. I disappeared into the waves of the desert sea and conducted my two ceremonies—one profane but very important, the other sacred and also very important. The sacred and the profane, for the Huichol, like everything else, is *todos unidos,* all united. Of course, I used my special peyote knife to dig out a hole for the scraps. I gently placed the dry peyote skin into the earth. I sprinkled in some tobacco and a Mexican coin, then bent my face down into the hole and thanked the spirit of the medicine for my good visions and teachings. When I was through with my prayers, I covered up the hole and patted down the dirt so no one could tell this spot had been disturbed. Then I stood up. I immediately froze. I was lost! I couldn't see back to our campsite! I was groggy, tired, and disoriented, and I had no idea from which direction I had come. I looked around for a telltale landmark to differentiate one area from another, something I could recognize. Nothing but sameness in whatever direction I looked. Just as my panic started to take off into the stratosphere, I noticed a wisp of smoke rise up from the floor of the desert. "Oh man, hallelujah," I said out loud, "Grandpa Fire is still cooking and still helping me out, showing me the way home. *Pam'pa Dios,* Tatewari!" Laughing at my own carelessness and giddy for being saved, I walked back to camp extremely grateful for those who had been feeding Old Grandpa while I was out getting lost.

When I reached our campsite, I shook out my sleeping bag and spread it out on the ground. Now I was ready to do some serious napping. I took off my medicine bags and looked inside for my tobacco pouch. I wanted to thank Tatewari for helping me find my way back from the ocean of desert. I found the tobacco but to my great dismay, I noticed there was no peyote knife! It was gone. I had forgotten to pick it up and put it back in my bag after digging the hole. I stood up and looked out into the desert. Then I burst out laughing at the absurdity of the situation. My knife blade was three inches long. It was stuck in the ground. The handle, which was sticking up, was made of wood, in exactly the color of the branches and bushes that amply fill the desert. Finding a needle in a haystack would be no problem compared to this challenge.

As I considered my options, a familiar pessimism began to emerge. *Why even try? You'll never find it. Just let it go. It's just a knife. You're exhausted. There is no way in hell that you'll ever see that knife again.* But then another part of my mind spoke up: *Hey, wait a minute. Don't give up so easily. One little obstacle and you're ready to fold up your tent. Remember, anything is possible with the Great Spirit's help. Go out there and hunt for your knife in the same way that you hunted for the peyote. Call in Kauyumari. Give thanks for its help in your life and explain what you need. Sing the Deer Song. See a positive vision of finding the knife and being thankful. Try your hardest, but let go of results.*

I thought about a favorite quote of mine from the psychiatrist Victor

The immense desert of Wiricuta

Frankel, who was a concentration camp inmate during World War II: "Everything can be taken from a man but one thing: the last of the human freedoms—to choose one's attitude in any given set of circumstances, to choose one's own way." Taking charge of my attitude, I took a few moments to clean out my negative thoughts by sending them into the serpent of the fire. Then I called in Kauyumari. After thanking it for all its gifts, I asked it to help me find the knife. *I don't have the slightest idea which way to go,* I said. *So I surrender to you. I will let you lead me.*

Then I meandered off into the great desert sea. At least this time I remembered to orient myself so I wouldn't get lost. Maybe I wouldn't find my knife, but at least I'd save myself the embarrassment, and danger, of getting lost.

I had no plan regarding which direction to look. I just went wherever my body was pulled. Sometimes I'd walk in a circle, my eyes on the ground, searching and singing. Back and forth went my footsteps and the voices in my head. *You're a fool. You'll never find it. Give up and go back to camp and relax. Its no big deal, it's just a dumb knife.* When that voice spoke, I acknowledged its presence but then sent it on its way. *Keep your faith strong,* said the other voice. *Anything is possible with Spirit's presence and help. Keep going forward with your heart and mind open, keep giving it your best. Appreciate the beauty of the desert. Right now is all you've got.* I kept walking, watching, stopping to wipe the sweat off my brow. *Whew, I don't recognize a thing, it all looks the same.*

I stepped over a bleached-out log. *Now I know I didn't come this way before, I never saw that log when I was out here burying the peyote.* Frustrated, I walked around a big sage bush that was taller than me, and boom—there it was, standing upright in the sand like a proud warrior radiating golden waves of *kupuri.* It was like a science fiction movie where something inanimate magically comes alive. The aura from the knife pulsated a good ten feet in every direction. "Who writes the script for this stuff?" I said out loud. Then I heard Kauyumari's now familiar voice transmitted telepathically from the energy vibrations of the field around the knife: *If you follow me in a respectful way, I will always show you how to walk. This is how it will be for you from now on. Others, or even your own mind, may tell you something is impossible. But in your heart, if you feel energy to go for it, open your mind and see a positive outcome. It is an open ball game until you close the door. You have been led to your knife in this way to show you how to go about things in a good way. Give it your best shot but always without attachment to the final results. Release with faith and trust into the bigger hands. Then go forward honoring the step that is right in front of you. This is your medicine path. The Spirit is with you always.* Vaya con Dios.

I sank to my knees filled with prayers of gratitude. Joy surged through every molecule of my being. How long I was there I do not know. Finally, the intensity began to ebb. I picked up the knife, stood up, and slowly walked back to camp. "No one is going to believe this," I muttered. But it doesn't matter, I realized. I know it happened. Now I have to. carry this teaching out of Wiricuta and back into my life. "Thank you, Great Spirit," I said aloud, "for this strong medicine. Help me to remember this always, help me to remember you always." As I walked, I repeatedly touched the knife in my bag to reassure myself that it really was there. When I reached my sleeping bag, I climbed in, filled with excitement but also with exhaustion. Within minutes, I was out cold.

The experience of miraculously finding my knife in the desert left a strong imprint. Like earlier experiences mountain climbing, it dramatically showed me the power of intentionality and right relationship, the power of the human mind to open or close doors. *Truly,* I thought, *it's a whole new ball game when I align my will with the will of the Great Mystery. The possibilities are beyond what I can even imagine and I understand that I will never find out what is possible unless I go for it with 100 percent effort and 100 percent unattachment.* It's a demanding challenge, but we live in demanding times. However, solutions to the dilemmas of our times will not be found on the same channel of consciousness from which they arose in the first place.

You know what metaphorical knives, or challenges, you yourself have buried out in the seemingly infinite desert. Perhaps they are challenges in the area of health and healing, of body or of relationship; perhaps they are in the area of greater self-realization or in gaining greater prosperity and success; perhaps in the area of transforming repressive institutions or social or economic conditions; it is all of this, perhaps; or it is something else. You also know your attitudes about it. Listen within yourself to see how my experience in the desert of Wiricuta might speak to you.

In my travels and work with people from all classes of life, I see that almost all of us have unconsciously bought into a radically impoverished notion of who we are and what we are capable of doing and being. Bottom line is that humanity has a much greater potential for effectively applied creativity, joy, love, happiness, intelligence, and compassion than has been actualized historically. In Western society, with its emphasis on separation and individualism, we are both spiritually malnourished and culturally deprived. We suffer from lack of supportive community and transcendent vision that unifies us with something greater than our egos. Along with these lacks, we also suffer in ignorance of practical tools and understanding by which to bring our highest visions to fruition.

My experiences of solar vision opened a perceptual lens to see that we are all children of the light, i.e., the sun. Christians are told that God loved us so much that He gave us His only begotten son. This is an accurate statement translated metaphorically, for life on this planet is born out of the light-giving energy of the sun radiating into the earth and oceans. In the cosmic realm, the sun is our father, the earth is our mother. The light of the sun is in turn a manifestation of the light behind it, so to speak, and the source of the sun, the Great Cosmic Mystery, is God. God so loved us He gave us His only begotten son—the *sun*. The sun in turn gave us its light, its sunlight, i.e., its *son*, to show us what we are and how to live. Within each of us is this light. Even the Western tradition recognizes this. What do we call our abdominal region in Latin? The *solar plexus*, the place of light. And where is it? Right in the center of our being! Jesus, a human manifestation of one who joined totally with the light, referred to this quite clearly: "I and my Father are one. The Kingdom of Heaven is within," he gently reminded us.

Literally, as well as in mythic terms, we do in fact have the son of the sun within us at the essence level of who and what we are. To know this as an existential, experiential *fact*, not a belief, a wish, or a desire, is to know true prosperity, and "the peace that passeth understanding." This is the great knife hidden out in the desert that we are all searching for through relationships and acquisitions. It is interesting to note that it was into the desert that Jesus went for his place of pilgrimage and testing. His faith was strong and he found his knife. Then he came back into the world of humanity and used it to heal by affirming truth cutting away untruth.

When we treat ourselves as the sacred beings we are, with respect, caring, kindness, compassion, love, and nurturance, we open a doorway by which the Great Spirit can act in and through us with love. Thus, our lives and our relationships can prosper from the inside out. This love from the Great Spirit never leaves us. Yet we shut it out when we act in unloving ways toward ourselves or toward others. It reminds me of a Buddhist story where a disciple asked the master: "How can I ever get emancipated?" The master answered: "Who has ever put you in bondage?"

If our choice in this life is to gain release from self-imposed bondage and actualize greater health, healing, wellness, real prosperity, and realization of our true nature, it can start with remembering that we are children of the light. If we choose to follow this path of light in our actions, then the wisdom of the Huichol path offers one model of how to proceed.

I remember the words of the shaman when we stopped in a small pueblo to pick up supplies and water. The sun was setting just as we parked our vans in the central plaza. We got out to discuss who was going to go into which store to get supplies so that we could get done and out of town as soon as possible. The Huichol didn't like being in town after Taupa went down. They wanted to be back out on the land, around Tatewari. Our deliberations were dragging on as the gringos debated one plan after another. Finally the shaman chastised us for taking so long: "We must get back to Tatewari. That is where we are safe, with our Grandfather watching out for us. During the day we stay with Taupa, Father Sun. At night we must be with Tatewari. This is how we live—stay with the light." I'd never heard it put so succinctly before, but it certainly fit with the practice that I had come to know during my time of being with the Huichol.

Every morning upon awakening, our first duty was to go to the fire and make an offering, purify ourselves, and offer our prayers to Father Sun and to the Sacred Directions. At night when we made camp, the first task, even before unpacking, was to start up the fire and once again purify and make an offering—each man, woman, and child gave a stick to Grandpa Fire and circled the light-giving flames. Only then did we set about the chores of making camp.

All of my shamanic homework assignments were centered upon connecting with light and keeping that connection going. Greeting the rising sun each day was number one—extending appreciation and filling up with *kupuri* for the day. "There is a ceremony going on all the time on Taupa. The gods and goddesses are celebrating, singing and dancing, praying, chanting. When we give our prayers back to them, it helps give them strength, and they give it back to us," explained Prem Das on my first pilgrimage. During my apprenticeship, I had to take my special medicine objects out to get the *kupuri* of the newborn sun every day. In this way, they were fortified to help strengthen me in facing the challenges of my life. After my prayers to the sun, I came inside and lit a purified candle. This was my "little Tatewari" to whom I would send my prayers and from which they'd travel out to my family and loved ones. I was instructed to do this every day, wherever I went. "Every day the sun comes up and blesses you. So it is a good thing to get up and say thank you. It strengthens you and helps you grow. Like the corn plants, grow straight up toward the light and raise up your arms and give thanks. It is a good way to live."

I have been following this practice for many years. As a pragmatist, I use what works and I "don't fix what ain't broken." My prayers with the sun and the candle set my orientation at the critical time of starting a new day, when we not only choose how we will dress but what identity we will carry forth into the world. I notice that when I choose not to do this practice with the sun and candle, what I am really doing is giving the negative programs in my unconscious the power to take me wherever they want. This has led me over too many cliffs.

Instead, I retake the reins by lining up with the light. This practice sets me up to notice more quickly when I forget and veer off course through judgment, fear, not being present in the moment, and through identification of my totality with ego. When I fall, as I do many times every day, I recall my intention to align with light, pick myself up, and get back on the trail again. It sounds simple. But it is the core of an ongoing personal mastery practice that produces results—stay with the light, day and night, bring it into the dark places, celebrate it, give thanks.

The light is intelligence, it is a giveaway from the Great Spirit bringing high octane fuel to fill up the tanks. By continuing this attunement practice, the *kupuri* increasingly enters body, mind, and spirit, bringing with it illuminating guidance, healing love, and the warm, good feeling of knowing that the Great Spirit is present always. Greater riches has no one. To work most effectively, of course, this sense of spiritual prosperity must be carried into all aspects of one's life. Nothing must be left out, for if it is, it can become a hole in the bucket from which the hard-earned profits can leak away. Compassion, kindness, insight, and love pay dividends always. Sustained focus takes mental discipline, without which there can be no freedom. Without focused intentionality to open to the gifts of the Great Mystery through humility and surrender, the riches of true prosperity fall through the cracks. The prayer of an unknown Confederate soldier beautifully illustrated the power of humility and surrender in obtaining true prosperity:

I asked for strength that I might achieve;
I was made weak that I might learn humbly to obey.
I asked for health that I might do greater things;
I was given infirmity that I might do better things.
I asked for riches that I might be happy;
I was given poverty that I might be wise.
I asked for power that I might have the praise of men;
I was given weakness that I might feel
the need of God.
I asked for all things that I might enjoy life;
I was given life that I might enjoy all things.
I got nothing that I had asked for, but everything that I
had hoped for.
Almost despite myself my unspoken prayers were answered;
I am, among all men, most richly blessed.

To be "most richly blessed" by a blossoming garden is not, however, the end of the process. There is still the task of taking the flowers into the acts of our daily lives, for without this integration, the blossoms soon fade from sight and from mind. Idries Shah, in *Tales of the Dervishes,* shares a wisdom story that illuminates this continuing process and how to do it in a good way.

God decided to become visible to a king and a peasant and sent an angel to inform them of the blessed event.

"O King," the angel announced, "God has deigned to be revealed to you in whatever manner you wish. In what form do you want God to appear?"

Seated on his throne and surrounded by awe-struck subjects, the king proclaimed, "How else would I wish to see God save in majesty and power? Show God to us in the full glory of power."

God granted his wish and appeared as a bolt of lightning that instantly pulverized the king and his court. Not even a cinder remained.

Photo by Mark Montgomery

Blending with Mother Earth

The angel then manifested herself to a peasant, saying, "God deigns to be revealed to you in whatever manner you desire. How do you wish to see God?"

Scratching his head and puzzling a long while, the peasant finally said, "I am a poor man and not worthy to see God face to face. But if it is God's will to be revealed to me, let it be in those things with which I am familiar. Let me see God in the earth I plough, the water I drink, the food I eat. Let me see God in the faces of my family and neighbors."

God granted the peasant his wish, and he lived a long and happy life. May God grant you the same!

8

᭟᭟

Resanctifying Daily Life

It is not what we do that makes us holy;
it is making holy what we do.

MEISTER ECKHARDT

I n ancient Mesoamerica, Quetzalcoatl was a Christ-like, archetypal figure of mythic proportions, a cultural hero teaching the ways of love, respect, and harmony with all of creation. When he died, betrayed by trickery, his demise signaled the loss of the sacred. It was said in prophecy that his spirit would return at some time in the future and that when it did, it would signal the return of spirit to the peoples of the earth. The vision on my first Huichol pilgrimage in 1981 of the eagle, representing the celestial powers, with the serpent, representing the earth powers, for the journey into transcendental oneness with the light of cosmic consciousness, alerted me to Quetzalcoatl's return. With the vision came an assignment: *You are an emissary for an ancient wisdom struggling to be heard in a culture that has lost respect for the sacred. You were initiated into the sacred way of the shaman over twenty thousand years ago. You are becoming who you are. This knowledge has been encoded in you ever since. Now is the time to bring it alive. You must use it to revise your life. You must bring Spirit into all of your activities. You will eventually work with people who are leaders of transnational corporations. You do not have expertise in business, but you do know how to access the sacred. This is what they have forgotten. Do not seek this out. Go on with your daily life. It will come*

179

to you as you honor what is given to you now. Quetzalcoatl returns.

I feel very uncomfortable revealing these experiences because they sound so strange. Are they the ramblings of a *machugigna,* a nut? Or is there something to them? Personally, I take them all with a grain of salt. What I can use, I use. What I can't use in addressing my life challenges, I release back into the Mystery. With that preface, I want to talk about an even stranger phenomena, that of shamanic encounters with extraterrestrial forms of intelligence. My first experience of this order took place in 1983 during an all-night Native American healing ceremony in Northern California. Healing energy swirled around the tipi, touching all who were there with its power, beauty, and presence. It continued on this way for several hours with singing, praying, chanting, and drumming. Then it seemed to reach some kind of required critical mass and suddenly rose up in the form of a flying circular disk and flew out through an opening at the top of the tipi, spiraling up into the night sky. I watched as it zoomed away, spinning off other circles of pulsating disks of light as it went. The disks looked exactly like flying saucers. They spread out in all directions, and in my altered state I could see them circling the planet. I watched in fascination as they spun down from the sky into gatherings where people were praying together for healing. Their presence brought *kupuri,* guidance, and inspiration, from the central fire in the tipi to all those who were open to receiving it.

Then I saw a shaman alone in the dark night of a jungle. He was in deep communion, drumming and chanting, praying for his people. I watched a rainbow beam of energy emanate from his body and extend straight up into the sky. I followed the path of this energy up into the black night until it entered a vortex of flashing lights. I saw that the lights were flashing from a control panel on the ceiling of a huge flying saucer high up in the stratosphere. It was communicating with the shaman; they were working together. The shaman's ceremony was a means of activating a complex communication system between an interstellar entity and planet earth. I watched in fascination until, suddenly, my mind was lifted out of my cranium and transported up to the ship, where it slowly merged into the ceiling panel. This panel was also in communion with a huge energy field in a distant galaxy. My mind was then transported beyond the speed of light from the spaceship to this distant galaxy, where some kind of psychic surgery was performed. During the procedure, I felt absolutely no pain. It was all energy transformation. When the procedure was completed, my mind was instantaneously transferred back to the spaceship, then back into my body here on earth, and I "heard" the following words: *It is not for you to know or understand what has taken place. Just know that the shamans of light throughout the history of your planet have been working with us. What you speak of as "the upper world" is the realm of your higher self but it is beyond the range of your imagination. Your job is to stay open to it. Information has been placed inside of you that will come forth as it is needed. You cannot hold on to it. You are simply a receiver and channel through which it expresses itself.*

Is it all delusion? Is it communication with beings from outer space or intelligence from another dimension? *Quien sabe?* Who knows? I focus my attention on the daily occurrences of my life and what the waves of the Great Mystery wash up onto the shore where I sit with my observing witness. I especially notice what I am doing, or perhaps more appropriately, what I'm "being used" to do. I track the consequences of what I see and feel during my experience, and I also notice the feedback of others and the consequences they experience. Here is an example of what I mean:

I asked the same medicine man who helped me through my bout with poison oak to visit a class I was teaching at a local junior college, which prepared people to go out on a quest. He brought ten or twelve of his people with him. With intimidating ferocity, he spoke about the sacredness of the quest, the sweat lodge ceremony, and Native American spirituality. "This is not for fun and games. When you go out on a quest and you humble yourself, when you suffer and give away of your self and pay attention, day and night, to the many ways the Great Spirit can speak to you through the forces of nature, then you may receive a vision. It may be a dream, an animal, a voice, a presence sent to help you if you are truly sincere and patient. But in receiving this gift, you also incur greater responsibility in life, which you carry right up to your death. Do not go any farther if you are not willing to carry this responsibility all of your days. You must be careful, you must be respectful. The Great Spirit is watching your every move and your every thought. It is strong medicine."

After the class, I went out to dinner with the medicine man and his people. I was very disturbed. I personalized all he had said to the students, thinking he was criticizing me, saying I shouldn't be taking people out on quests. I told him of my concerns. "No," he said. "You understand, you have respect. You are a bridge builder between cultures. It is important for you to do this work. Keep taking the people who are ready, who are sincere. Take them into the sweat lodge, take them out on quest. Help them to learn the teachings of Mother Earth and the Great Spirit. Help them to learn that when they hurt the earth, they hurt themselves, and when they hurt themselves, they hurt the earth. Help them to walk the Good Red Road. We are all related. We must all learn to live together in harmony with the laws of nature. Then we will survive."

I continued on my path. Today what the "voices" told me long ago about working with corporate executives has come true. Sometimes I am invited out to a company's headquarters to work on-site, using ceremony and ritual. Sometimes they fly here to Northern California and I take them through a sweat ceremony by the Pacific Ocean. We watch the sun sink into the sea, then enter the lodge, a dome-shaped structure with a framework of willow branches covered by blankets and tarps. Inside, it is dark, the womb of Mother Earth. We take off our clothes, get down on the ground and crawl in on our hands and knees. We sit on the bare earth around a hole dug into the center. It is the passageway down into the lower world. Soon red hot rocks heated in the ceremonial fire outside (the "stone people," the oldest people on the planet) are brought into the lodge and placed in the hole. When each stone has been properly thanked, greeted, and blessed, the flap is closed, plunging the occupants into pitch darkness. Nothing can be seen except the shimmering rocks radiating heat and medicine into the lodge.

Soon, water is poured onto the glowing rocks and they "breathe." Steam shoots out and the purification gets intense. Four rounds of prayers and sweating are conducted in this way, one round for each of the surrounding directions. Physical bodies are cleansed by the steam, while emotions, psyche, and spirits are cleansed by the power of prayer. Inside the womb-like structure, there is no separation by age, color, size, sex, or economic or social status. All are as infants together inside the womb of our Mother Earth, seeking cleansing, healing, and renewal. When the ceremony is completed hours later, participants emerge revitalized to walk a healing path as children of the earth.

At a recent sweat, a CEO of an international consulting and training company was in great despair at having lost his spirituality along the way to his material success. In the third round, I saw Spirit shoot into the lodge and enter his body. He jerked upward and burst into tears, sobbing in joy for the return of Spirit in his life. He thanked me profusely for his healing. I took in his words of thanks but I explained to him that it was to the wisdom elders, to the wisdom ways themselves, and to the indigenous people throughout the world still struggling to maintain their age-old teachings that we owed our thanks and our prayers. I taught him a thankfulness song, and with rattle and drum we sang and prayed together. Afterward, I emphasized the importance of regular thankfulness prayers and how this practice forms the basis for the resanctification of daily life. I also emphasized the importance of protecting the earth and her places of sacred power and of protecting the rights and very life of the indigenous people struggling against the forces of oppression that threaten their ceremonies by robbing them of their sacred sites. "You are a leader," I said. "You must remember that we are sacred beings. When we forget this basic truth, we dishonor ourselves and all of life. We cut ourselves off from our innate wisdom, creativity, happiness, and our potentials for leading more fulfilling and meaningful lives. When we remember our true nature—Spirit at the center of self and at the center of everyone and everything—and when we make room for its presence in our everyday lives, we create an opening for it to work through us in a healing way. Then we can listen for guidance on how to create lifestyles that contribute to healing Mother Earth and the full community of life." The executive listened to my words without responding. I wondered how he was taking them but I didn't want to intrude on his silence. Some time later I found out. He referred a close colleague who was also interested in learning about "shamanic healing ways."

At this point it is important to mention that saying yes to all requests for help is not always the right thing to do. Sometimes it is just as important to say no as it is to say yes. I learned about this from the medicine man who came to my quest class years before and who had helped me deal with my poison oak attack. "Just because someone asks for your help, it doesn't mean it is right for you to give it. Don't let your ego be the one that answers. You don't know what is best for another person. But the Great Spirit does. Take some time to go off by yourself and ask for guidance about what you are supposed to do. Listen for the Great Spirit's counsel. Sometimes you are not the person or your medicine is not the right medicine for what they need. Pray on it. Dream on it."

A short time after this counsel, a dramatic river experience vividly brought home the power of his words. The year was 1974 and I was directing the Wilderness Treatment Program with heroin addicts, and white water river running was an important and exciting component of our program. We'd start people on less challenging rivers and for those who did well and wanted more challenge, we moved them up eventually to the Tuolumne River. The Tuolumne is considered one of the best white water challenges in the Western United States. It is not for the meek or the inexperienced. One spring, when the river was running fairly high, I put together a strong crew and was looking forward to a good run. At the last minute, a friend from elementary school days was out visiting from the East Coast and called me up to say hello. I thought he would enjoy the river run and invited him to join us. He had no experience with this kind of outing but with the rest of the crew strong in that regard, I figured we could carry him and it would be all right.

But at the last moment, one of our crew had to drop out and we were one person short. Several experienced folks from the program all wanted to go. We only did this particular run once per year, so it was a special opportunity. Then a reporter from a local paper asked if he could go on the trip and then write a story about the wilderness program. I was concerned about his lack of experience and knew that two inexperienced people would weaken our crew past the point of safety. When we hit rough sections of the river, we would need everyone on the boat working smoothly as a team under stress. We couldn't afford anyone freaking out, especially when trying to avoid the hole at the bottom of Clavey Falls, which I had already been in for a frightening period of time when I thought I was going to die, discussed in an earlier chapter.

I was in a quandary. I knew the reporter's story would bring good publicity to the program, highlighting our successful work with addicts using wilderness as healer. I also knew I would be taking a risk and endangering our whole crew by taking him on. My conflict was intensified by an insidious influence that I didn't want to face: I didn't want to be seen as a *bad guy* by saying no to the reporter. At the time, I didn't have the ego strength to deny him the trip and risk his ill will. I wanted to be liked more than anything else. It was a dangerous hole in my bucket. I ended up saying yes against my better judgment, and along he came.

All went well until we hit the last hundred yards on the swoop heading toward the falls. The momentum of the river is tremendous at this time, heading toward the drop off. If you hit the falls just right, you sail over the hole and catch downstream water that sweeps you out of danger. Well, we were out of synch. We went over the falls sideways and the hole caught the back portion of the boat. The captain and I were in the back. The hole's massive power started to suck the boat into its swirling maw. "Hard forward!" the captain screamed. Everyone dug their paddles into the waves and pulled with all their might. Ever so slowly, the boat started to inch forward out from the grip of the hole. "Pull!" yelled our captain. We pulled like maniacs. Huge waves washed over the bow. The boat stopped in mid-air. Just when the outcome could go in either direction, the two inexperienced rafters freaked out and stopped paddling.

In that instant, we lost our power and the rear of the boat dropped into the hole. The captain and I were instantly sucked down and the rest of the crew washed overboard by huge waves crashing over the falls and into our boat. Remembering my long-ago lesson about surrendering into the downward pull, I released into it without resistance. Once again, I was sucked down into the raging maw and after what seemed like an eternity, was shot out of the hole and into the downstream current. I struggled to shore, shaken but glad to be alive, and pulled myself onto dry ground. Catching my breath, I scanned upstream and downstream to count heads. One by one, I saw the various members of our crew sprawled like wet rats on both sides of the river. But someone was missing—my friend.

Frantically, I searched up and down the river calling out his name as hard as I could. No answer. He wasn't there—no one had seen him. Panic hit. *Oh my God, he's gone. Drowned.* I'd have to call his parents who lived one block from my parents back East, people I had known almost all my life, and tell them their son was dead and that it was all my fault! Just because I wasn't strong enough to say no when I should have. It was my weakness that had killed their son!

I was devastated. I saw the whole phone call in my mind—how his parents would react when I gave them the news. Their oldest son was gone. Dead. And it was all my fault. His family was ruined. I was ruined. The wilderness program was ruined. It was a total disaster. In the middle of this calamitous scenario, I suddenly heard a high-pitched yell: "Help me. I'm stuck!" It came from above. I looked up and saw him twenty-five feet up a steep rock face, holding on for dear life. Somehow in the adrenaline rush of what had happened, he scrambled up the rock as high as he could go. Now he was stuck and couldn't get down. I don't think I was ever happier to see anyone than I was in that moment. Relieved and grateful, I burst into laughter. I learned an incredibly important lesson that day: to say no when it needs to be said. It can literally save a life! Today my yes is amply strengthened by an ability to say no when judgment or guidance calls for it. The Clavey Falls hole is a teacher that really gets its point across. As for my friend, we coached him down from the rock face, and to this day I don't think he's ever been out on a river again.

Since then, I try to remember to listen for guidance whenever a situation presents itself for healing. While doing so always helps, it still doesn't guarantee smooth sailing. A number of years ago, when I was invited up to Portland, Oregon, to lead a workshop on shamanic healing, I listened for inner guidance on what to do and got the go-ahead, so I told them okay. I sent the organizers some materials to draw on in writing up their publicity flyers. I expected some back and forth dialogue with them before they printed up the final flyers so that I could see what they were writing and make sure it was accurate. A few weeks later, I was taken aback when I received their completed brochure in the mail, saying, incorrectly, that I would be conducting "Native American Ceremonies."

I knew if Native people saw what they had written, they would be upset and rightly so. I was upset myself. In my work, I use what I have been taught and authorized by my elders to do, but I never claim it is Native American ceremony. I simply say, "This is what I have been shown by my teachers. It has power and meaning for me in a way that nothing else I have tried or know about does. I try to use it in a respectful way, for healing, for guidance, and for strengthening me to walk the best path I can in this life."

But it was too late to change what had been written. It had already been mailed out. When I flew to Portland a few days later, they met me at the airport. "We have a problem," they exclaimed. "A group of Native American people are upset about what you are doing and threaten to picket your workshop. They want to meet with you beforehand." I had expected something like this ever since I'd read their flyer. I was anxious but also curious to see where these people were really at. If they were really into medicine work, I trusted they would see not just my "outer robes," but also be able to read my heart and know what was there—my love and respect for the ways of Mother Earth and the Great Spirit. I thought of a saying I'd heard years before: "When the going gets tough, you get what you practice." In my daily prayers at home, I worked with the power of the South, faith and trust, in surrendering into Great Spirit's hands. Now was a good time to put it into practice under pressure. "Great," I said. "Let's go meet them." We grabbed a bite to eat and then went to the retreat site, where a Lakota pipe holder and a woman were waiting for us.

He was a solidly built man and very strong in physical presence. He didn't say a word when we were introduced, just nodded. The woman was the initial spokesperson. He sat down, closed his eyes, and went inside to listen from his looks-within place. I welcomed that. I knew that if he was open, he would know that I was walking the Good Red Road in the best way that I knew, trying to serve Great Spirit by following the directions I had been given on my quests and pilgrimages. I had nothing to hide.

The woman spoke of how upset they were, then wanted to know what I actually did, who I had worked with, and what authority I had to do what I was doing. I opened my heart and let the words flow. I explained how I got involved with shamanism, my visionary experiences during my quests in the mountains, and how I was working with others to bring them to Spirit in ways that had been meaningful for me. I spoke of the great respect I had for the old ways of Turtle Island and that I believed they held the answers for how Western society needed to change if life was to continue on these lands in a good way. I spoke of the elders I had worked with, what exactly I was doing, and how I felt about it. During this time, I focused on keeping my heart wide open. I wanted to be seen directly with no defenses or blocks. "This is not a game for me," I explained. "It is not a passing fad. It is my life. I am not trying to be something I am not. I use these ways because they help me to be the best me I can be. They speak to my soul. I believe the great powers of the universe are given by the Creator for all people to know and acknowledge and pay respectful homage to. This is what I try to do." Then I told them of my daily thanksgiving rituals and how it is the best way to live that I know. It speaks to my heart, to my spirit, to my entire being.

"Ever since I was a little boy," I continued, "I've loved nature and wanted nothing more than to be in it. I loved walking in the woods alone. In school, I always sat by the window wishing I could be out there instead of inside listening to words that held no interest for me. Western religion and philosophy held no meaning for me. They had no power. It wasn't until I discovered the native ways of this land that I finally found something that made sense to me, that spoke to me, and that I could respect. The ways of respectful relationship with all living things, with the wind, the sun, the animals, the earth, the plants—with all of creation and with the Great Sacred Mystery that underlies it all—this is my religion. This is my life." I continued, "In my work with others, I see they are also hungry for deeper connection with Spirit. They too are lost and are looking for a way that speaks to their deeper being. I share with them what I know, what Spirit has taught me, and some are helped by this. I ask on my quests if this is what Spirit wants me to be doing. The answer so far always comes back yes. So I do the best I can, sharing what I have been taught, trying to go on in a good way as a channel for Great Spirit in the world."

After I had expressed myself, I paused to see if they wanted me to continue. The woman nodded so I went on. "I know that all nonindigenous people who come to this land from elsewhere bring with them a tradition and religion from their country of origin. I believe it is important to honor this and to carry it on when it is good medicine. My people go back thousands of years to the Twelve Tribes of Israel. I am a tribal man. My ancestors, the Hebrews, were a tribal people who went out into the desert and up onto sacred mountains to seek vision and to commune with God. I am following the tradition of my ancestral roots with the quests that I do. But," I emphasized, "I feel that it is vitally important to connect with the spirit of the land where my family has now lived and died for three generations. I have to listen to its voice in order to learn how to walk in balance with the rhythms of Mother Earth here in my new home. I am trying to do this in the best way that I know how, the way I have been shown by teachers I respect. I am trying to do this in right relationship with Spirit and all the living circle of life. This is my path."

When I finished speaking, there was a long period of silence. I sat back in my chair and released into the Great Spirit's hands. I waited patiently, breathing in, breathing out. *Thank you Great Spirit, for right now,* I prayed in silence. *Help me to open to your presence and to your will. I surrender to you and whatever it is that serves you and the greatest good. Ho. May it be so.*

Finally, the man raised his head and spoke: "I see that we are doing the same work. I see that we are brothers on this path of life. I see in your heart that you are doing the work of Great Spirit. It is a good thing. I am glad that we have met. I want to support you in what you are doing. Tomorrow I would like to bring my buffalo skull as an altar and with my helpers do a pipe ceremony for you and your people. But first there is one thing that I must ask you to consider. You call what you are doing when you take people up to the mountains a vision quest. I see that Spirit has guided you to do this work and you should keep doing it, but it is not right that you call it a vision quest. You do not carry the *chanunpa wakan,* the sacred pipe. You do not use the *inipi,* the sweat lodge, before you go to the mountains. You are not trained by a Lakota elder in the specifics of the *hanblecheyapi,* the lamenting for a vision. So it is disrespectful for you to call what you do a vision quest. It is not for me to tell you what to do. But I hope you will think about what I say. Listen to the counsel of the Great Spirit. Then let us talk about this later."

I took his words to a deep place within me. "Thank you for listening to me and for listening to my heart. I appreciate all you have given me and I will go off alone now to be with what you have said." Then I went to meditate and pray. In my room, I reached out for help. *Help me, Great Spirit, I come to you seeking your will. If you do not want me to be doing this work, let me know and I will let it go. For I know it only works to the extent that it is truly serving you. If it is something that you want me to keep doing, help me to see how to do it in a good way, a way that is respectful to the Lakota and to all Native people. You have shown me the power of fasting and praying alone in the mountains. I have shared it with others and I have seen them come back to a respectful relationship with Mother Earth. But perhaps I am fooling myself. Perhaps you no longer want me to do this. I am confused. I surrender to you.*

After my prayer, I sat very still, just being open and listening. All I could hear was the beat of my heart and the crickets chirping loudly outside my window. Ten minutes went by, fifteen, then twenty. Then I felt a presence and heard the following words. *Keep going on your path. Keep taking people to the mountains to pray and to be with me. But the words of the brother are true. It is not right for you to call what you do a vision quest. Honor what is true. It is a quest for vision. Speak those words.*

A Quest for Vision. Yes, it felt right. It wasn't just a matter of semantics. It was analogous to the difference between non-Catholics calling their spiritual work a Mass versus calling it a sacred communion ritual with Holy Spirit. *I do take people on quests for vision. That's perfectly true,* I thought. *It's accurate and I need to stand solid behind what is true.* I felt clear in what I had to do. I went back to the Lakota pipe holder and told him what had come through my prayers. He listened attentively, then nodded and said, "Ho, this is a good thing. I thank you for your listening. Tomorrow we will smoke the pipe together and give thanks to the Great Spirit. We have work to do together." In that moment, I felt our hearts join as one.

The next morning at the ceremony, the Lakota pipe holder gave me a beautiful Pendleton blanket. We smoked the *chanunpa* and sealed our relationship. He gave me a leather pouch with powdered earth from Bear Butte, the sacred vision quest site of his people. "Give this to your people when you take them out to pray. It will help them on their quest." I carry him and the medicine he gave me in my prayers to this day.

The experience in Oregon heightened my sensitivity to the issue of non-Native people using shamanic ways. Many Native American people today are very upset with Anglos using shamanic practices. In looking at Native people's anger toward Anglo shamanic practice, it is important to recognize the historical context from which it springs—five hundred years of holocaust directed toward the indigenous peoples of the Americas by the invading force from Europe. We have taken their land, their lives, their children, and now, many feel, we are trying to take their religion.

My religious heritage is Jewish. I lost relatives to Hitler's genocide and I lost relatives fighting against it. This history of prejudice, discrimination, persecution, and violence is a part of who I am. My roots also include a long history of standing up against oppression and supporting justice for all peoples, a tradition of which I am proud. Yet while I value and respect my people's history, I do not feel connected with its religious practice. My way is of the earth, the way of listening to nature. I have found it amongst the shamanic people who still live according to the earth-based spiritual-ity of their ancestors. It is these people who face an even greater holocaust than the one faced by mine, and it is still going on today. The genocidal murder of fifty million men, women, and children. The theft of land, the desecration of religious ceremony, the abduction and forced socializa-tion of children according to the white man's ways, the destruction of languages, the destruction of ways of life thousands of years old—this and much more has been the plight of Native people on the American continent since the invasion force from Western Europe first hit these shores. It has not yet stopped. The result of this carnage today threatens the rest of the entire life support system of the planet. What can possibly help us bring healing to oppressed people and to an oppressed earth and ecosystem? I believe one pathway involves an exploration of the consciousness that existed on this land before its violation. No, we can't literally go backward, but we can resensitize ourselves to a consciousness of right relationship with the spirit of Turtle Island, which is what North America is called by some of the indigenous people of the Northeast. We can then use this consciousness to guide us in blending with appropriate technology and strategies of sustainable development to produce enough for "all our need, but not our greed," as Mahatma Gandhi used to say. One way to learn how to live on this continent in respectful right relationship is to listen to its original inhabitants, the ones who have been following their "original instructions" from Spirit on how to be here in a respectful manner. They are the original ecopsychologists, the very first deep ecologists. We should not seek to copy Native people and be something we are not, but instead endeavor to learn from them, and with them, in cooperative partnership with sensitivity, respect, and humility, how to create a way of life that is in harmony with all the forces of creation and the spirit of this land.

First, we have to listen, then we have to learn how to give back. As psychologist Richard Katz, who has worked with indigenous peoples around the world, puts it, "When Westerners learn indigenous healing, what's important is not how they conduct the rituals, but how they conduct their lives. Only a true exchange, built upon mutual respect and accountability, can be our guide. Rather than focusing on which rituals to import and how, we can struggle to be good human beings."

To be good human beings, we must not continue with the pattern of take, take, and more take. We must address the fact that over fifty million Native American men, women, and children have died as the result of the European invasion force in the last five hundred years. Yet, there is no memorial in Washington, D.C., as there is for the Jews who lost their lives to the Nazi holocaust, or for the Americans who died in Vietnam. Ours is a collective denial of historical genocide and it contributes to our reluctance to address the oppressive forces directed against Native American sovereignty today.

Forces such as a 1990 Supreme Court decision (Smith vs. the State of Oregon) that threatened the constitutionally guaranteed right to freedom of religion by allowing states to deny members of the Native American Church the right to use the sacrament of peyote in their services.

Forces of oppression such as the fact that religious sites used for millennia by Native people—mountains, deserts, rivers, canyons, forests, the equivalent of our temples, churches, mosques, and synagogues—are increasingly being lost to civilization's progress. That is, they are paved over, logged, polluted, made into tourist spots like Disneyland, ski resorts, or shopping malls. Alcoholism, suicide, unemployment, and a median death rate of fifty-five years old among Native people all testify to the efficacy of the genocide and oppression still active today. It is vitally important that non-Native people, especially those who feel they have been helped by Native American spirituality, become educated and involved in working to rectify these conditions of injustice, discrimination, and oppression. To not do so means we are in collusion with continuing the historical rape and pillage of Native peoples—taking without giving back while their lives and land are destroyed for the sake of greed and power. We need to join together with all oppressed peoples of the Americas in creating a society that respects the integrity and intelligence of indigenous wisdom ways while simultaneously protecting their sovereignty, sacred rites and ways of worship.

This is not to deny that the ancient historico-cultural roots of non-indigenous peoples of America have something to offer in the way of earth-based spirituality. There was a time when we all sat around the fire, singing, praying, and shamanically dancing with the spirits of animal, plant, wind, sky, sun, and moon. But it is important to recognize that those wisdom ways did not evolve here on this land. Just as the human body emits different electrical charges at its different anatomical points, so, too, does Mother Earth put out different energies at different parts of her body. These energies are part of the spiritual identity of a specific place and location. As such, they convey guidance on how to live in harmony with the forces present in that specific locale. The creation stories of aboriginal people, the very language they speak, are manifestations of these energy forces, which are themselves forms of intelligence, moving through human biological systems instructing them on the dynamics of right relationship.

Thus, it is vitally important for immigrants from Europe, Asia, Africa, and elsewhere to honor their ancestral religions, but it is also vitally important to pay sensitive attention to the "instructions" from indigenous peoples on how to live in ecological balance with the places of power that constitute the spiritual heritage and "working order" of these lands we call North and South America. The sacred places of power, the spirit of the lakes, the rivers, the mountains, the forests, the rocks, the animals, the play of the seasons—they all are the manifestation of cosmic intelligence and they all communicate their teachings to those who have ears to hear and hearts to feel. They open not by command or through force or manipulation, nor can they be bought or bribed by material gifts. They open themselves up to sincerity, to heartfelt prayers, to humility and patience, and to a genuine willingness to listen with respect, along with commitment to act on what is given for the well-being of the full circle of life.

Traditional indigenous peoples of this land, like the Huichol, still remember how to live this way. From their example, we can learn, not to be Indians, but how to become more of who we are and how to blossom in this fertile land of Turtle Island for the benefit of all our relations. We can learn from them how to live here in creative, respectful partnership characterized by interaction patterns of sacred reciprocity with all the living, and with all who have crossed over but whose bones make up this land and whose spirits still look out for their descendants and their places of worship. To do this requires us to resanctify our lives. It means to realize that there is something more purposeful, more important, and more meaningful than living a life based primarily on accumulating material possessions. It means remembering that the essence of who and what we are is spirit relating to a universe of spirit. Following psychologist Abe Maslow's recognition that "the sacred is in the ordinary that is to be found in one's daily life," it is imperative that we take time to look at how we greet spirit each day.

How do you give thanks for the breath that enters you when you first awake, a breath you did not create? How do you give thanks for the beauty and gifts of the earth beneath you, which feed and house you? How do you give thanks to, celebrate, and honor the natural rhythms of your life cycle and that of your family and friends? How do you honor the natural rhythms of the seasons around you? How do you use ritual, ceremony, art, dance, song, silence, and sound to enrich and express your appreciation and give back to the creative source from which all the gifts come? And how do you give back to the land and spirit where you live so that balance is maintained for future generations? How do you build supportive, truth-telling, caring communities of people responsibly addressing the challenges of the time and place where you live? How do you honor the Native people and sacred places of power in your geographic region? How do you use the daily acts of living to help you wake up to greater consciousness, to greater aliveness, to greater and more responsible involvement with the interrelated forms of life that inhabit the land where you live? How do you support the dignity and well-being of the children, old people, and minority members of your community? Do you have a guiding vision for your life, and how do you build the personal power to follow that vision to its fulfillment?

These questions address the basis of resanctifying daily life. It's not about blindly following someone else's ritual or someone else's religion or spiritual practice. We each need to find our own way, one that connects with the integrity of our deeper being and with the life of the human and nonhuman community around us in a respectful and life-promoting manner. It is a fitting challenge for those of us living at the close of the twentieth century. Should we fail, the future looms as a cancerous growth, bringing increasing violence, destruction, and a continuing erosion of human decency and compassion. Listen to the encouragement of poet Rainer Rilke who says: "You must give birth to your images. They are the future waiting to be born. . . . Fear not the strangeness you feel . . . the future must enter into you long before it happens."

I'm a realistic optimist. I think the possibilities for transforming the planet are infinite. Why? Because I know that we are not alone. We are children of the light, we are made in our Creator's image of infinite spirit and infinite creativity. If we turn to Spirit for guidance, if we practice patience, humility, and mindful surrender, if we quest with respect, we will receive that which we need for our lives, just as it has been throughout humanity's history of people seeking vision in time of great need and cultural crisis. But we must hold this as our intention and energize its presence in our awareness. We need practices that train us to call forth our highest selves when the going gets rough, when chaos, fear, anger, guilt, and reactivity hit with full force.

If we do not cultivate loving kindness and skillful action born of the wisdom that we are all related, it will not automatically appear when most needed. It must be consciously planted in the garden of our mind as a "seed of intention" each day. Then it needs to be nurtured and fertilized with the waters of faith and trust throughout the day. Vigilance is required as well, to pull out the weeds of despair, pessimism, ignorance, cynicism, doubt, and negativity, which can cut off healthy growth. We, humanity, most definitely have within us, individually and collectively, the seed potential of creating healthy gardens for the entire human family, but it will only birth out of conscious action to resanctify our lives, our families, our communities, our social institutions, and our relationships to the natural world.

It is a formidable challenge, especially to try and go it by yourself. Human beings are meant to live in supportive communities where people share their heart path truth with one another and where they pray for each other and for the greatest good to come through the opening that is their collective. To the extent that we no longer live that way, we are culturally deprived and suffer as a result. Having experienced this mode of life for short periods of time with the Huichol and other indigenous peoples I have spent time with, I have felt its power and have missed it even more when I returned to this country.

Thus, I excitedly welcomed a special gift that came to me on Christmas Eve in 1986. I was awakened in the middle of the night by a voice that told me to pick up my dream journal and write down what I was to be told. Groggily, I sat up and turned on the light next to the bed. I picked up the pen and wrote down the following words: "You are to start an organization called Wakan, which is a word from the Oglala Sioux language, which translates roughly as 'sacred.' WAKAN, Inc., is a spiritually based educational organization dedicated to the premise that all life is sacred. Our goal is to provide programs that help participants find and remember what is sacred to their highest awareness, and to empower the ability to realize and incorporate the sacred in all aspects of life. This includes personally, professionally, socially, in the corporate marketplace, in the political arena, at home with family, and in all relationships. Services, programs, and educational materials are to help participants WALK ON A PATH OF HEART, a path with purpose and meaning inspiring all whom it touches upon."

After writing this down in my journal, I turned off the light and went back to sleep. Upon awakening the next day, I wondered if I had dreamed the whole thing or if I really had heard a voice and written down what it said. I opened up my journal and there it was. After one year of incubation, Wakan was born into the world as a nonprofit federally tax-exempt organization whose purpose was exactly what the Christmas Eve dictation said that it should be. It started with a monthly drumming circle where people who felt called came together to speak out the truth of their hearts, give thanks to the seven powers through ritual and ceremony, then create an energy field through the sound of the drum and rattle, dance, song or chant, that anyone could draw on for healing, inspiration, or power.

There is a certain level of healing that only comes through community and if we do not have the community, we pay the price. And many of us pay the price and keep paying it. Wakan has grown in response to that need for earth-based spiritual community and over the years has evolved to an extended, spiritually bonded energy field that supports its members in realizing that the essence of our being is love, that we are all joined, and that we are all related on the spiritual level of who and what we are—always. Today Wakan has a quarterly newsletter, *Sacred Reflections,* with subscribers from all over the country. The monthly drumming circle sometimes draws sixty or more people and its facilitation has been taken up by rotating members of the community. Separate support groups for men and women, a couples group, parenting workshops, men's retreats, women's retreats, mixed retreats, river trips, pilgrimages to sacred sites around the world, a yearly one-week retreat on the island of Kauai, a rites of passage program for children, adolescents, and young adults, quests for vision, as well as quarterly retreats at the time of solstice and equinoxes, have all become regular aspects of Wakan. There is also an outreach program that has gone into senior citizen homes and abuse shelters to help create healing ceremonies, and that raises money and supplies for various causes that contribute to Native American education, health, and medical well-being, along with protection of sacred sites and indigenous sovereignty issues. Wakan works with local and nonlocal Native American groups through political activism and support of cultural integrity, and in whatever other ways it can help address the injustices still being done and promote healing of the sacred circle of life. (See the Wakan apology statement in the final appendix.)

There are open meetings where all who are interested can attend and provide input to decisions affecting the community. More people are stepping into leadership positions, taking initiative to "birth through" what they are interested in having Wakan focus its attention on. We are

The bear looks—within.
Woodcut by Dennis Murphy

looking for property to establish a land base for responsible, sustainable community living in harmony with the spirit of place. As time passes and members go through the cycles of babies being born, young people being initiated into responsible adulthood, marriages, divorces, career changes, retirement, and deaths through illness and accident, we are learning what it means to be in caring relationships where people are committed to being there for each other. We are teaching each other how to do it, as students and teachers to one another, no one individual the final authority, but using a council process that enables each voice to be listened to and heard. We stay with it until we reach a "felt consensus," then act in a joined way, *todos unidos*. It takes a lot of patience, a lot of trust and faith in the Great Mystery, and a willingness to face and own your own shadow instead of projecting it onto someone else. But the effort is worth it. Wakan is growing in a good way, through the gift of dedicated people seeking to integrate and honor spirit in the acts of their daily living for the good of all.

9

∴∽∿∼∵

Today's Hunter
The Spiritual Warrior

*In the oldest religion, everything was alive, not
supernaturally, but naturally alive. There were only
deeper and deeper streams of life, vibrations of life more
and more vast. So rocks were alive, but a mountain had a
deeper, vaster life than a rock, and it was much harder for
a man to bring his spirit, or his energy, into contact with
the life of a mountain, as from a great standing well of
life, than it was to come into contact with a rock. And he
had to put forth a greater religious effort.*

D. H. LAWRENCE

This is a story about a rock, a mountain, and a hunting spirit that misses its mark and thereby calls up a *greater religious effort.*

The August sun was baking hot and heavy as we stepped out of my car in the Sierra foothills of Northern California. Waves of heat shimmered from the parched earth. Everything else was still. Trees. Bushes. Flowers. I was with three young men in their early twenties. They had joined me to visit an Apache friend of mine who lived here on a patch of land filled with scrub oak, manzanita bushes, and madrone trees whose shiny red bark glistened in the scorching sunlight. We'd come up at my friend's invitation to purify in his *inipi,* the sweat lodge, then in the morning follow him up onto the hills behind his house to spend time alone seeking vision for our lives.

We stayed in the shade of his porch until the sun went down. His visiting friends, also Apache, went home about eleven that night. It was very interesting to hear them talk about the Apache side of history: what for "white eyes" had been defeats to Geronimo and Cochise were for them glorious victories. They were proud to tell us of these great battles won by their ancestors against the might of the U.S. Army. But they wished us well with our sweat and our quest, then departed. We followed my friend behind his house to the cleared area his prayer flags designated as sacred grounds. With prayers to the four directions, he started the ceremonial fire. Slowly, he added the elders, the holy stone people, onto the burning logs, then covered them with additional pieces of wood until they were completely embedded in flames.

We sat around the fire for hours, listening to my friend's guidance on how to be with the sweat lodge ceremony and the quest. "Keep your concentration strong, stay with the light of the fire," he counseled. "Remember your purpose, what it is you are seeking to purify, what it is you are seeking. Fight off sleep." It was easier said than done. My muscles ached from sitting so long. Fatigue after the long drive up and sitting around waiting in the wilting heat, plus the late hour, all began to take their toll. I struggled to keep my eyelids open and not succumb to the seductiveness of sleep. Finally, about one-thirty in the morning, my friend went into the lodge to purify it with some sweetgrass. Then he came out and did the same with us, wafting the delicious-smelling smoke over our bodies and praying for a successful sweat. His prayers bore fruit—the lodge was very hot and we sweated all night long.

Each of us cleansed and opened our minds, bodies, feelings, and spirits. In the pitch dark of the womblike lodge, we entered into another consciousness. Boundaries of time, space, and form dissolved. The ancestors were present. Animal spirits visited, bringing their medicine and teachings. Toward the end, however, I was so drained I didn't know if I could continue with another round. When the flap finally opened, we went outside to hose down. I was greatly relieved to finally see the light of predawn coming over the horizon. *Whew, we made it!*

After leading a sunrise ceremony, my friend guided us through the woods and fields to the top of the tallest foothill in the area. It was about six hundred feet high. From there, we could survey the entire surrounding valley, which was just waking up as the light of this new day brought its blessings to the land. This particular spot had long been used by the local indigenous people for questing and ceremonies. Now it was our turn. Each of us was led to a spot and dropped off. I was the last one. I felt called to the very top. A boulder fifteen feet high and eighty feet or so in circumference was calling my name. My friend dropped me off there with some final prayers, and then I was alone.

I took out some tobacco and purified it with sage. Then I offered it up to the spirits of the mountain and to the people whose ancestral grounds had been here for eons. I asked their permission to be there and for guidance on how to do so in a respectful way. I stood up and began to walk around the perimeter of the mighty rock, perhaps the grandfather of those we had used in the sweat lodge. I offered the tobacco as I went, thanking all the animal and plant spirits for allowing me to come into their living room. I explained that I would try and be as respectful as I could and leave their homes in good shape when I left. I didn't get ten steps before I ran into foot-high piles of smashed whiskey bottles, rusty beer cans, cigarettes butts, and empty cigarette packages. I was incensed. *Those sons of bitches,* I ranted and raved for several minutes in an outburst of passion and pain. But then I began to hear a soft voice, which gradually got through my cursing and self-righteous judgments toward the perpetrators of the mess at my feet. It grew louder: *I remember when you and your buddies in high school would go out to Great Falls in Virginia,* the voice said. *You'd drink all night, get in fights, and totally trash the area. How many beer bottles did you leave in your wake? You are here now criticizing those who made this mess. Most probably it was young men just like you, doing exactly what you were doing at their age. Drop your self-righteousness. Look deeper. This is part of your quest medicine.*

Like it or not, I was looking at the refuse of my own unconscious youth. The voice went on: *The young people came to this mountaintop for the same reason you did, seeking to alter their consciousness. They came without benefit of any knowledge passed on to them by their culture on how to do this in a responsible manner, but that fact didn't make their desire go away. They just worked with what they had—cigarettes and booze. You had the advantage of coming up here with the help of a tradition that knows how to teach its young people to alter their consciousness in a healthy and responsible way, with the sweat lodge, the praying, the fasting, the isolation, the ritual, and use of ceremony that helps you wake up. The youth who trashed this place were hunting for something to bring meaning to their lives, and they left here without having found it, for booze will never bring them what they are looking for.*

Don't waste your energy on blame and attack, the voice went on. *Instead, recognize your brotherhood with them. Recognize that there is a major need here that is not being fulfilled, just like it wasn't in your life when you were a teenager. These young people need to be exposed to wisdom ways that help them find what they are hunting for, and which enable them to feel empowered from the inside out. They need techniques and traditions that help them feel good about themselves while connecting them to the power, beauty, and teachings of the natural world. This spot is a place of power. Their intuition took them to a good place. Acknowledge that. But don't stop there. It is your job to help them learn how to be here in a way that shows them the interconnectedness of all life and how to work with it to promote healing, balance, and fulfillment of their own lives. That's a better use of your energy than tramping around hollering and raising a ruckus.*

Humbled, I climbed to the top of the boulder. Except for coming down to piss, I stayed on that rock for the following twenty-four hours. Exposed to the boiling heat, dehydrated from the sweating, and exhausted from sending my prayers out to the six powers and to the Creator, I asked for strength to make it to the nighttime when darkness would bring relief from the heat. When Father Sun set down over the western horizon, I stood up and raised my arms to the heavens. I steadied myself to keep from falling over, which wasn't easy because the top of the boulder rose to a platform that was just a few feet wide. I was woozy and could barely stand. But I wanted to reach as high as I could and thank the Sky Father for the cooling embrace of evening.

I grounded myself by sending roots deep into the rock and pulling up some of its strength, then looked upward. Cottony clouds billowed languidly across the sky. I watched them slowly change shape, enjoying the grace of their movement. Suddenly, I saw the image of an eagle. It was as big as an apartment building. I gazed at it in awe. Immense power radiated from its wings. Immediately, words burst out of my mouth: *"Ho, thank you Great Spirit, thank you, Great Eagle Spirit. Help me to fly with you, to see over great distances, clear and accurate, to see what Great Spirit would have me see. Thank you for the guidance about helping young people. Help me to open to your light and your wisdom, showing me how to do it in a way that is truly healing."* Tears streamed down my face. I felt blessed to be seeing what I was seeing, feeling what I was feeling. I strained to keep my eyes open and catch it all. I knew it was *wakan*.

My excitement at seeing the vision of the eagle totally revitalized me. I stood up even straighter, singing out praises and thanksgiving with all my might. Then I watched as the image slowly began to fade. Soon the sky was back to its former state, with billowing clouds turning darker as the light faded away and the night began to descend. I knew that I was being watched and cared for by the elders. I knew too that they were teaching me, so for the rest of the night I gave thanks and prayed for the strength to walk the path of a spiritual warrior, knowing, loving, and serving Great Spirit's will with all that came my way. *Help me to be a good hunter, hunting you in everyone, everything, everywhere, all the time.* I prayed. Then I lay down on the rock for a few fitful moments of uncomfortable rest.

In the morning, I welcomed in Father Sun and gave thanks for the blessings of the new day. Then I took from my medicine bag a scrap of paper on which I'd written a quote from the book *Black Elk Speaks* by Joseph Niehardt. I read the words slowly and deliberately, taking them in one breath at a time. I wanted to remember them when I returned to the lowlands and the challenges that lay ahead: "We should understand well that all things are the work of the Great Spirit. We should know that he is within all things, the trees, the grasses, the rivers, the mountains, and all the four-legged animals, and the winged people; and even more important, we should understand all this deeply in our hearts, then we will be and act and live as he intends."

Upon reading each sentence in deep meditation, I thought again on the young people who had left such a mess at this place of sacred power. In my slowed down pace, I could now see how Spirit was working in the midst of all the garbage. I saw that the young people were hunting here and had missed their mark, just as we all hunt for something—for jobs, higher wages, promotions, status, power, love, sex, friendship, intimate partners, security, recognition, our own souls, meaning, success, inner peace—and sometimes miss our mark.

We are all hunters, and in the process of hunting we all take life. It is unavoidable in being alive. Even those who do not eat meat are hunters. Each breath takes in life and swallows it up alive. Each step upon the earth takes life. No, the question isn't whether we take life or not, the question is whether we take it consciously and whether we give something back in exchange. But in our modern society, we too often forget, as Black Elk put it so well, that "the work of the Great Spirit . . . is within all things . . ." Thus, we go about our hunting, our taking of life, in an entirely secular way, a way that produces imbalance and disharmony even in those cases where we get what we were after. Why? Because we hunt with an extractive consciousness socialized into us by a society that emphasizes taking, getting, and accumulating material wealth.

Our culture trains us to believe that bigger is better and that economic expansion is the answer to all our problems. Those whose participation in the consumption-consumer treadmill is barred or weakened by discrimination through racism, sexism, ageism, or lack of marketable educational skills, language, and knowledge, all too often end up hurting, frustrated, and desperate, and at times resorting to criminal behavior to get the material goods that they have pushed in their face by aggressive media marketing in every direction one looks. As author Helena Norberg-Hodge puts it so succinctly, "the price of never-ending economic growth and material prosperity has been spiritual and social impoverishment, psychological insecurity, and the loss of cultural vitality."

In shamanic and hunting cultures that still remember their spiritual roots, the hunt does not begin with the pursuit of game. It begins in an I/thou communion with Spirit. The hunters are clear about their purpose: they hunt for food to feed the family, they hunt to sustain the life of their community. The Huichol hunt the deer for its meat as well as for its blood, which they sprinkle on their ceremonial objects and carry to Wiricuta. First, the spirit of the deer is called in by the shaman. It is thanked for past gifts and honored in song and dance at ceremonial gatherings. Then it is told why the people need it to sacrifice itself on their behalf. The spirit of the deer listens to this, to the hearts of the people, to the shaman speaking of how the deer spirit will be honored in future ceremonies, how there will be prayers for its spirit, for the life of its family. It listens to how its tail, antlers, and skin will be used in a sacred way, its flesh will be eaten for the life of the Huichol to continue on, its blood will be sprinkled on the prayer arrows and other offerings left at the holy places along the pilgrimage trail. Then it makes a final decision based on its feeling about the prayers of the people requesting its aid.

Meanwhile, the hunter will purify, fast, and promise to honor the deer's spirit in death and carry on its spiritual gifts with his own life. The spirit of the hunted animal sees whether this particular hunter has honored previous promises and obligations. If not, then why should the spirit believe the promises now? If yes, then the spirit is more likely to offer itself up on the day of the hunt. If this is not done correctly and with integrity, then it matters little if the person is the greatest hunter of all, the animal will not appear. Or, if it does show up and experiences a dishonoring of its spirit, then it will not offer itself up on future hunts.

Another factor to consider is that the hunting of large game—whales, elephants, buffalo, etc.—was frequently a cooperative venture. The hunter's survival was dependent on each person doing his job and backing up others. There was a strong element of trust in the person working behind you, next to you, in front of you. This web of cooperation and community consciousness extended into the sharing of the kill. Old people, children, nursing mothers, and widows often were fed first. The bounty was shared amongst the most vulnerable so the people might live. The paramount concern was the promotion and continuation of balance and harmony among all participating parties, seen and unseen. There was respect and responsibility, asking for permission, giving back, sharing, thanksgiving at all stages of the process. Appreciation of the sacred was at the center.

How far we have strayed from this practice today! Frank Waters, in his beautiful book *The Man Who Killed the Deer,* about a Hopi man struggling to live as an Indian within the laws of the dominant society, speaks eloquently to this loss:

There is no such thing as a simple thing. One drops a pebble into a pool, but the ripples travel far. One picks up a little stone in the mountains, one of the little stones called Lagrimas de Cristo— and look! It is shaped like a star; the sloping mountain is full of stars as the sloping sky. Or take a kernel of corn. Plant it in Our Mother Earth with the sweat of your body, with what you know of the times and seasons, with your proper prayers. And with your strength and manhood Our Father Sun multiplies and gives it back into your flesh. What then is this kernel of corn? It is not a simple thing.

Nothing is simple and alone. We are not separate and alone. The breathing mountains, the living stones, each blade of grass, the clouds, the rain, each star, the beasts, the birds and the invisible spirits of the air—we are all one, indivisible. Nothing that any one of us does but affects us all.

So I would have you look upon this thing not as a separate simple thing, but as a stone which is a star in the firmament of earth, as a ripple in a pool, as a kernel of corn. I would have you consider how it fits into the pattern of the whole. How far its influence may spread. What it may grow into . . .

So there is something else to consider. The deer. It is dead. In the old days we all remember, we did not go out on a hunt lightly. We said to the deer we were going to kill, "We know your life is as precious as ours. We know that we are both children of the same Great True Ones. We know that we are all one life on the same Mother Earth, beneath the same plains of the sky. But we also know that one life must sometimes give way to another so that the one great life of all may continue unbroken. So we ask your permission, we seek your consent to this killing."

Ceremonially we said this, and we sprinkled meal of corn pollen to Our Father Sun. And when we killed the deer we laid his head toward the East, and sprinkled his head with meal and pollen. And we dropped drops of his blood and bits of his flesh on the ground for Our Mother Earth. This was proper so. For then when we too built its flesh into our flesh, when we walked in the moccasins of its skin, when we danced in its robe and antlers, we knew that the life of the deer was continued in our life, as it in turn was continued in the one life all around us, below us and above us.

We knew the deer knew this and was satisfied. But this deer's permission was not obtained. What have we done to this deer, our brother? What have we done to ourselves? For we are all bound together, and our touch upon one travels through all to return to us again. Let us not forget the deer.

We have forgotten both the deer and the spirit, which is also dear. We have fallen prey to equating our well-being with the well-being of our material economy. But the acquisition of material wealth is not enough. I have worked with a number of millionaires in my private practice and coaching work, and most assuredly, their wealth did not bring them happiness or peace of mind. One client, a CEO of a computer startup company, had wealth but complained often of the lack of meaning in his life. I have heard this same complaint from many "successful" people. This is because our cultural emphasis on materialism does not engage our deepest yearnings and highest values nor encourage what is worth doing for our soul growth. Thus, it leaves in the dust what is one of the most important functions that a healthy society provides for its citizenry—the opportunity to contribute in a meaningful, soulful way that brings self-satisfaction as well as appreciation and affirmation from others.

What is needed today is a lesson in how to restore awareness that spirit is present always in the center of everything, everywhere, all the time and within everyone. The positive warrior qualities of courage, determination, sacrifice, and discipline, plus love for that which it offers its life to defend, are precisely what is called for to open the heart of humankind and to free up its visionary imagination and drive to create win-win outcomes for the full circle of life. This is the best medicine to heal the violence, the injustice, the fear, the ignorance, the prejudice, the greed. Each individual is responsible for developing their medicine gifts and power. We each need to find and walk our own heart path, transforming our attitudes and behaviors to serve all of humanity and all of life. This is the path of the heart warrior, committed to protect and steward the sacred biodiversity of life on this planet.

Open-hearted, spiritual hunters use the psychospiritual technology and metaphor of the shaman as a model by which to energize their own access to the state specific knowledge and abilities that will be most helpful to them in their hunt. They choose the state of consciousness with the attendant knowledge and capacities most appropriate for the challenge at hand. A challenge might be, like mine, to create healthy and meaningful rites of passage for young people. Other challenges may range from finding a job or a life partner to finding solutions to one of the many environmental and social problems of today's world. Many of us are seeking a way to live by deeper truth and vision; others are looking for ways to run a business, build team and organizational solidarity, and to develop responsible, effective, and healthy leadership for the institutions of our society. Whatever you are hunting for in your personal life, your family, or your community, know that you have infinite creativity, infinite intelligence, and infinite holographic consciousness available to help you in your hunt.

Respect—respect for the great mystery of creation and doing all within human power to live in harmony and balance with its ever-changing rhythms and cycles—is vital for successful long-term hunting, and this important dynamic is well understood by the hunter, the heart warrior, and the shaman. As in mountain climbing, real victory is not in how high you climb, for you never conquer a mountain, even when you stand on its summit, but in experiencing the process of full effort without attachment to outcome or form.

Successful hunting in the spiritual sense is based on the amount of personal power one has developed, which itself is a manifestation of a trained and disciplined will developed through working consciously with mindfulness—paying full attention to the truth of what is. This will is then aligned and attuned with the flow of the great Tao in the moment through the practice of focused surrender. It is strengthened through awareness that one's personal power and the amount of time remaining between now and the time of death is all that one ever really possesses. This awareness enables one to use time wisely. Ironically, Western culture teaches us how to "kill time," yet right-now time is all we ever have.

Wise hunters use time to stalk and count coup on the tyrants of their lives. "Counting coup" is a Plains Indian practice in which combatant warriors get so close to the enemy that they can reach out and touch them with a "coup stick," then quickly duck out of harm's way and return to a place of safety. The fact that they got so close means that they could have easily killed their enemy but instead chose the more dangerous and courageous course of just touching them. There is greater honor in counting coup, which demonstrates the prowess of the warrior, than in taking a life.

Stalking and counting coup in today's world involves consciously observing the process of your mind by being present for what is taking place. This practice enables you to make a conscious choice of what you want to experience—peace or pain, love or fear, separation or connection with the presence of spirit. It helps you to observe the inner tyrants—judgment, anger, fear, etc.—as well as the outer tyrants of daily life, those persons or situations that push your buttons and show you where you are attached, fearful, or stuck. Stalking enables you to see how these tyrants are "fed," where they derive their energy, so that the energy can be refocused and used for counting coup. Thus, one can shift out of the learned helplessness of victim state, repossess personal power, and use that power to create responses to any situation that will help successful realization of goals, i.e., the objects of the hunt.

I remember stalking and counting coup on a mountain climb up the Cathedral Range of the High Sierra in September in 1972. I was second on the rope, and we were ascending a very thin pinnacle with steep exposure. Eric, who worked with me in the wilderness project with heroin addicts and who was an excellent, experienced climber, was finishing up the last pitch. I sat on a knife ridge with one leg on one side of the mountain and the other leg dangling over the other side. Eric was above me and out of sight. I could hear his voice and feel the rope moving through my hands. Winter cold was on its way, slowly sapping my strength. I couldn't take my eyes off the dizzying heights that in a few moments I would be climbing. I looked at the route in front of me leading up to a small ledge fifteen feet over my head. There was more beyond that; that's where Eric was now, but I couldn't see it. I'd deal with that if and when I got to it. But getting to it was problematic. As I scanned the crack for holds and a climbing strategy, my terror increased. Below was empty space, then, far below, the boulder-strewn ground. With my thoughts racing in this nonproductive manner, by the time Eric gained the summit and yelled out that it was my turn to climb, there just wasn't much juice left for me to do anything.

Nevertheless, I set out. Climbing with frantic, jerky movements, I hoped to cover the scary part quickly. Despite my trembling, I actually made it successfully up the crack. I reached out with my left hand and grabbed the top of the ledge. *Hallelujah, a solid hold!* I reached up with my right hand, but just as it touched the hold, I lost my grip and went shooting off into space. Fortunately, Eric's belay held and I only fell five feet or so until the rope went taut and I knew my end had not yet come. Hanging there gasping in relief, I felt like a big flounder on the end of a fishing line. I was exhausted and in no shape to climb any more, so we descended and walked back to camp. I felt that I was a failure—just when I'd made it over the hardest part, I'd lost it, and all my efforts were for naught.

I decided to "stalk" my experience with grim objectivity. In my mind's eye, I reviewed in minute detail everything that had happened. I quickly saw the obvious: I'd let my mind run amuck with fear-based negative thinking, which completely drained my willpower. Reviewing the movie in slow motion, I saw that the instant I put my hands on the ledge, my fingers went numb from the cold and my mind snapped. I had never been in that kind of situation before, I hadn't expected it, and I couldn't handle it when it happened—I lost my composure and my grip on the mountain at the same time. I realized that the real cause of my fall was not the fact that my hands were numb and couldn't feel what they were touching. If I had kept my wits about me, I could have compensated for that without a problem. No, the real reason I fell was because the unexpected information of numb hands caused me to lose the power of my focused will. I dropped my *kupuri*. If I hadn't lost it, I could have told my hands to hang on to the rock like claws even if they couldn't feel it. Then I could have successfully pulled my way up to the ledge and the rewards of a safe perch. But my mind was not strong enough to hold its concentration under the unexpected pressure. I realized then that I needed to add something to my daily practice to strengthen my will, something physical that required overcoming self-imposed obstacles of inertia, laziness, and wanting the easy way out. I decided to use the discipline of daily runs, working up to a twenty-six-mile marathon, as my vehicle for developing willpower and staying with it for sustained periods of time under all kinds of physical conditions. I would develop my will to the point where I could count coup on my fear-prone mind, thereby empowering myself to successfully climb the mountains of my life. I added running to my daily practice of yoga and meditation and have kept it up to this day.

It worked. I've made it up to the top of many summits. I've still got more to go, but now I know the process of successful mountain climbing. I've learned to empower myself as the hero figure of my own mythic story. I've run two marathons and achieved my goal of being able to finish with a sprint and go out dancing with Andrea that very same night. I used the tuning of my body to tune my mind. Reflecting on the fruits of my stalking process regarding my fall from the mountain, I recognize how it was a *nierica,* a doorway for growth. It helped me realize even more the importance of a regular discipline and that internal freedom cannot be realized without it. The pain of my first big mountain climbing fall turned out to be a real boon; it helped me learn to use personal power to confront, subdue, and transform my inner demons.

Bodies and wills are instruments that need to be kept in sound operating order. To achieve greater attunement with higher self and the transformation required by the increasing rate of change that characterizes the twenty-first century, it is important to stay true to one's highest calling. In facing this challenge, it is helpful to remember the teachings of shamans and subatomic physicists about the nature of the universe—that it is all a dance of vibrating energy. Years ago, in a visionary state, I was shown that everything in the universe has its own rate of vibration, or "song." All material objects and all nonmaterial manifestations of creation, even thoughts and feelings, have their own vibratory rate. The vision showed me what all shamans know—that using the instrument of your own body to find and reproduce a particular vibratory rate dissolves mind-created barriers of separation. When the shaman finds and "sings the song" of a person or situation, the shaman can then join with the subject, gain entry into it, and thus influence what is taking place. So chanting, singing, and sound making plays a great role in the elicitation of trance states used by the shaman to hunt power, knowledge, and healing. The shaman sees the energy pattern of the reality, attunes to its vibrational rate by "singing the right song," and thereby resonates with it via the process of entrainment. Once "inside," the shaman facilitates change by altering the vibrational rate from within. These sounds are the sacred songs, the *icaros,* which the shaman uses as a surgeon uses a scalpel.

Shamans know, through their discipline of control and focused attention in extreme situations, that life is about power. They empower themselves through communion with vehicles of power in nature. Shamans hunt by exploring, interacting, and eventually gaining alliance with the net of power that animates the universe. They learn its operational laws through direct experience and they learn how to work with these laws to accomplish their aims. The hardship of learning in shamanic initiatory ordeals, which involve confronting demonic adversaries and turning them into allies and teachers, culls out the weak and the unprepared and strengthens the power of the survivors. During the trials of their

Photo by Larain Boyll

Tacho doing a sunrise ceremony in a sacred cave

apprenticeship, shamans work toward mastery in balance, equilibrium, and right presence of mind through the practice of applied power.

The initial call to power takes shamans into archetypal encounters, first with death and dismemberment, then into the numinous world of spirit entities, climaxing in their realization of their own spiritual identity. They find their deeper life purpose by facing death, which is a prerequisite to shamanic vision, power, and wisdom. From the ashes of death comes resurrection of a new being, guided by insight, understanding, and teachings from wise spiritual elders. Shamans learn how to enter into the union of opposites, the sacred marriage, thus transcending polarities that are experienced in ordinary states of awareness as being in opposition to one another. They learn how to willfully ascend and descend the axis mundi, the Cosmic World Tree, into the upper world or lower world. And finally, they learn to bring the fruits of their journey back into the middle world to be of service herein—reshaping the dream and the dreamers. In perhaps more recognizable terms, they come to purpose in a sustained path of balance, success, productivity, and effectiveness.

Shamans are spiritual hunters, heart-path warriors seeking and actualizing a transcendent vision through a disciplined practice that focuses their consciousness, their intentionality, and their behavior into service of the numinous powers that animate this mysterious universe that is our home. It behooves all who seek deeper healing, understanding, power, health, prosperity, meaning, success, and enjoyment in life to learn from the model of the hero's journey taken by shamans since time immemorial.

Seek deeper vision, develop a personal mastery practice based on mindful, conscious choice of what you want to experience in your life. Develop personal power to befriend shadow forces, close holes in the bucket, and cultivate courageous communion with higher self. Build inner strength to the point where individual will can surrender to the presence and will of the Great Mystery. Be its servant, a channel for its will, a vehicle through which it can work, serving the greatest good of all. Protect and nurture the garden and carry its bounty out into the world to feed the people. Ask the ultimate question: "Do I want to know the Great Spirit's will for me?" Your answer will show you how far along you are on the heart path of the spiritual hunter.

10

~·~·~

The Sacred Marriage

It must be pointed out that the underlying principle in
nature's unique law between the pair of opposites, Yin and
Yang, conceived as essentially one, or as two co-existent
poles of one indivisible whole . . . is harmony, balance or
equilibrium. . . . To gain awareness of this oneness . . . is
precisely man's raison d'être.

WEN-SHAN HUANG,
THE WEB THAT HAS NO WEAVER

I am sitting in a dark room directly across from an elaborately prepared
altar. The house is in a rural, wooded area in Northern California.
The only light is from flickering candles placed on either side of
numerous vases, each filled with bunches of red and white carnations.
The occasion is an all-night ceremony called a *velada,* a night vigil, led
by a visiting Mazateca shaman. The Mazatecas live in the Oaxaca region
of southern Mexico and use psilocybin-containing mushrooms as a sacrament in the *velada* ceremony. Under the guidance, prayers, and purifica-
tions of Doña Julieta, a fifty-eight-year-old *curandera,* or healer, we are
each handed a dosage of the sacrament. She then goes to the front of the
altar, kneels down, and begins a long prayer in her native language. I have
been studying with her for several weeks now, sitting in with her daily
as she works with individuals who come to her for healing or guidance.
After each session, she explains what she was doing. For some of the healings, she brings me in to join her and her apprentice of eighteen years,

216

Camila, a long-haired beauty who works with Tibetan medicine as well as the herbs and ways of the Mazateca. The *velada* is the culmination of our work together.

Now it is in full swing. A beam of energy is emanating from the center of the altar, taking me into a state of bliss. All dualities are resolved. Tension, fear, and thoughts and images of separation are dissolved. There is only love. I look at Camila and Doña Julieta and they smile beatifically, their radiance adding to my bliss. *My God,* I think, *if it is this good from across the room, I wonder what it is like close up.* I also want a closer view to see just exactly where this beam of energy is coming from. I check with Doña Julieta and she motions that it is okay for me to approach the altar. Sending grounding energy down to my wobbly legs, I slowly stand up.

Each step closer brings stronger radiance from the altar. Powerful, rose-colored waves of energy pulse out from a little five-by-seven card. The card is a *nierica,* a doorway. On the other side, I see the vast space of infinite universe filled with the presence of the Sacred Mother, the feminine principle of creation. The energy pulsing through the open doorway is the unconditional love of the mother who is there for us always. I see that she never sleeps, she never rests, she never turns her back on us. Tears roll down my cheeks as I feel how loved I am by this Holy Mother.

I focus my vision on the card at the center of the altar to see what is printed on it. It is a picture of the Virgin of Guadalupe, a patron saint *de las Indios pobres de Mexico,* of the poor Indian people of Mexico. I know intuitively that she is the feminine counterpart of the visions of Jesus that I have seen twice before, and that this vision initiates a sacred marriage between the cosmic male and the cosmic female. I am consumed by Guadalupe's gentle, ever-present, unconditional love. *This is the holy feminine, the Goddess, the true lover of all creation. This is what is missing in today's world, this is what is so sorely needed to heal our wounds and open us up to love.* I open myself up as a container to be filled with her love, then extend it outward to Doña Julieta and fellow participants in our circle, then out as healing into the world. *Thank you, Holy Mother, for your unconditional love and forgiveness, for opening me up to see you in all your glory and light. Thank you for being here for us. Thank you for You.*

The sacred marriage

In the midst of my bliss, I hear one of my companions call me. I turn around and find him lying on the ground. Tom is a large, well-built man of fifty-one who was a scholarship football player in college and who maintained his physical prowess through regular fitness training. But he also has major back problems. "Ho Tomás," he calls, "I could use some healing energy in my back. Could you help me out?" I walk over and kneel down, place my hand on his back and use my arm as an extension conduit for the loving light of Guadalupe to flow into him. Breathing in, breathing out, no words. Just pouring in the love of the Mother to one of her sons.

As the love flows in, his back muscles soften and begin to release.

I can see into his past and how in order to be tough, much like me, he had to learn to tighten up, literally. His stomach muscles had to be tight so when he was punched in the belly, his armor would protect him and the blow would not take his breath away. He had to toughen up on the athletic field so that he could play when he was hurt; only a wimp would complain about anything less than a broken arm. In other words, he had to disregard the body's wisdom messages about pain and continue on in the behavior that caused the pain to begin with.

In this tightening process, the belly is a primary area of holding. It locks in "unmanly" feelings of tenderness, gentleness, compassion, and softness, lest they get out and brand you as a wimp or even worse, a fag. Don't be vulnerable. Be strong. Be assertive. Nice guys finish last. Whew. It doesn't leave much room to breath, and given this poisonous conditioning

Photo by Mark Montgomery

Macho persona

of mind and body, it is no small wonder that so many men have lower back problems as my friend was experiencing during the *velada*. For as the stomach tightens up, it is the back muscles behind it that are doing the real work of holding it all in. Keep that going for too long and your back is going to "feed back" information that something is drastically wrong, i.e. lower back pain. While it is important to know how to "suck it up and go for it" when that is what's really needed, it doesn't make for a healthy lifestyle to live in that state constantly. The key here is to consciously choose the response appropriate to the situation and not be stuck in the "hard warrior" program when it is not needed. Otherwise, you are constantly living in a state of distress, waiting in readiness to defend yourself from the next attack by destroying the perceived enemy.

Tom's back pain was archetypal in nature in that he was carrying the burden of being a man in Western society and paying the price for it where the stress hit him hardest. Repressing gentleness extracts a tremendous toll on men and on society. We die on the average seven years before women, in part because we wreak violence on ourselves unconsciously. We also wreak violence on women, children, and the earth. We make war on the feminine because we are so alienated from our own internal feminine, or *anima,* and threatened by anything or anyone who reminds us of it. Until we come to terms with the female energies within us all, women, children, and Mother Earth all pay the price.

For a boy trying to live in this pathological state of male identity, the absolutely worst energy to let in is that of the loving mother, for it is soft and thus a threat to his developing hard maleness. Yet it is the energy of the loving spiritual mother, the Goddess, the energy that I was receiving from the *velada* and the *Virgen de Guadalupe,* that is so necessary to heal the hard male. Tom's back was in knots. We are all tied up in knots and act it out on self and others. The soft, gentle love of the Sacred Mother undoes these knots, allowing healing *kupuri* to flow through unblocked passageways.

The dominant masculine with its emphasis on control, force, and an analytical, linear mode of sequential consciousness is pathologically out of balance. Not that masculine energy is bad per se—what is bad is ignorance of who and what we truly are. In this ignorance and fear, the beauty of the masculine gets poisoned and we are all the losers for it. We need to bring the masculine and the feminine into conscious, cooperative, respectful partnership, a partnership of equals working together synergistically to birth a creativity that cannot be achieved by either one working alone. This is the sacred marriage, the joining of the inner feminine, the *anima,* with the inner masculine, the *animus,* in harmony and balance, in love and with joy. When it is achieved internally, it also manifests externally. The increasing emergence of the sacred feminine through goddess imagery such as my experience with the Virgin of Guadalupe is moving us toward healing our imbalance through the experience of a sacred marriage. Kwan Yin, the Chinese goddess of mercy and compassion, is another female deity I have seen in visions twice in the past few years. In both visions, she radiated love and showered me with her healing touch. When she finished, she merged her transformational healing gifts into my body, which gently smoothed out all the tension knots in my back and shoulders.

The primal male energy is that of thrust and assertion. It is built into the evolutionary hard wiring of the system. The primal female energy is that of receptivity and receiving, harmonizing with the flow of Tao. Yin and yang. Yang and yin. It is through the joining of these two energies that new life is produced. Our universe is an erotic one, cosmically making love with itself on all levels, from the micro to the macro, to produce the world(s) of physicality. Without this dance, there would be no physical universe. Consider life on our planet. Current astronomical theory postulates that billions of years ago, our cooling earth was bombarded by comets from outer space bringing in the rudiments necessary for life to appear. In mythopoetic terms, our feminine receptive earth was "impregnated" by the infusion of masculine, sperm-like comets from the far reaches of the great beyond. In this joining of masculine and feminine, new life burst forth, something neither one could have achieved on its own.

On the level of the individual, the energies of the masculine and the feminine are present in both men and women. We each have the potential for both receptivity and assertion within us. One is usually dominant

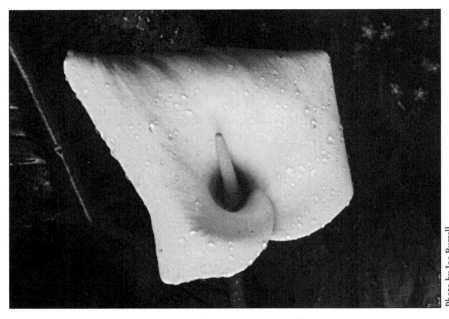

Photo by Joe Burrell

Sensuality of nature—masculine

over the other by virtue of birth and social conditioning. One is not better than the other. Both have their positive aspects and, if misused, their shadow or destructive aspects. The life-preserving, evolutionary challenge is to bring to fruition the best of each and make the blend with its opposite in sacred joining of harmonious balance. The transcultural quest for vision provides a good model of how to bring these seemingly contradictory qualities into cooperative partnership.

Questers are immersed in nature while cultivating a state of receptivity and awareness to all that transpires, both internally and externally. Emphasis is placed on observing and listening to the intelligence of natural rhythms. Wherever the questers turn their attention, they see only the truth of nature, the truth of the Tao, the truth of what God and Goddess have made through their union. The natural world is constantly communicating. It teaches, models, and demonstrates how to be in harmony and balance with all its forces. This information is available to anyone who pays attention, who takes the time to retreat to the mountains, the forests, the oceans, and the rivers still unspoiled by humans. The sun shines equally on all people, rich or poor, black or white. The wind blows equally on all things, big and small, short or tall. Through the gift of the feminine—the receptive listening—the doorway opens to receive the teachings. With patience, vigilance, and attention, questers experience deeper insight and understanding of how the universe works and how they can work with it for health, happiness, and true prosperity.

Photo by Joe Burrell

Sensuality of nature—feminine

After being alone in nature practicing emptiness and sustained observation, questers return filled up with the fruit of their perceptions. Then they must take the next, and hardest, step—the path of action in alignment with their vision so they can successfully manifest it in their lives. The moving forward, the extension outward into the world, calls for the masculine energy. But to be in right relationship, the actions of masculine strength and power must be grounded in the womb of the receptive feminine. The rational mind is used as a tool in service to the feminine wisdom that births life and knows what is necessary to sustain and nourish it. The male energy is used in stewardship of life, in protection and reverence of life, and in doing all it can to provide that which is necessary for this fruition to be achieved. Intuitive listening to body of self, body of earth, body of feelings, dreams, visions—i.e., deeper mind of the wisdom elders speaking through the individual—helps keep us on track so that our actions can be ones that honor and bless the Sacred Hoop and the Sacred Mother.

In Hawaii on New Year's Day of 1976, I climbed a holy mountain to offer prayers. At the top, I found trash remains of previous climbers lying all about. The message hit me immediately: *Pick it up and carry it down with you. This too is part of your job. Don't complain about it. Don't judge others who leave it lying around. They are asleep, much as you have been. Do what you can to raise consciousness about not leaving trash but know you are never going to be totally successful in seeing it all cleaned up in your lifetime. To really walk a healing path, recognize and accept that part of the walk is being a garbage man, not just psychologically, or spiritually, but physically too. It's not glamorous or exciting, but it is necessary. Send love out to those who made the mess. Pray for them to wake up and learn to respect Mother Earth. Teach a better way by living it. Deal with your own garbage first, then you will be more effective in helping others deal with theirs.*

It wasn't what I expected to find atop this holy mountain on the first day of the new year, but I got that I really was a garbage man and I might as well do it in good spirit. It's my observation that most of the trash I see in nature has been left there by boys, teenagers, or men, i.e., the masculine dishonoring the feminine. Our hearts are closed, our vision is myopic. We are suffering in our minds, our bodies, and our souls. We need both the support and teaching of healthy masculine models and we need an infusion of the healthy feminine to help us develop more loving relationships with ourselves, each other, and with life, relationships that merge the feminine and the masculine in a marriage of cooperative partnership.

As I sat on the steep summit meditating on these thoughts, a thick grey mist swirled in from the peaks to the northwest, enveloping me in a dripping wet, cold fog. I left the summit and hiked rapidly down the mountain to get warm. The fog reminded me of another wet mist, one I'd sat down in and surrendered into on a vision quest on the Northern

California coast in the fall of 1975. I had been hiking over the land seeking guidance for where to do my quest. In the thick fog, I had become
disoriented and lost my way. I stopped to rest and collect myself. I put
on a warm jacket and leaned back against a boulder. My eyes felt heavy,
my body weary from the previous night's late sweat lodge. Soon my eyes
closed and a whole adventure story unfurled beneath my eyelids. It began
with the image of a little boy.

The boy looked about five or six years old. He was sitting on a carpet
with a bearded old man. The carpet rose up into the mist, moving through
time and space. Finally, the clouds began to clear and below him the boy
could make out the shape of a huge stone castle. He saw the inhabitants
of the castle and its surrounding lands and he sensed they were in great
despair. As the carpet began to descend, it shrank in size. The little boy
and the old man shrank as well, smaller than your smallest fingernail.

Traveling through time and space
Drawing by Ilsa Pinkson

Unnoticed because of their diminutive size, they walked through the castle and saw the unhappiness.

The king was a miserable old coot, mean, selfish, petty, and cruel. He cared for no one but himself and his own greed. The people of this castle land were all close to starvation, brutalized by the king's guards, and in constant fear for their lives. In fact, just as the boy and the old man landed, an execution was about to take place. One of the king's subjects had killed a deer from the king's royal forest to feed his starving family. The king had forbid any hunting in his land except for that which would enrich his larder. The blade of the executioner was just starting to rise above the head of the poor father. The little boy was horrified. He was confused as well. "Why is he acting that way? Why is he so mean?" he asked the old man. "Because his heart is imprisoned in a block of ice," replied the old man. "You can free him from his imprisonment if you want. It is up to you." The little boy responded quickly, "But how can I do that?"

THE KING WAS A MEAN AND BITTER MAN...

The mean king
Drawing by Ilsa Pinkson

The old man reached down to his side, opened up a leather pouch, and pulled out a pinch of powder. He sprinkled it on the little boy and himself. Instantly, the boy and the old man were inside the king's body, traveling toward his heart. When they reached the heart, the boy saw that what the old man had said was true; the king's heart was surrounded by a huge iceberg. "Send him your love," said the old man. "Use your breath to open your heart and then send everything you've got right smack dab into the iceberg. Do it quickly."

The little boy took a deep breath and brought it right down into his heart, which opened like the petals of a flower receiving the warm rays of a new day's light. His heart became a radiant burst of light and he sent it right into the iceberg. "That's it!" yelled the old man excitedly. When the first ray of the little boy's love hit the iceberg, it immediately began to melt. As the boy continued sending his love, the iceberg began dissolving. "Keep it up," said the old man. The little boy did precisely that until there was only a small piece of the iceberg left, then in a final *swoosh* it too was gone.

THE ICE SHUDDERED... AND BEGAN TO MELT

Melting ice
Drawing by Ilsa Pinkson

The wave of water from the melting ice propelled the little boy and the old man out of the king's body and they landed right in front of the executioner's stand. The glistening blade was on its deadly arc downward at the very instant the ice melted. Suddenly, the king shouted, "Stop!" The executioner was barely able to halt his blade just inches from the quivering head of the terrified prisoner. The king fell to his knees, sobbing. "Please, my people, forgive me for all the pain and suffering I have caused you. I don't know what was wrong with me, but now I feel free. I am a new man. Release this poor fellow. Release food from my royal larder, release my gold and jewels in my royal treasury. Use it all to feed the people, to build new homes and whatever it is that the people need. Let the royal physician be available to all. Use my soldiers to help grow and harvest crops, to plant fruit trees and flowers, and to heal our land. Ring out the bells, call all the people to a great celebration. From this day forth the realm of Castleland will be one of peace, of love, and of prosperity for all!"

The healed heart
Drawing by Ilsa Pinkson

Upon hearing this news, the people were stunned at the sudden reversal of their fate. But after a few moments of watching the king's tears and feeling his genuine love, they raised their voices in song and soon all the people of Castleland were celebrating in the streets and fields. The little boy and the old man, seeing their work was done, went back to the carpet, which rose slowly back up into the sky. Weary after all the excitement, the boy laid his head down on the old man's knee to rest. "Why did all that happen?" he asked. The old man looked kindly down at the boy. "It's why we are here for our time on earth," he replied. "We were just doing our job, changing darkness and fear into light. The king was imprisoned by his own fear and selfishness. You, my fine fellow, are a magician of love. That is what everyone is. They just forget it at times, like the king. Your gift is to remember your true magic and give it away, like you did when you melted the ice." The little boy felt warm inside. The cold, wet mist was all gone now; there was only the shining sun in a clear, blue sky. He closed his eyes and soon was fast asleep.

As the vision faded, I opened my eyes and saw that the sun was shining out here, too. I knew immediately where I was and my disorientation faded away just as the fog had faded away during the time of my inner journey.

Recalling this experience as I hiked rapidly down the fog enshrouded mountain in Hawaii, I thought about the juxtaposition of ideas hurtling through my mind: the challenge of making a sacred marriage with the garbage atop the summit, the initiatory teachings from a Wisdom Elder to a young boy, which shows him his own powers of transformation, and lastly, how each of us needs the love of the feminine, the Goddess, to heal our wounds and open our closed hearts, just as I had experienced with the vision of the Virgin of Guadalupe in the *velada*.

In healthy societies that remember wisdom ways, boys are initiated into adulthood by older men through rites of passage that open them to the life-honoring wisdom within their own true nature, which includes accessing the receptive, intuitive feminine. Through these rites and the example of positive role models, they learn how to tap into and use their beautiful masculine strengths in service to Higher Will through serving their tribe and all of life. Girls are initiated by the onset of their menses into the rhythms of life and death and are honored by the other members of their tribal group at this sacred occasion. But we are sadly lacking in such rites in the dominant society of today, and we suffer for their lack. We must birth them anew. Both boys and girls must learn that they are *all* sacred beings. They must learn that within them are the energies of the other, and they must learn how to honor them both internally and externally. They must learn how to respectfully join with the other in a cooperative partnership of equals, through friendship, as colleagues, as lovers and marriage partners when appropriate, and in creating healthy families and communities and places of work and play. Successful sacred marriage on the inner plane enables us to work skillfully together toward win-win outcomes. In this way, we can utilize the gifts each brings to the table to feed the hungry, raise healthy children, develop healthy communities, and heal the wounds of the earth.

Photo by Larain Boyll

Tacho blessing young boy at sunrise in Wiricuta

The rites of passage necessary to produce these kinds of outcomes must themselves come from a merging of the feminine and masculine qualities as already discussed with the model of the vision quest.

The rites always involve the interfacing dynamics of the active and the receptive, the listening and the doing, the introspection and the extroversion, the yin and the yang. Each rite has a masculine component—some kind of physically testing challenge facing the unknown, which requires the participant to show up and take some kind of action. Yet each rite also involves a feminine aspect—dealing with feelings, being vulnerable, surrendering control to a power greater than the ego self and ego mind, and tuning into and using intuitive wisdom. After the challenge, the participant spends a period of time in solitude and reflection with the receptive feminine, the womb within, to observe what new growth is being birthed as a result of the experience and what kind of nourishment it needs in order to mature and blossom. I think of a line from the poetry of Rumi and how well it expresses this time of introspective listening: "I have lived on the lip of insanity, wanting to know reasons, knocking on a door. It opens. I've been knocking from the inside!" The feminine and the masculine, working cooperatively—this is the sacred marriage. Without this respectful partnership, there is disharmony and turmoil. With it, the possibilities are infinite.

Grandmother Guadalupe,
spiritual grandmother of the author

Photo by John Catalin

The sacred marriage needs to occur in everyone. Then we will be able to treat each other as human beings were meant to be treated, with respect, caring, and kindness, knowing that what we give to another, we give to ourselves. A significant sacred marriage for me took place during a guided drum journey. My feminine spoke with gentle power: *I am the Spider Woman weaving my webs of gossamer and lace. I am the Receiving One. I am the Old One, the one who remembers. I am the Birther and Celebrator, who loves life and celebrates it in all. I want to blossom myself to all that the Goddess had created me to be with joy in my heart as I travel my path. I am woman born out of the marriage of Above and Below. I am Gloria. I love my mother's body in all her forms. I love to lie on her belly and walk barefoot on her moist flesh. I am soft and gentle. I love the sensuous and the erotic, to dance wildly with my long hair twirling all around me. I love to listen to the stars twinkle in the cosmic night. I'm impulsive and wild, and I can be a terror, using my feminine wiles or my claws to get what I want or to protect myself or those I love. I am an open pipeline to the Mysteries, through my womb, through my vagina, through my feelings, and through my dreams and intuition. I am ecstatic Warrior Woman. I am the wild horse galloping across the plain. I am the wind whistling across the tundra.*

When Gloria was finished speaking, she mounted a golden horse and rode up onto the top of a hill. Far off in the distance, I could see another rider approaching. I realized that it was my masculine side, my *animus*. I watched in fascination as the two rode toward each other over the rolling foothills. My journal entry describes what happened next:

"We come over a rise from separate directions and almost crash into one another. Our eyes meet as our horses rear up on their hind legs, snorting and bellowing. We struggle to stay mounted. Gradually, they calm down. We look into each other's eyes. Who is this one? Where did you come from? we both wonder. No words are spoken. We dismount and walk toward each other. The energy builds as we get closer. It hits us both at once: I am looking into myself, my long-lost soul partner. Where have you been? The figures merge into one another. There is no longer separation. Sparks fly. Rainbows explode. A voice speaks: 'We are now

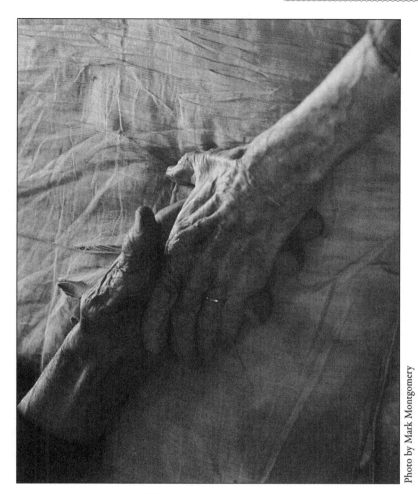

Photo by Mark Montgomery

The power of connection

more than the joining of two. We are a bridge, a doorway to the infinite! We are a song of bliss!'"

I was still filled with the power and beauty from this drum journey of sacred joining when, a short time later, I went to visit the home of a friend whose daughter was a gifted artist. While waiting for dinner to be served, I wandered through the rooms of the house. In one room, I found a pile of pen and ink sketches made by the daughter. I casually looked through them, then stopped short. Here was a drawing of Gloria, the one I had seen in my vision. I ran with the drawing into the kitchen and explained what it meant to me. She and her daughter were both delighted to give it to me as a present. I took it home and put it up on my altar. It sits there to this day, over thirty years now. Every morning, I greet her as I do my prayers.

Ho Virgen de Guadalupe, Kuan Yin, Gloria. Thank you for your light and your unconditional, healing love. Thank you for the gift of the feminine energy, the gift of feelings, of intuition, of the dream power. Thank you for your strength pouring out your love no matter what. Thank you for always being there. Help me to open myself to you, Holy Mother, your compassion and your tenderness, help me to bring it into the places within me that need it, and to be a channel for your healing touch to whomever you would have me send it to in the course of this day. Ho. May it be so.

11

Coyote Teachings

The Universe as Trickster

The world we perceive is a dream we learn to have from a script we have not written.

SILVAN TOMKINS

The clown, the fool, the *heyoka* contrary who brings the law of levity to balance the law of gravity, the one who upsets the apple cart just when you're planning to open up for business, who busts seriousness, arrogance, and feelings of certainty, confidence, and self-importance; who runs through your campsite and pisses in the fire just as you are about to sit down to enjoy your hot bowl of soup—ah yes, the coyote! Just when you think you know what's going on, when you think your theory of the universe is ontologically tight, look out, here comes coyote to humble and humiliate, to embarrass and wreak havoc. It does sacred work reminding you that it is all mystery and that whatever you think you know, it doesn't amount to a hill of beans compared to what you don't know. The coyote says, "Stay humble, Jack. It's a movin', jumpin', jivin', livin', breathin' big ole mystery, and the more you get to thinking you've got it all down clean and neat, the more I'll be comin' around to let you know it's a happenin' fact that you don't know doodly! Stay open, pay attention, and don't try to lock it up in tight boxes of meaning and knowing! It's bigger than you, boy, and grander than you can even imagine!"

Photo by Andrea Pinkson

Coyote, the trickster

All of which goes to say, my notes and outlines and quotes and stories and anecdotes and remembrances and plans for this chapter disappeared. Just vanished. I looked everywhere for them. *Nada.* Nothing. Really. I can't find them anywhere. All I could find were some coyote droppings. I think I'll put them in the garden and use them for fertilizer. The plants will know what to do with them! Oops! Wait a minute, the coyote just peeked out from behind a coyote bush . . .

Back again. I ran over to try and catch it but it was too quick for me. All I found was a piece of parchment with some writing on it.

Here's what it said:

After the enlightened cave-yogi and songmaster Milarepa left this world, a scrap of rice paper was found inscribed with his handwriting. His ascetic followers were astounded, for it stated that beneath a nearby boulder was buried all the gold that the ascetic Mila had hoarded during his life. A few eager disciples dug around and under that large rock. In the earth they discovered a ragged cloth bundle. Opening the knotted bundle with shaking hands, they discovered only a lump of dried shit. There was another scribbled note as well. It said: "If you understand my teaching so little that you actually believed I ever valued or hoarded gold, you are truly heirs to my shit."

The note was signed, "The Laughing Vajra, Milarepa." (Jack Kornfield in *A Path with Heart*)

12

~~~

Blossoming the Flowers

Most live their lives without much recognition of the
enormity available in the shared spaciousness of being . . .
in which we are always interconnected.

STEPHEN AND ONDREA LEVINE,

ACKNOWLEDGING THE BELOVED

O n the day I was born, New York City was shut down by a
major snowstorm. Somehow, my father got out and bought
a gift for my mother to celebrate my birth. The gift was a
porcelain bull, purple in color and six and a half inches long, five inches
in height. Growing up, I'd occasionally notice the bull sitting on a bookshelf but never took an interest in it. My mother never said a word about
it. Forty years later, while visiting my parents' home in Maryland, I was
struck by a desire to have something that had been physically connected
with my long dead father. He didn't leave much of material worth behind
him; he was an activist, a doer, not an accumulator. Mostly, he left books.
While perusing his library, I noticed the bull sitting in a corner. I asked
my mother if I could have it and she said yes. I didn't feel a particularly
strong connection with it, but then there wasn't that much to choose
from, so off it went back home with me to California, where I put it on

a bookshelf in my office. Once again, it got shuttled out of conscious awareness and languished in obscurity in the back shadows of the shelf. It wasn't until the final years of my apprenticeship with the Huichol that the bull came off the shelf and into a prominent position in my psyche and my life.

Photo by Joe Burrell

El Toro

In an interesting incidence of synchronicity, the bull my father bought almost half a century ago became the symbol of what I had to face to complete my apprenticeship and earn the equivalent of my undergraduate degree in Huichol shamanism. The occasion was the Bull Ceremony, a completion ceremony held in the shaman's village after the return from my fifth pilgrimage.

I didn't know anything about the Bull Ceremony when I first started my involvement with the Huichol medicine path. But then I didn't know much about anything in those days. I just knew intuitively that it was a path I needed to walk on as best I could no matter where it was taking me. During the course of my journey, I was fortunate to be helped by a gringo couple, Larain and Bob Boyll, who were with me on all my pilgrimages except my last one because by then they had "graduated." After my last pilgrimage with them, they stayed on in Mexico while I returned to the States, and they went through their Bull Ceremony, completing their apprenticeship. When they returned, they called me up to tell me all about it. As I listened to their report, I became increasingly disturbed, for I knew where it was headed and I didn't like it—in order for me to complete my apprenticeship, I too would have to sponsor and take part in a Bull Ceremony.

It is important to mention here that ever since I had my first realization of the interconnectedness of creation and started meditating, I have tried to do no harm to any living being. I apologize when I kill a mosquito or step on an ant because I believe the words of the elders who say that all life has equal value in the eyes of the Creator. If you take life, they state emphatically, do it consciously and give something back. This is the way of respect. If you want respect for your own life, you need to give it to all others. One way I have tried to honor this is to not eat meat. Since 1968, I haven't had meat except for the occasions where venison has been offered as part of a ceremony. Once I ate some bear meat in a ceremonial manner because it is one of my main power animals and taking a piece of its body into my own helped me connect with its medicine. Other than that, *nada*. Occasionally, I'll eat fish or fowl if it hasn't been polluted with chemicals. But every time I eat, I thank the spirit of that which I am eating, for its life and its gift to me, and I pray for the life of its family. I learned long ago that someday a force greater than my own will take my life and that when this time comes, I want to be treated with respect. I want someone to thank me for my life and pray for my family, so I must do the same for all others.

Mainly, though, I try to take as little life as possible. So when I heard that I had to take another being's life, directly by hand and using only a knife, I seriously considered not going through with it. But I knew I had a year to prepare for whatever I decided to do, and that meant some serious homework, work to do down deep inside where I really live—my inner home. I had to confront a number of major issues that fell in one of two categories. First, what warrants taking the life of the bull? How important is this shamanic work to me, and how important is the medicine path of the Huichol, which I have been following these past years? Am I willing to trade it for the life of another being who has as much importance in the Great Spirit's eyes as does my own?

The second order of questioning had to do with my own squeamishness about the actual physical act of taking the bull's life, plus taking the life of a turkey, both of whose throats I would have to cut. With the bull, it would be even worse: I would have to cut an opening in its throat, then thrust my knife through its long, thick neck down into its torso to finally reach its heart. Then I would have to cut into the center of the bull's heart and hold my knife there until the bull died. *Whew!* I don't like blood to begin with, let alone blood I am responsible for drawing. I don't like killing anything. For years I have been trying to make myself more gentle, not harder, which is what I felt I would have to do if I were going to successfully kill the bull.

All year long I grappled with these issues. I'd visualize the entire process of buying the bull, getting to know it, spending time with it, explaining to it what I was going to do and why. Then I'd force myself to see all the details of taking the bull's life. I'd concentrate on facing every feeling, thought, and sensation that came up in response. Midway through this process, I realized the obvious, that I was already in intimate relationship with the spirit of the bull—we had already begun working together.

During this time, I reflected on my feelings about my work with the Huichol and what it meant to me. My experiences with what they and the plant and animal and spirit elders had taught me was priceless. Through it all, I gained entry into a tradition as old as humanity, among people who still remember the life-preserving teachings of nature and how to commune directly with its wisdom. I wondered if all I had learned would somehow be lost if I did not follow through with what I had to do. At some time during that twelve months of rumination, I made the decision that I would go ahead with it. I communicated this to the bull in my prayers and meditation. I treated the bull exactly as I would have liked to be treated—I told it the truth. I made offerings to its spirit, thanked it for its life, prayed for its family, and asked for its forgiveness.

This of course was all in my mind's eye; I had no idea of how I would show up when the time came for the actual ritual. I had no idea how the bull would be secured, where to actually cut, how to make the cut, and many other questions. The answers to these questions would have to wait. I couldn't figure them out beforehand and worrying about them was producing more and more anxiety. Exercising the faith muscle once again, I let them go, trusting that the Great Spirit would help me as I needed it. I also realized that I trusted the Huichol. They had brought me this far and what I'd learned had served me well. With faith, I accepted that this was the right thing for me to do, and if not, if Great Spirit wanted something different, it would be revealed to me.

Each day, as I greeted Taupa, Father Sun, and as I welcomed in Tatewari, Spirit of the Fire, when I lit a candle in prayer, I sent thanks to my Huichol elders—the shamans who were leading me down the same trail they and their ancestors had taken for thousands of years before them. I prayed in thankfulness for all their gifts, for the life and protection of their people, and for guidance and strength to do what was called up for me to do. I relived my initial 1981 journey with the Huichol, when I first entered their energy field. I remembered how at home I felt with them, more so than I felt with people from the culture I had grown up in. These feelings grew in intensity until, midway through my apprenticeship, I felt torn in two—feeling more connected with the Huichol than with my own culture. I felt I could only survive if I stayed in Mexico and didn't return to the States at all. I didn't know what to do.

But it was on that pilgrimage that I received the message that I was to be a bridge builder between cultures and between states of consciousness. I saw that the reason the medicine teachings were given to me, the reason I had been initiated in the way that I had been—my father's death exposing me to the truth of impermanence and propelling me to seek deeper truth and finding it in shamanic cultures—was so I could learn and bring back into my culture the transformational teachings of how to face the darkness of death and loss, sorrow and pain, and transmute their energies into psychospiritual "fertilizer" for the growth of healthy blossoming plants and flowers. At an early age, I was touched by death in such a way that I could not deny its power. Its touch led me to shamanism, which in turn initiated me into mystical rites of passage. Through these journeys, I learned that fear of death is really ego's fear of dissolution. My visionary experiences of ego loss and union with Great Spirit's unconditional love helped me move past the fear of death and into a daily appreciation of the numinous. It was a journey from death to new life. Through it, I realized that my life task was to help people find and nourish their souls, thus honoring the truth of their higher identity—beings of light here to serve the will of the Great Mystery. I saw that I was also to give back to the Huichol in some way that would be of benefit to them and the struggles they were facing with Western monophasic culture bearing down on them in their mountain retreat. My faith grew stronger while my questions and doubts began to shrink, empowered by the vision of the heart in the fire, by the blossoming flowers in my heart, and by finding my lost knife in the wilderness of the desert. After this pilgrimage, I was eager to return *á el norte,* to the North, and to whatever situations the Mystery brought my way for the purpose of learning, growing, and serving.

As the time grew closer for my completion pilgrimage, my prayers took on greater intensity. In my body, my mind, and my spirit, I felt the power of what lay ahead of me touching me more intimately each day. The night before I left, I dreamed I was in a small boat with a group of others. Huge waves rose up, shaking the boat like a leaf in the wind. I worked desperately to get the others off safely before the boat sank, taking me with it in its slow, swirling descent into the depths of the sea. As I drifted downward, I heard these words: *Release into it, let go, surrender.*

The next day as I loaded up my gear for the trip, I thought about the dream and how it was showing me a way to approach this pilgrimage in right relationship: *In order to serve the greater good, you must die and let go of your old self and sink down into the depths. There you will receive.* I was mulling this over on the bus to the airport when out the window I saw a big rainbow. I almost jumped out of my seat in happiness for this omen. I knew immediately it was a bridge to the elders and the teachings of the healing rainbow energy of which they so frequently spoke to me. *Stay focused,* I thought. Using the colors of the rainbow, I dropped deeper into my intention: *To complete! To surrender into the depths of Great Mystery on all levels and all ways. To open to and be with the wisdom elders for however they guide me on my heart path. To discover, own, and empower the medicine gifts that Great Spirit "lends" to me to carry in this life. To bring it all back home to integrate, act on, and honor for the greatest good of all in unattached, loving service to Higher Will.*

As the colors of the rainbow faded into the sky, I picked up my journal from my first pilgrimage in 1981 and began to read through my notes. I was shocked to read the very first entry, about a dream I had the night before I left. In this dream, I was also on a boat with other people. Big waves came up and overturned the boat, dumping everyone into the powerful currents, including me. The same dream the night before the beginning and the night before the ending! I reflected on the one significant change: in the first dream, all the people on the boat were dumped into the big currents. In the second dream, eleven years later, I was to offer myself up for the good of the people and sink deeper into the depths of what awaited me there. The *nierica* was opening wider and wider.

It wasn't until midway on the pilgrimage that I got the full significance of what the dreamtime was telling me, and by that time, many adventures had already taken place. Ten of us gringos assembled at Guadalupe's rancho on the outskirts of a small pueblo just south of Tepic. For several days, we camped out there while preparations for the pilgrimage were completed. Each person made a number of different kinds of prayer arrows to be offered at various holy places along the way. We sat in a loosely assembled circle watching the Huichol make their offerings and listening to their instructions on how to best make ours. Tacho, the male shaman for this pilgrimage, told me that I had to make an additional offering, a yarn painting modeled after the Huichol ones, which are made by inlaying yarn onto wax melted on a flat board. My assignment was to make a two-headed eagle, representative of the sun and wisdom, the Way of Sol, which I'd bring to Wiricuta. My efforts were clumsy compared to the artistry of the Huichol, but they all offered encouragement and told me how well I was doing.

Photo by John Catalin

Guadalupe making offerings

With the help of my longtime Huichol brother, Presciliano, with whom I have traveled this pilgrimage path for many journeys and whose children I have watched growing up, I purchased the many items needed to "complete." In addition to buying the bull and its food, I had to buy a turkey, two long, white, tapered candles from a funeral home, firecrackers, and of course, plenty of chocolate, cigarillos, regular white candles, and firewood, both for the rancho while we were on the road, and for the road itself, where firewood might be hard to find when we stopped in the wee hours of the morning looking for a good camping spot in the dark.

During the first few nights of preparations, my dreams were quite active, showing me again the importance of listening to the intuitive feminine and taming my shadow-reactivity, triggered when fearful or frustrated. One dream told me about El Toro, the bull: *When you take its life, do so with compassion, respect, and with full consciousness. Do not take it with fear or trembling, for then the bull will suffer. Do it with full force, full strength, full love for the bull and what it is offering to you and the people.*

The next morning, I sat down close to the bull but out of range of the rope it was tethered to in the middle of a nearby pasture. I did a prayer smoke to the bull and told it who I was, what I was going to do, and why. I thanked it for its life and for its sacrifice, and I cried as I asked its forgiveness. I prayed for its family and thanked them all for their gift. The bull's head was decorated with a lei of flowers and ribbons that the Huichol had placed on its horns. *When,* I wondered, *did they do that? It wasn't there when we went to sleep last night.* There were more surprises to come.

On the last night in the rancho before leaving on the pilgrimage, we stayed up around the sacred fire alternately socializing and holding parting ceremonies. Actually, it's all a ceremony for the Huichol, who do not separate the sacred and the profane as we do in the West. Joking and talking are interspersed with prayers, singing, dancing, and ritual. Tacho, the shaman leading this pilgrimage, gave me my new name, as he did for each Huichol. The other gringos would be named during the actual pilgrimage. Naming is an important part of preparation. You are expected to recite your lengthy Huichol name in future ceremonies and you will be a laughingstock if you cannot remember it. The shaman "sees" the name for each person through psychic vision and each person eagerly awaits to see what it will be. Tacho closed his eyes and peered within when he came to me. After a while, he opened his eyes and recited my new Huichol name. I wrote it down so I wouldn't forget it. It has to do with feeding the fire so that its light, with help from the *kupuri* of Father Sun, can fertilize the flowers of my life and help others to do the same. I smiled at Tacho and Guadalupe. *"Pam'pa Dios,"* I said happily. I liked my new name; it reminded me of what I need to do—stay conscious of the light, nurture it, then use its medicine to make the *tutus* blossom.

In addition to the naming ceremony, we were each given a specific position—around the fire, where we sat in the vans as we drove, which van went first—which were all strictly maintained throughout our time together. This has to do with spiritual protocol. The first van was the head, antlers, and eyes of Kauyumari, who leads the way. The second van, which was mine, the *iyari,* was the heart of Kauyumari and was holding the two shamans and their immediate families. The last van, *cola,* was the tail of Kauyumari. Each was blessed in ceremony that night and on each successive morning until we returned.

In the wee hours around that last night fire, Tacho casually leaned over and told me that I had to cut off one of the bull's ears and attach it to my main prayer arrow. Everyone else, he said, would take some of the blood from the bull's severed ear to bless their arrows and all their ceremonial gifts, just as Tacho would do with the blood of a deer that was especially hunted for the occasion of the pilgrimage. Upon hearing what I had to do, I promptly panicked, wondering how one goes about removing the ear of a live bull. I tried to stall for time but two Huichol men motioned me to stand up and follow them. We approached the bull, which rose abruptly from its slumber, sensing we were up to no good. As we got closer, the bull started thrashing the air with its horns. My mind was running amuck in fourth gear: *How am I supposed to get close to a charging, kicking bull, lashing out madly with its sharp horns and powerful hooves? What should I do?* I wondered desperately.

I looked to the Huichol men for clues. They feinted toward the bull and jumped back just as its sharp horns swished dangerously close. I stood ready with my knife but without a clue about what to do. Just then my old buddy Ruck, the one who saved me from drowning years before when we were scuba diving off the Marin County shore and who was on his first sojourn with the Huichol, bolted out of nowhere and grabbed the bull's tail. The bull turned his head to see what was causing the disturbance. In that instant, two Huichol men raced in and grabbed the bull by the neck. Then Max, my other buddy, who was on his second pilgrimage, joined the fray. Then another Huichol man jumped in and they wrestled the bull to the ground. *"Pronto!"* they yelled. I swooped in to the fallen bull, grabbed its ear while mumbling a prayer asking for forgiveness, then sliced through the soft flesh, severing the ear in two. I expected the bull to go crazy when I made the cut, but it didn't even flinch. Blood spurted all over but the bull acted as if nothing had happened. I thanked it for its gift and stepped back quickly with my trophy. The Huichol roared in approval.

We got back to the fire and Tacho took the severed ear and dripped its blood on all the offerings while he prayed for a safe and successful pilgrimage. When he finished his prayers and all those going on the pilgrimage had blessed their ceremonial gear, he handed the ear back to me with instructions to attach it to my prayer arrow and carry it with me to Wiricuta. I took the ear and looked back at the bull. It was now standing up again, busily engaged in eating a meal and looked fine. But I was pounding with adrenaline. It didn't help that I could see the bull's death coming closer. I wondered how I would do when it came time to take more than an ear. Softly, I apologized to El Toro for any pain I caused it and thanked it again for its gift. *I'll carry your power and spirit to the Holy Land and there I will pray for you and your people,* I promised.

We set out the next morning, our three vans arranged in proper order and with a final blessing from Tacho and a line of waving Huichol. On the road, the coyote became quite active. Cars broke down in the middle of nowhere, drivers lost their keys, people got sick, gringos did things out of ignorance that aren't supposed to be done, which Tacho said I had to "undo" with various ceremonial acts. Nervous about getting to Wiricuta, I pushed the other drivers to go faster and stop less. People were angry with me, which led to an impromptu encounter group on the main street of a little pueblo. They told me to stop pushing so hard and I knew they were right. I was in goal-driven behavior so deep that I had lost touch with enjoying the process of getting there. I was in fear and out of balance. My masculine "push-program" was in full swing.

I felt like a failure, that I'd ruined the trip for everyone. My tension increased tenfold when Guadalupe emphatically stated her feelings as well. *"Vamanos,"* she said. "We need to get out of this town as soon as we buy supplies. We have to get back to Tatewari. Here we are in danger. Taupa is gone and we are in darkness. With Tatewari we will be okay."

Guadalupe's words helped me to remember spirit's presence and to slow down. It came right in the nick of time, for as we started to pull out of town, with me now going very slowly and paying attention to everything, two kids on bicycles roared around a corner and crashed into the dusty street right in front of the car I was driving. If I'd been going any faster, I wouldn't have stopped in time and the kids would have been history. *Whew, Great Spirit, thanks for the slow-down message.* From that moment on, I surrendered to Kauyumari. *You lead the way, Deer Spirit. You do a much better job than I. Thank you for your protection and your guidance. Lead us forward with your wisdom.*

Surrender was the ticket throughout the rest of the pilgrimage, especially at Tateimatinieri, the Grandmother Springs in the middle of the desert. When I first came to these springs in 1981, it took us most of the day to get there. We had rented a big flatbed truck to bushwhack us in.

Guadalupe praying

Photo by John Catalin

We crowded onto the back of the truck, packed together like sardines. There was no road and it was a slow, nerve-wracking, bouncy ride. Several times, the truck almost overturned. It was especially rough since all of us first-timers were blindfolded and had been ever since we had been taken through the ceremonial gateway at Jaikitenieh. We remained blindfolded until we arrived at the springs and received its holy waters. Only then were the blindfolds removed and we could face out across the desert to the holy land of Wiricuta, our next and culminating destination.

This time, there was a dirt road to the springs and the going was much easier. Of course, coyote made another appearance and we got lost for a while, leading to an extra night out before reaching the springs. At least this time I didn't have to wear a blindfold. It was a tough go for the first-timers, though. Tension tightened their faces, their moods were foul, and it was a long night. The next day, we got back on the right trail and made it to the springs by mid-afternoon. The Springs of Tateimatinieri are one of the holiest places for the Huichol. Here we received the blessings of its waters, drank some of it, and had a bowlful poured on our heads to the cries of delight from the others. Everyone was included in this—babies, elders, children, all of the Huichol, and all of the gringos. Afterward, everyone found a place around the springs and left prayer offerings for the sacred grandmothers who live below it. Arrows, coins, votive bowls, crackers, chocolate, and flickering candles lined the banks. Sacred water was sprinkled on everything. It was a time of great reverence.

Just as I was in the middle of my prayers, Tacho called me over and motioned me to sit down before him. This had never been done to me before at this place, but then I had never been the one who was completing. Throughout the pilgrimage, I was expected to sit next to Tacho and Guadalupe, watching their every move and being available to them to serve however they needed. I saw with satisfaction that over the years I had figuratively worked my way up from the back of the bus to the position of sitting right behind the driver, the shaman. In a way, though, this was the hot seat, for I had little if any time for myself. I had to be at their beck and call at all times; if they needed something done and I wasn't there to do it, the whole show stopped until I got with the program.

Being in the front of the bus had its advantages; it was a prime location for learning. I had never been in such intimate interaction with the shaman before except for certain times during ceremony. Now, I was with them continually, and I observed the minutia of all they did. Tacho or Guadalupe repeatedly leaned over and explained what they were doing and why. Tacho taught me specific chants for healing, gave instructions on the proper way to conduct various ceremonies, and provided spiritual guidance to help me understand my rich visionary experiences over the years. I ate it up.

When Tacho called me over to kneel down before him at Tateimatinieri, I instantly remembered the surrender teachings of my dream about the sinking boat. *This is the time,* I said to myself. *Let go entirely. Release. Drop into the deeper currents and let them take you into the Mystery.* I closed my eyes and dropped down. I could hear Tacho chanting and I could feel his feather wands, his *muwieri,* passing over my body, opening my *chakras.* The next moment, I was sucked down into the bowels of the earth. Deeper and deeper I plunged until I finally reached solid ground. There was a circle of twenty-four Huichol elders, almost all of them old women plus two or three old men, dressed in their beautiful ceremonial clothing. I knew immediately they were the Grandmothers of the Springs. In the center of the circle, Tatewari was proudly dancing. I was excited to be there and touched when they said they were expecting me.

They welcomed me warmly into their circle. Their faces were radiating rainbow-like energy in an aura as bright as the flames of Tatewari. They showed me how they listen to the prayers and offerings of those who come to the springs. They look into the heart of each person. They see into the person's life, past and future, and they see what is for that person's greatest good. For those who they feel are sincere and deserving, they call up Tatei Nakaway, Great Grandmother Growth, who lives even deeper in the earth, and she comes to fulfill their requests, rising up and into the life of the person who is praying, bringing her mysterious growth power. They showed me how they do this and how to include it in my own shamanic practice. They taught

Photo by John Catalin

Sacred kupuri blessings from the Grandmother Springs

me how to call them up when I am doing healing work and how they in turn would then call up Tatei Nakaway and she would bring her power to the healing ceremony.

Far away I could still hear Tacho chanting, but I was no longer there with him, I was with the grandmothers, gratefully receiving their teachings. When they were finished, they blessed me, then turned to the sacred fire and listened to its beautiful singing. Then I felt a tug in my belly. Something was calling me back. The next thing I knew, I was up on the surface kneeling before Tacho. *"Finito,"* he said. *"No mas."* I opened my eyes and looked into his wizened face. He looked like Yoda in the movie *Star Wars.* Did the old man know where I had just been? He motioned me back to my place by the springs. His eyes twinkled and he laughed out loud.

We left the springs shortly thereafter, my head still spinning with the impact of my journey to the underworld and the medicine teachings of the grandmothers. *I haven't even taken any peyote!* I thought. *This is one of the strongest experiences I have ever had.* I felt totally blessed and loved, and profusely thanked the spirits of the springs for their wonderful gift.

The next day, we arrived in Wiricuta just before nightfall. I felt relieved to finally be there, like a mother hen who has gotten her chicks back to the safety of the coop. I felt at home here, though the power is immense and constant vigilance is mandatory. But I was overwhelmed with joy at being back—I loved seeing the sparse foothills, the rolling mountains, the desert itself, all familiar to me, old friends I've been through the wars with on previous hunts. This place has shown me my life and how to access the power to live it in a good way.

But there was no time for reminiscing, for no sooner did our feet hit the ground than Tacho and Guadalupe gathered us all together for prayers and blessings. Then we were sent out to hunt for medicine before night descended and impaired our vision. At first, there was nothing to be found. We fanned out in all directions, walking slowly across the desert floor, searching out our elusive prey. The going was slow for the gringos, but the Huichol soon began locating the "tracks of the deer." Enthusiasm mounted. Each person stood by what they found without picking it. Finally, Tacho called us to gather around him. He stalked and shot a ceremonial arrow into the ground next to the "deer." Joyful and excited, we knelt before it and offered our prayers, joining with those of Tacho and Guadalupe. We had found our game and would eat of the sacred communion medicine to renew our lives. Because it was almost dark and we needed to harvest more medicine, Tacho sent us right back out to gather as many plants as we could while the light allowed it. Domingo, one of the oldest of the Huichol, a sweet and gentle man, asked if he could borrow my knife. This was my special knife saved from previous pilgrimages and I prized it dearly. My heart ached but there was no question of what I must do. This was my kind grandfather, who had showed me the way on this and previous journeys. *"Si abuelo, es para ti,"* this is for you, *"con mucho gusto,"* with much pleasure.

I walked with Domingo as he carefully dug up his beloved prize,

Photo by Trout Black

Domingo, Huichol elder

excitedly praising each one, his eyes sparkling. Carefully, he left enough root still in the earth to produce more "little babies." Before long, it was too dark to differentiate peyote from flat rocks, so we headed back to camp and gathered at the shaman's altar around the "fallen deer." Under the shaman's directions, we lit our candles and offered our arrows, bowls, money, chocolate, and the other gifts that we brought here in thankfulness for our lives and for our families. The velvety desert darkness was illuminated only by the candles, the shining stars now emerging in the clear night, and our hearts bursting with excitement, and anticipation.

Tacho cut the cactus into little pieces and blessed each one, then placed a piece of it—the sacred footsteps of Kauyumari—into each of our mouths. As we took the flesh in, he prayed aloud for our lives and for good visions here at Wiricuta. Usually, the taste of the peyote is quite bitter. Even the Huichol faces grimace when they chew it. But tonight its taste was sweet. "Eat," said the Huichol. "It is good for you. It will help your heart open. Brush it over your eyes and your face, hold it over your heart. Take it all the way down inside your belly. It is life. It is the holy food of the gods. It blesses you. It will make you sing and dance. We will do the deer dance around Tatewari."

Domingo looked over at me and smiled. *"Buena medicina hermano"*— good medicine brother, he said softly.

After we all chewed and swallowed our first bite, and after our prayers were finished, Tacho conducted a long blessing chant, and then we loaded on a fresh contribution of firewood and took our places around the first shaman, Grandpa Fire. We settled in for the evening— twenty-five of us—women and children, nursing babies, grandparents, gringos, and Huichol, shamans and *peyoteros*. We all ate as much or as little medicine as we chose. Even without the medicine, just being in this place of power was intense. And to come here with these ancient people in the way of the ancestors is a priceless gift. Over the course of the night, I ate ten plants. I wanted to learn as much as I could, go as deep as I could. With each plant I offered my prayers of thanksgiving and prayed for the life of the Huichol.

While the medicine was sweet and we ate a lot, the coyote messed with our heads once again—many of the gringos got nauseated and threw up. It was a hard night for many people. I too got very nauseated but didn't vomit. Instead, I felt a drowsy malaise that filled my bones and seductively invited me to lie back in my sleeping bag to catch some sorely needed sleep. *But no, I must not succumb. This is my graduation test—to fight through my tiredness and stay awake, stay present, for everything that happens.* Sick people needed help, Tacho and Guadalupe called out for me to go here, do that, prepare this. In between, they talked softly into my ear, telling me more about the shamanic work of the *mara'akame*. I was filled with fatigue and nausea; my eyelids felt like they weighed a thousand pounds. Staying up and being present was an ordeal, but it also brought me great joy. For this was what I had been seeking and praying for, guidance from the elders for my life path.

Whenever I looked up at Grandmother Moon to get a sense of the night's progression, it seemed like she hadn't moved the whole time we had been doing ceremony. With resignation, I accepted that my graduation night in Wiricuta was going to be a long one. On past pilgrimages, I could lie down and get some rest, even sleep for a bit in the early morning. But this time, there would be no rest. I marveled at the staying power of Tacho, who chanted for hours on end, then sang, told jokes, laughed, and prayed. He and Guadalupe and her two younger sisters, Manuela and Eberta, Tacho's wife, sang rounds back and forth to each other in a cosmic rendition of gods and goddesses serenading themselves through eternity. It was beautiful.

One of the things I appreciate more than ever as I reflect back on my experiences with the Huichol is the important role that preparation and ceremony contribute toward a successful interaction with the peyote. The discipline of saving the first bite of food when eating and putting it in the spirit bag, the ceremony where each person has to publicly name each and every lover from his or her entire life, daily morning and evening prayers around Tatewari, offering a stick as food for the fire, then cleansing off in the smoke, thanking Tatewari for its light and medicine and telling it why we are going to Wiricuta, the various fastings from food and drink, the long and exhausting hours and resultant sleep deprivation—all this and more served to break us down, open us up, focus our attention and motivation. It also provided us with a conceptual framework with which to understand what we were experiencing and what was to come with the help of the peyote. After all this experiential attunement, the medicine came in and gave us what we needed—not always what we desired or liked or were comfortable with, but always what we really needed to experience for our soul growth, and more often than not, in mysterious and testing ways.

My night-long ordeal at Wiricuta pushed me way past anything I'd done before. I struggled against exhaustion and nausea, trying to stay alert, aware, and available for service to the shamans and other elders. I didn't know if I was going to make it without collapsing. I prayed for strength from one moment to the next, and like every other time in my life when I have prayed from my heart, humbled myself, and surrendered to spirit's presence, I received support. Every time I closed my outer eyes and opened my spiritual ones, Kauyumari was there, dancing and sending out *kupuri*. Just when I felt that I couldn't go on one minute longer, a new power ally showed up, one I'd never even heard of before. It was a beautiful, golden deer, as big as an elk. Kauyumari del Oro danced above my head, sprinkling golden energy that revitalized my body and my spirit.

Throughout the rest of the night, my deer spirits appeared, disappeared, then reappeared, dancing gaily through rainbow-colored, flashing *niericas*. I felt their love and support. I couldn't have made it without them. It was wonderful and horrible at the same time. My malaise never backed off for an instant. *So what if you feel terrible?* I said to myself. *Stop indulging yourself. It is merely a distraction that you must overcome, irrelevant to the fact that this is your time to be present with every ounce of your attention. This may be the last night of ever being here. You may never see these beautiful mountains and sit with these beautiful people ever*

Author's painting:
Riding on the Back of Kauyumari

again. You may never sit this close to the mara'akame in this way and learn from them as you are doing now.

And learn I did—about initiation by ordeal, about suffering, and about staying with it by overriding whatever came up to get in the way of being present with an open heart. With the considerable help of my allies, I did manage to stay up the whole night. Tacho and Guadalupe taught me many things that long night and so did the dancing deer. Of course, it came with a price—more assignments for future ceremonies and rituals to do when certain situations revealed themselves.

I saw many beautiful things that night, but the most meaningful one of all was seeing the beauty of the interconnected circle that encompassed everything that took place. I saw Tacho and Guadalupe serving the people, I saw Spirit serving them, I saw the fire serving us all, I saw me serving the shamans, I saw the Spirit being served by our prayers, our offerings, our songs, and our hearts that were open to the teachings and testings of the medicine. It was a continuously revolving circle, a true medicine wheel weaving everyone and everything together in a cosmic dance of relationship: *todos unidos.* If one player drops the ball, the whole team suffers. When each player does his or her part, everything hums. Though physically exhausted, my spirit soared with the dancing deer.

Finally, after what seemed like forever, Grandmother Moon began her descent and the first rays of Taupa streaked silently over the horizon. "Hooray!" I hollered. *"Taupa viene,"* Father Sun is coming! My joy was short-lived however because the rising of Father Sun required a sacrifice in exchange for its gift. It was the end of the line for the turkey that had accompanied us on the pilgrimage. Each night, we had fed him and packed him up in the van when we left the following morning. This was his last morning and since I was the one completing, I was the one to make the sacrifice. The turkey was brought over to the fire and passed around the circle. Each person held the sacrificial knife to its neck. The shaman prayed over the turkey and when they were through, it came to me. In my year of preparation, I had been so involved with thinking about the bull, I'd forgotten to prepare myself for taking the turkey's life.

I looked at *wacalote* with great sadness, then explained what I had to do and asked its forgiveness. I offered tobacco and sprinkled water from the holy springs on its body and thanked it for its life. Tacho explained that the spirit of the turkey is called *tao* after its song, *"tao, tao, tao."* After its death, he explained, its spirit flies directly up into the newly birthing sun, Taupa. Taupa in turn gives its energy to Tatewari, the sacred fire. Tatewari in turn gives us its *kupuri,* its energy, as it had been doing each night, singing, guiding, and protecting us. The medicine of the fire gives us strength to open our hearts to the fertilizing power of the love energy that nurtures our *tutus,* our flowers. Then we give our thanks back to the fire and to the sun through our prayers, our songs, and our offerings, which include the life of the sacrificed turkey.

I tearfully picked up the knife while my Huichol *sobrino,* my nephew Guiliermo, stretched out the turkey's neck. *Wacalote* struggled to get away but Guiliermo held it tight. I had a borrowed knife since mine had been given to Domingo. It wasn't the sharpest, so when I started cutting the bird's neck, it took several moments of rough sawing back and forth before I was able to sever the bones and tendons. Blood spurted out all over me as *tao* jerked spasmodically. I was a wreck. Tears poured down my face mingling with the blood. *Pam'pa Dios, espiritu de tao, may you be one with Taupa. May you be in peace. I am sorry for any pain I caused you. But now your blood will mark my clothes and your flesh will feed the people. I will connect with your spirit each day when I do my sunrise prayers and I will remember you and your family. Pam'pa Dios, mi amigo.*

The blood of *tao* was used to bless the people's remaining sacred objects, while its body was taken away, only to appear a few moments later, plucked and ready to be cooked in the fire and eaten for breakfast. Each person had a bite, with the first piece of course given to Tatewari. The turkey, the fire, the sun, the people eating and praying and giving thanks, united in a cooperative flow, each doing its part in harmony and balance and respect for the other: this is the *buena medicina* that the Huichol spiritual path is all about.

After our ceremonial meal, everyone went back out into the "gardens" to pick more medicine. The surplus would be brought back to the Huichol villages and used throughout the year for healing rites and ceremonies. Only the peyote harvested in a sacred way on the pilgrimage to Wiricuta is used by the Huichol. There is no drug problem with the peyote; abuse does not exist. Their holistic usage pattern is a glue for the social cohesiveness of their community. It keeps them aligned with their historical and spiritual roots, thus providing continuity of meaningful purpose to their lives. This is a priceless gift that cannot be purchased nor satisfied through the acquisition of material goods.

I loved watching entire Huichol extended families, men and women, children and elders, all walking through the desert loading up their *bolsas* and straw baskets with the cactus that feeds their spiritual growth. They'd praise each plant they found but got especially excited with the families, groups of plants growing one out of the other in clusters. It was wonderful to watch the young children with their parents and grandparents, their aunts and uncles, all working together in the transmission of an ancient culture from one generation to the next. I was touched to witness and be a part of it all. The children were radiant, the elders were shining. I thought of the words of an old spiritual, ". . . there will be peace, in the valley, some day . . ."

The hunt was successful and we set out for home with full bags and full hearts. On the ride back through the wide deserts and twisting mountain roads of back-country Mexico, *cola,* our tail bus, broke down and Ruck and his assistants had to jury-rig a temporary repair out in the middle of nowhere with whatever odds and ends we could scrape together, including a safety pin. The brakes were barely working but we did a special prayer ceremony by the side of the road and asked for Kauyumari's protection to lead us safely back to the rancho. We set out not knowing how it would go. At twilight, we passed two coyotes standing by a busy intersection on the outskirts of Guadalajara. They disappeared in an instant but not before they gave us an approving nod—we were on the right trail! Twelve hours of hard driving later, we arrived at Guadalupe's at three in the morning. The brakes and safety pin worked just fine.

Upon our arrival, sleepy Huichol appeared from all directions to welcome us back. Despite the early hour, they greeted us with great joy and excitement. More Huichol had come in from surrounding villages, including old friends who had come in for the welcome home, and, as I found out later, for my "graduation rites." Ceremony, feasting, and dancing around Tatewari went on until mid-morning, when exhaustion and the hot sun took its toll. I fell asleep right there in the midst of it all with my hat over my eyes and my dirt-filled, blood-stained clothes matted to my body. I was feeling no pain.

When I woke up, the Huichol were already preparing for the two-hour ride to the ocean at San Blas. We weren't to wash our bodies or our clothes until we did our completion ceremony for the pilgrimage at the ocean. The dirt was considered holy, for it came from all of the sacred places we had visited. We had to carry it with us to Tatei Haramara, Great Grandmother Goddess of the Ocean. We packed up our ceremonial gear one more time, loaded it into the three vans and drove over the coastal mountains to the shore. There Tacho and Guadalupe led us in procession out to the waters where we each lit a candle. Facing Washetahaway, the rock offshore that marks the place where the gods and goddesses first came through the *nierica* and went on pilgrimage to find the center of this middle world, a journey we had just retraced, we offered our closing prayers and gifts. We planted our last prayer arrows where the waves ran up onto the wet sand, then erupted into joyous celebration and waded into the water, giving our holy dust to Tatei Haramara. How sweet it was to feel her wet, cooling touch.

Relaxing in the ocean's gentle swells, I thought of how much I had to be thankful for. There had been some close calls, but we were all back safely, the pilgrimage had been a success and the medicine teachings strong and full. When we returned to Guadalupe's later that afternoon, I was told that we would go right into the Bull Ceremony that evening. Usually there is a waiting time between returning from the pilgrimage and the Bull Ceremony, but this time we were going straight ahead. My stomach tightened as I got the news. No more relaxation. Time to get ready for what's next.

I went directly to the bull who, sans half an ear, sat contentedly tethered in the pasture. I sat down five feet away from the end of the rope. He looked up but didn't move. I took out a cigarillo from the pack I kept in my medicine bag for whenever I needed to do a prayer smoke. *"Ho, El Toro,"* I said to him as I lit the cigarillo and sent the smoke his way to carry my prayers. *Tonight I will be taking your life. I am sorry that I must do this, for I wish you no pain or suffering. I thank you for your life. Your body will feed many people who don't get to eat meat very often. Your strength will become their strength. I promise you your life will not be taken in vain. I will honor you for all my days. I will take your power and use it to serve the people in my life, just as you do in your death. May it be so.*

Early evening came and with it a growing swell of Huichol. All the men and boys went to a field where the stubs of recently harvested cornstalks poked up from the ground like sharp spikes. The bull came with us, secured carefully to the stout rope led by a Huichol man. Corn is a foundation of the Huichol way of life and they have many ceremonies to honor it. They grind the shucked corn kernels into a powder, then bake them into delicious tortillas, which form the mainstay of their diet. The children delighted in bringing us fresh tortillas even before we were out of our sleeping bags in the morning. *Fantastico!* But this field was now barren, a place of death. All the men and boys knelt down together. We were there to do a ceremony for the regeneration of life. The corn's life had been taken so the Huichol people could live. Now in sacred reciprocity, we were preparing to give back.

Tacho purified all the men because it is they, not the women, who take the life of the bull or of the deer. Candles were lit and following the shaman's prayers, *kupuri* was given back to Mother Earth, to fertilize her renewal of life for the crops of the next planting cycle. Afterward, we returned to Grandpa Fire and sat down in a huge circle, perhaps forty or more Huichol with a scattering of gringos. We stayed in that circle for the whole night—praying, singing, chanting, dancing. All the while I kept anxiously wondering, *Will I be strong enough when the time comes to face the bull? Will I be able to go through with it when I am eye to eye with this magnificent living creature? Will the Huichol help me or will I be expected to do it by myself?*

Trust that it will all work out, I kept repeating to myself. *Trust the Huichol, trust the Great Spirit. Just show up and do the best you can. Surrender into the experience. Be with the shaman, watch what they are doing. Follow them. Enjoy yourself. You may never be back this way again. Use the pressure to help you be present. This is your life. Be here! Enjoy it!*

And so it went, back and forth in my mind between worrying about what was going to happen and enjoying the camaraderie and growing power of the ceremony, which was building to a climax. At four o'clock in the morning, just when I could barely keep my eyes open, Tacho bent over in my direction and said softly, *"Ya es tiempo."* It's time. A chill ran through me although I was sweating from the heat of the fire. I sat there, frozen. In the blink of an eye, my *sobrino,* Guiliermo, and two other Huichol young men were by my side. One of them handed me a knife, since the one I had planned to use I had given to Domingo in Wiricuta. *"Andelez,"* they said. I gripped the knife in my right hand and picked up my medicine bag with my left. Max and Ruck, my stalwart *compadres,* stood up with me. Thank God, they weren't going to let me do this by myself!

The five of us left the light of the fire and walked toward the bull. El Toro jumped up as we approached and began to thrash its sharp horns, running back and forth as far its rope allowed. The post holding the other end of the rope started to wobble. *Oh man, what if it gets loose?* The two Huichol men must have had the same thought because one of them grabbed the bull's neck just as the horns swished dangerously close to his chest. He twisted its neck back and then Guiliermo, Ruck, and Max all jumped in and wrestled the bull to the ground. The Huichol quickly bound up the bull's legs and in an instant, there it was—the moment of truth.

I felt everyone's eyes on me and the hair on the back of my neck stood straight up. All of my senses were on red alert. I sat down in front of the bull. Our eyes met. His were wide and frantic. Mine were too. The whole universe boiled down to the bull and me. His body heaved from the toll of his exertion. I took out some purified tobacco and held it over my heart. Then I spoke to the bull. *"Dear Toro, our time has* come. *Forgive me, mi amigo, I must take your life to complete what I have committed to do long ago. I pray that your spirit goes straight into the light of the Great Spirit. Help me, Great Spirit, give me the strength to do what I must do as quickly and efficiently as possible so my brother does not have to suffer unnecessarily. Ho, Toro, with your help I will take in your power and use it every day to honor the medicine gifts and responsibilities that have been given to me on the Huichol path. Con su auyuda, with your help. Vaya con Dios."*

I gripped the knife and opened a fold in the loose skin of the bull's neck so I could insert the knife. At that moment time/space dimensionality collapsed and I suddenly felt the presence of my dead father, Fred, alive and well. He was there helping me, just when I really needed it! His strength joined with that of Ruck, Max, and my two Huichol helpers. Courage and determination poured into me as a surge of power bore me forward like a roaring tidal wave. I drove the knife in and downward, exactly where it needed to go, through the throat and into the chest cavity and heart. My forearms disappeared into the bull's massive chest. My face was now inches away from the bull. Our eyes locked together in the intimacy of death. Blood spurted out like water from a fire hydrant, splattering onto my chest.

"Cut his heart so he can die quickly!" yelled the Huichol. I twisted the knife back and forth with all my might, cutting into that mighty pulsing heart. Desperately, I thrust and cut and prayed for the bull's life to leave his body. Then I saw it. I saw death come and take him. I saw it in his eyes. I felt his last breath exit his struggling body and the spirit of El Toro flew from his heart into mine. It was only there for an instant, but in that moment I knew that I would never be the same person again, for now I carried some intangible part of the bull's power inside of me.

After the transmission of power, the bull's spirit shot up into the sky. I fell over backward in relief, pulling out the knife as I fell. Simultaneously, the Huichol set off a massive barrage of firecrackers that filled the night with explosions of sparkling light. Tacho reached out with a gourd to gather the bull's streaming blood. I was covered with it—my clothes, my medicine bag, my hands, and my arms. *"Vaya con Dios, Toro,"* I said out loud. "I will remember you every time I wear my Huichol clothes. Every time I open my bag, you will be there with me. I go forward with your strength. Be at peace, my friend. Thank you."

Tacho led us all back to the fire and each person lined up to receive a blessing of the bull's blood. My body was present physically, but my spirit was somewhere up in the night sky, with the firecrackers and the spirit of El Toro, shooting toward the celestial light. I felt exhausted, filled with sadness for the bull's death, but also joyful and awed because of my father's presence. My father's strength appeared for me just when I really needed it. Somehow, he had opened the door to all of this when he bought the porcelain bull half a century before on the day I was born. *Did he*

Photo by Max Poppers

Ruck, with the drying skin of El Toro

know then that his infant son would one day be involved in an act of power involving a bull with shamanic people in the mountains of Mexico? It was a pretty big stretch, but time in its usual sense of past, present, and future, no longer existed; it had all fused together. I saw how my father's death long ago had freed him up to be with me whenever I needed him. He, like the spirit of El Toro, was free, and both were now somehow inside of me as well. *Todos unidos.*

Meanwhile, back at the fire, I was escorted to the seat of honor amidst enthusiastic, back-slapping accolades from the Huichol: *"Buen trabajo,"* good work; *"que bueno, que bueno."* I moved in a daze, multidimensional realities floating before me. I watched Guiliermo and his father, José, skin the bull so quickly and so efficiently that within forty-five minutes there was nothing left except a neatly stacked hide and the blood-stained earth. The fresh meat of the bull was given first to the fire, then to the shaman, and then to everyone there. Its blood went into the cornfields and to the special candles that served as my graduation certificate. I was fed a ceremonial meal that consisted of tortillas made with the meat of the bull and washed down with *tisquino,* the bitter-tasting Huichol beverage made from fermented corn.

As I sat there eating and drinking and watching the merriment around me, I felt a strange detachment from it all. I could feel changes deep within me. My body still looked the same. My driver's license was the same. But something way down inside was different. I didn't understand it at all, I still don't, but a part of me died along with the bull. I passed through some kind of threshold. I was now the person whom Tacho had named on the first night of the pilgrimage—the one who feeds the sacred fire for the growth of the *tutus,* the flowers. It had come alive inside me, empowered by the life force transmitted by the bull and by my father. A new being within me now looked out at the world with a different perspective, through the eyes of a *mara'akame,* a shaman. It was a whole new world.

Since that time, I see even more clearly how everything that comes in life has a doorway, a *nierica,* that can bring continuing transformation if we find the key to unlocking it. One year exactly after my completion ceremony, my dear friend Ruck was killed in a tragic accident. He worked

Photo by Max Poppers

The morning after the Bull Ceremony

as a tree trimmer and one day his extension pole accidentally hit a power line eight feet above his head. Boom—a flash of lightning took him out in an instant, knocking out the power in the surrounding neighborhood as well. He had to be cut down from the ropes that held him in the tree, his arms outstretched to the sky as if he were in prayer reaching out to the Great Spirit. I went into a state of shock when I got the news. I couldn't believe that someone so robust, so full of life, so vital and alive, could be gone in an instant. Not Ruck, it couldn't be. But sadly it was true.

I sat with his body at the mortuary for three days along with his partner, Josi, his two daughters, Joi and Mia, and his stepson, Tim. We sang, prayed, drummed, and chanted his spirit down the river of death through the western doorway into rebirth with the light of the Great Spirit. I miss him dearly. I light a candle for him when I enter my office each day. His picture sits right next to the light. That's where he always liked to be, next to the light.

His sudden death dramatically reinforces the teaching that we don't have forever in these bodies. Our time on this planet hangs by a fragile thread that can break in any given moment. Right now is *the* time to be fully living our authentic heart path life. Each of us is called to bring forth our deeper vision and birth it into the world. Sing your song. Dance your dance. Celebrate *now!* Heal the sacred circle. May it be so.

POMPARIOS TO YOU, DEAR READER. I WISH YOU *BUENA MEDICINA.*
VAYA CON DIOS.

Tomás

WISDOM WAY OF THE SUN
TUTU MEHJHEAWOWUNEA

Friend, hope not for truth while you are alive.
Jump into experience while you are alive.
What you call salvation belongs to the time before
    death.
If you don't break your ropes while you are alive,
Do you think ghosts will do it after?
The idea that the soul will join with the ecstatic
just because the body is rotting
that is fantasy
what is found now is found then.
If you find nothing now, you will
simply end up with an empty apartment
in the city of death.
If you make love with the divine now,
then in the next life
You will have the face of satisfied desire.

RUMI

Acknowledgments

Many people contributed to the birthing of this book through prayers, encouragement, love, financial support, and belief in its worth. I thank you all from my heart. The baby is alive and well; the flowers are blossoming; the summit has been gained; the race has been completed. Now the fruits of the work go forward in whatever way the winds of the Great Mystery carry it.

Special thanks to Andrea, my life partner and medicine teacher, and my daughters Kimberly and Nicole, all three of whose grace, patience, love, forgiveness, and support while living with a man possessed, writing a book, made it all possible.

Thanks to Eric Ahola for teaching me to keep going until the summit is reached. Thanks to my mother Ruth, my two wonderful fathers, Fred and Ray, my always supportive sisters Ilsa and Briane, and my Grandmother Sarah and Grandfather Nathan for being my first teachers about love and support. Special thanks to Cissa Kelly for her generous support years ago when I first started writing this book, to Brother Ben Dixon, for his spiritual and financial support from beyond this life, and to Michael Allen for his generous gift for final publication.

Special thanks also to Marsha Richmond, Jeanette Walshe, Rob Moore, Kresser Deitsch, Earlene Karp, and Barbara St. Andrews, who each contributed to the writing of this book and who died before it was finished.

And thanks to the members of the Shamanic Healing and Empowerment Group and other members of the Wakan community whose courage, trust, love, and support have given me an extended family to work together with in blossoming our mutual flowers:

Harry Allen, Don Leonard, Martin Bernbaum, Mary Frandina, Barry Flicker, Diane Soash, Cindy Flaherty, Ken Norton, Jeff Anderson, Liz Allen, Leonard Leinow, Nancy Binzen, Lion Goodman, Karen Roberts, Margaret Morrison Watson, Susan Leonard, Jerry Luger, Sharon Norman, Mike Lerner, Alan Stout, Gene Kunitomi, Marilyn Riley, John Littleton, Kelle Olwyler, Becca Goeking Nofte, Scott Patton, Mary and Steve Knecht, Van Metaxis, Kay Garrick, Clark Grove, Pat Nalley, Annie Deichtman, Janice Greenberg, Margie Jamin, Ross Herbertson, Sue Adams, Michelle and Norm Groleau, Ellen Lerner, Nick Sica, Janet Goodman, Trout Black, Maria Rosa Kauffman, John Catalin, Maggie Meyer, Vita Rose, Sandy Barrett, Janica Fox, Norm Smookler, Ron Tilden, John Gladstein, Susan Greene, Christina Hammond, Jim Schuenemann, Diana Saint James, Lewie Sheridan, Tom Herrington, Gary Topper, Sue Herbertson, Cynthia Penhallow, Toni Bernbaum, Linda Sheridan, John Van Liew, Teddy Olwyler, Rick Kutten, Terumi Oikawa Leinow, David Dotlich, Doug Elwood and son Carter, Nikko Morris, Paul Ehrlich, Annelise Schinzinger, Nancy Corser, Ron Demmers, Mark Goldberg, Maia Silver, Ann Riley, Stewart Munroe, Charlie Setzler, Chris and Ruth Thorsen, Kenny Jimenez, and Max Poppers for being there when it counted.

Gratitude and appreciation to Tom and Flame Lutes, Penelope Moore, Nancy Iverson, Avon Mattison, Phil Bryson, Rich Yensen, Donna Dryer, Don Gowey, Stephen Rosen, Carol Hill, Paul Handleman, Doug Maxwell, Elizabeth Shepard, William Pemberton, Anne Stine, Hal Kramer, Bill Collins, Steven and Meredith Foster, Ed Thrift Jr., Julia Weaver, Alan Levin, Val Skonie, Carol Frank, Cass Adams, Joanie Misrack, Mira Foxman, Brendan Gilmore, J'aime Schelz, Jeff Cash, Rich Van Horn, Marilyn Robinson, Steven Marshank, Sasha and Ann Schulgin, Paul and Cheryl Shohan, Sharon Pair Taylor, Jerry Jampolsky and Diane Cirrincioni, Ralph Metzner, Terrence McKenna, Joel Alter, Marty Kent, Hyla Cass, Faustin Bray, Aida Hinojosa, Cheri Quincy, Kathie Eaton, John Perry, Kat Harrison, Josi Taylor, Jane English, Dennis Murphy, and Sandy Scull.

Many thanks to Prem Das, Bob Boyll, and Larain Boyll for opening the doorway to the Huichol people and keeping it open in the early years, and of course to the shamans of the Huichol, the *mara'akame,* with whom I studied—Doña Andrea, Guadalupe de la Cruz Rios, and Eustacio Perez, along with the members of my Huichol extended family, Jose and Paula, Presciliano and Maria Feliz, Domingo and Manuela, Chevalo and Cuka, Imalia and Lalo, Javier, Remaldo and Guiliermo, and to all their children. Also to Doña Julieta of the Mazateca and her apprentice Camila Martinez. *Muchas gracias.*

And finally, acknowledgment to Michael Saint James, whose spirit, organizational skills, creativity, encouragement, and publishing expertise made the book a reality in this world, along with the wonderful editing help of Jean Schiffman.

Thank you all for a healthy birthing, including those whose names I have forgotten to list but whose contributions are in my heart.

.·.·~.~.·.

Medicine Wheel of the Four Niericas

The medicine wheel is a mandalic, symbolic map, a cartography of psycho-physical-spiritual space. It represents a multidimensional, interpenetrating web of relationships that are constantly in communion with each other. It exists simultaneously in a vertical axis and a horizontal one, as well as in a continuum of past, present, and future. Anyone can make a medicine wheel. Mine is the result of direct, personal experience through over a quarter of a century seeking deeper vision, insight, and understanding of "how it all works." "It" refers to the Tao, the flow of the universe, nature—seen and unseen. It is all a work in progress.

This Medicine Wheel of the Four Niericas, or doorways, serves as an opening by which to consciously enter the cyclic, time-space unfolding of Great Mystery through a practice of respectful, harmonious, right-relationship with all of creation. It is based on the belief that the universe is alive, conscious, intelligent, and always communicating its wisdom to whoever makes the effort to listen to its myriad unfoldings of cosmic guidance.

It *is* power and it manifests its power in different ways, each one bringing its own quality of being, teaching, information, and challenge or testing. Thus each direction of the wheel, each *nierica,* is a field of energy that has its unique qualities, opportunities, and responsibilities. To move around the wheel, learning about and working with each of these four great teachers, is to step out of the comfort zone and step onto a path that will carry you onward for the rest of your days. It is my hope that this map will help you discover your own cartography, one that evolves out of your direct experience in nature and therefore has power for you in all that you do.

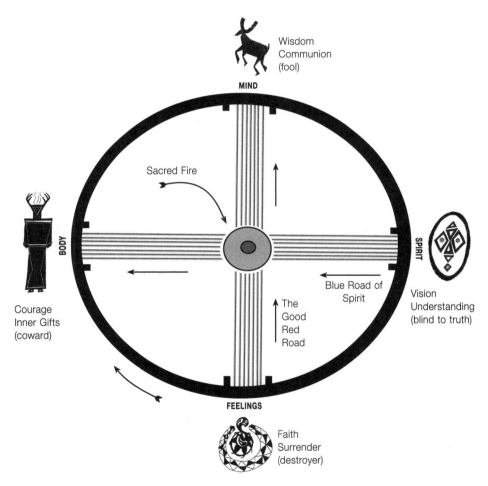

The Medicine Wheel of the Four Niericas is a
"Process Map" for exploring the operative laws of how
nature and the universe work

THE GOAL

To walk in balance on a respectful, right relationship, healing heart path with all of creation up to the time of completion.

INQUIRY QUESTIONS FOR WORKING WITH THE FOUR DIRECTIONS

The East
The Visionary—Power of Illumination—Golden Eagle

Task: Flying high like the eagle, gaining expanded, clear vision of greater truth. Connecting with the power of birthing sun cutting through darkness reminding us of our true nature—illumination. Being a light-bearer.

> How do I honor truth in my life?
>
> How do I dishonor truth in my life?
>
> What vision or purpose do I follow in my life now?
>
> How am I, or how can I be, a visionary bringing inspiration of expanded possibilities?

Shadow: Constricted, earth-bound myopic who doesn't know truth and follows no vision except the whims of ego and unconscious reactivity; i.e., a mechanical person.

Assignment: Greet the rising Father Sun upon your own arising. Start the day by attuning with the light. Find something true in nature. Thank it. Dialogue with it to explore what it might teach you about truth.

The South
The Healer—Power of Faith and Trust—Serpent

Task: To shed the old that no longer serves healthy living, and surrender to the new, the unknown, with the faith and trust of the innocent young child. Attunement with feelings. Healing with love.

What do you have faith in?

What do you trust?

What do you need to shed?

What needs healing in your life?

How are you a destroyer in your life?

How are you, or can you be, a healer?

Shadow: The Destroyer; subverting, wrecking, denying, repressing, blocking, killing.

Assignment: Cultivate faith, trust, and your ability to consciously surrender control in a responsible manner. Find something in nature that teaches you about healing. Thank it. Then dialogue with it to see what it can teach you about realizing your own healing potential.

The West

The Warrior—Power of the Looks-Within Place—Black Panther—Bear

Task: To enter the place of introspection to face and befriend your fears, shadow forces, and eventual death, turning them all into allies and advisors, thereby mining the treasures they guard.

What are your worst fears?

What kind of relationship do you have with your death? Your shadow? With relatives and friends who have died?

What do you need to face in your life?

How are you, or can you be, a warrior in your life?

What gives you courage?

Shadow: Wimpy coward, shut down in fear, constricted; existing but not really living the truth of who you are.

Assignment: Call up the power of the bear to journey within using the ferocity of the panther to help you face your darkness and access the gifts of your deeper being. Find something in nature you dislike— what does it remind you of in you? Thank it, and ask what it can teach you about your own death.

The North
Elder-Leader-Teacher—Power of Wisdom—Deer Spirit

Task: Communion with higher self, wisdom grandmothers and grand-fathers, guides, living and in spirit. Bringing through their guiding wisdom for the benefit of the community, healing and growing the people.

> What are the wisdom teachings that you follow in your life?
>
> What does wisdom mean to you?
>
> Who are the wisdom teachers of your life?
>
> How do you close off to ignore, or dishonor wisdom?
>
> How do you act out the fool?
>
> What are the wisdom teachings of your own historical-cultural, tribal past?
>
> How are you, or can you be, a wisdom leader and teacher in your own life?

Shadow: The Idiot, the dummy, the ignorant fool who follows delusion as reality.

Assignment: Face the North and give heart-felt appreciation to the power and bearers of wisdom in your life. Sit down humbly at their knee and ask for their guidance. Find something in nature that has wisdom. Thank it, then ask for guidance on how to develop that quality in yourself.

The Center
In the center of the sacred circle is the Great Mystery, the Holy Spirit, represented by Grandfather Fire, what the Huichol people call Tatewari, the First Shaman. Everything emanates from the center. It is the Source. It is present in all things, all places, all people, all situations, all the time. It has been always, it will be always. Its essence is unconditional love, infinite wisdom, peace and illumination. At the deepest core of our being, we are one with the center and all of creation that births from it. We are all related.

MOVEMENT AROUND THE WHEEL

Movement around this wheel starts with clockwise motion following the path of the sun. Each direction interfaces with its opposite side, so the light gathered in the East helps one enter the darkness in the West. The surrendering work of the South helps one open to communion with wisdom from the North. The South-North axis is called the *Good Red Road*. The East-West axis is called the *Good Blue Road*. The spirit of new life enters this world through the eastern doorway and it leaves at the time of physical death through the western one. During the course of a lifetime, by continuously working your way around the medicine wheel, touching and being touched by the power, teachings, and testings of each direction, the mysterious process of growth is activated and nourished.

The wheel is a synergistic energy vortex that fuels and feeds upon itself. It is an infinite source of intelligence that follows you wherever you go. It is always present. It is always surrounding you. You are never alone.

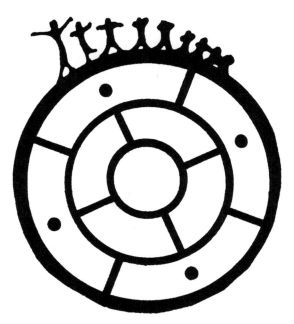

"The people come forth," drawing by the author

Resanctifying Daily Life through Ritual and Ceremony

The purpose of ritual and ceremonial practice is to bring consciously chosen, focused attention to attune with Spirit as a living presence. Clarity of purpose and process, along with attitudes of respect, humility, receptivity and full personal presence, are of vital importance in preparation and performance of ritual acts in a responsible manner. Assume that the depth of your sincerity and commitment is witnessed by Spirit and that this "reading" has a great deal to do with the outcome of the act.

Take nothing for granted save that you are loved, there is no such thing as a separate thing, everything is connected, for every action there is a reaction, and that Spirit-Nature-Tao knows best. See each act of the ritual as a seed that will bear a consequence. Pay careful attention to the seeds you plant, for that which you sow, you will surely reap. Remember that what you give to the ritual, you give to yourself. The ultimate purpose is to help you become the fullest and healthiest expression of all that is within you as potentiality in a way that is for your greatest good and the greatest good of the community of life.

DAILY PRACTICE

1. Purification and sunrise prayers: Creating sacred space within body and physical area offering smoke of cleansing herbs and heart-felt thanksgiving to the above, below, around powers and to the Great Spirit Mystery at the center from which all of creation manifests. Centering, grounding, empowerment practice; lining up with the light to start your day.

2. Mindfulness work with meditative breath, posture, movement, sound, stretching, and physical exercise for physical power and cardiovascular, respiratory conditioning. Your mind-body is an instrument of great sensitivity and intelligence and requires regular tuning to keep it in top operating order.

3. Lighting candles and goal setting with positive imagery and visualization techniques using the *kupuri* or chi (energy) built up by the first two practices.

4. Breakfast-lunch-dinner prayers to connect with the source of life and spiritual nourishment to complement the physical nourishment, holding hands with others present sending out thankfulness prayers.

5. Sunset meditation giving thanks for gifts, teachings, blessings of the day, releasing what needs to be let go, and opening to the energies/rhythms of the night.

6. Inviting gifts from the dreamtime by invoking it and placing dream journal by your bedside.

WEEKLY PRACTICE

1. House purification using cleansing herbs with open window to free dwelling space of old or unwanted energies.

2. Vehicle purification to cleanse and create protection shield on inside and outside, especially before long trips, or after any kind of accident or harrowing experience.

3. Workplace purification and prayers bringing in Spirit's presence for the work of the day and cleansing out energy of earlier interactions so space can be clean and new for the next situation.

4. Regular sacred circle work with drumming, prayers, and heart-truth sharing with equal time for respectful listening for each person present.

YEARLY PRACTICE

1. Seasonal ceremonies honoring and attuning with the rhythms and teachings of the winter and summer solstice and the fall and spring equinox in community with others.

2. Annual quest for vision in wilderness setting to get back to the roots for renewal, re-creation, healing, and spiritual empowerment.

3. New Year Prayer Arrow Ceremony with all family members helping create a ceremonial arrow embodying thankfulness for the gifts of the year and prayers for the new year. Arrow is planted at your home into the body of Mother Earth, or at the ocean, a river, a mountain, or other place of power.

OCCASION-SPECIFIC PRACTICES

1. Birthing and naming ceremonies
2. Dying, death, and mourning rituals along with appropriate memorial services
3. Weddings
4. Rites of initiation for children, adolescents, midlife, and becoming an elder
5. Graduations
6. Birthdays
7. Life changes such as job promotions, partnership changes, children leaving home, moving to new home, retirement, etc.

APPENDIX 3

⌇⌇⌇⌇

Wakan Community Philosophy

Wakan is an intimate community of individuals who are supporting each member's healing and growth on all levels of being through a deepening connection with all our relations. We hold Mother Earth and all of creation as united in a sacred circle of mutual interdependence and responsibility. We seek to create respectful "right relationship" with all our relations walking as lightly as we can, protecting and honoring the natural world and its inhabitants. We value vision in our lives and the power necessary to actualize it in a loving, unattached service to the Higher Will of the Great Mystery. We strive to walk in balance on a healing heart path of love for all of Creation, all those who have crossed over, and for all those yet to come.

We acknowledge the life-affirming wisdom teachings of indigenous peoples and support their application in facing the challenges of the modern world. We actively support the struggles of Native Peoples to survive and flourish in a world of respectful diversity and shared common interests, such as the health of Mother Earth's air, water, body, and spirit. Wakan is involved through fundraising; clothing and medical supplies contributions; political activism defending indigenous people's sovereignty, sacred sites, and freedom of religion.

We offer the support of a committed community with Spirit at its center gathering together for celebratory rituals, rites of passage, and seasonal ceremonies to help blossom the flowers that are within us all. Predicated on a shamanic, Earth-based spirituality, we support and define eco-psychological health and wellness for all in terms of the larger environment of which we are all a part.

AN APOLOGY TO THE INDIGENOUS PEOPLE OF THIS LAND

The members of the Wakan community want to express our deepest and heartfelt apology for the genocide and abuse your cultures have suffered at the hands of our ancestors, who invaded this land some 500 years ago. We apologize for our own role and for the actions of our relatives who have initiated and perpetuated this holocaust. Your lands have been stolen, your peoples murdered, your cultures devastated, and your belief systems suppressed. We recognize that the oppression of Native Americans continues into present time in the form of racist attitudes, institutionalized poverty, lack of opportunity, inferior education, inadequate healthcare, refusal to settle land claims, environmental desecration, and continuing efforts to deny religious freedom.

We understand that Native Peoples respectfully stewarded this land for thousands of years before the European invasion and maintained a sacred relationship with the Earth Mother. We honor the profound Earth-centered wisdom embodied in your cultures, in your languages, and in your sacred practices. We believe this knowledge is critical to the transformation of Western consciousness for the survival of all living things through to the seventh generation ahead.

We wish to shed the veil of cultural denial that has masked the truth for too long now. We are no longer willing to stand by silently as a part of the problem. We choose to take an active stand in support of justice for our indigenous relatives both here and around the globe. We ask that you accept this humble apology so that we can join together as part of the solution to the enormous challenges that face the healthy survival of all beings.

About the Author

Photo by Marilyn Riley

The author, 1985

Photo by Andrea Pinkson

The author, 2007

Tom Pinkson was born in the heart of New York City in 1945. The death of his father when he was four years old set him on a path of exploration beginning with psychosomatic illness and juvenile delinquency, but eventually took him to the far reaches of the Amazon jungle, the Andes mountains, and to an eleven-year apprenticeship with a group of Huichol Indian shamans of north central Mexico. Seeking deeper truth about the mysteries of life and death, he sought out numerous shamanic medicine teachers who initiated him into new realms.

During this time, Tom earned three college degrees, including a Ph.D. in psychology. His doctoral dissertation, "A Quest for Vision," described his successful work with heroin addicts in the early 1970s using a wilderness treatment program of mountain climbing, river running, snow camping, ski touring, and vision quests in the High Sierra. The quests continue to this day, with people coming from all over the United States to join him on these powerful experiences of solitude and adventure.

From working with drug addicts, he went on to help start one of the first hospice programs in the United States, offering support services to the terminally ill. He was invited by Jerry Jampolsky to join the Center for Attitudinal Healing in Sausalito, California, to work with children facing life-threatening illness. Tom worked with the center as a clinical consultant for thirty-two years.

Walking in two worlds, the shamanic world of indigenous spirituality and the Western world of a practicing psychologist, consultant, teacher, public speaker, and high-performance coach to business executives and health professionals, Tom serves as a bridge-builder, bringing what he calls *The Teachings of the Elders* into practical applications within the modern, urban setting. From major corporations to pediatric oncology units within prestigious cancer treatment centers; from the academic world to rites of passage work with children, adolescents, and adults; the dying process and subsequent work of grief, mourning, and rebirth, Tom has successfully brought in wisdom teachings from the elders that have had dramatic impact on people's lives.

Tom also "tills the garden" through numerous workshops, retreats, and pilgrimages to sacred places of power throughout the world, including Bali, Peru, Brazil, Hawaii, Mexico, and Ireland. He is the founder and president of a nonprofit, spiritually based educational community, Wakan, which offers a variety of programs and services to help people find and remember what is sacred in their lives. He has appeared on international television and radio, written numerous articles, and produced video and audio recordings on attitudinal healing and shamanism.

His most recent work, through A New Vision of Aging, focuses on conscious aging and training workshops to help people learn the attitudes and behaviors that build emotional, physical, and spiritual resilience for meeting the challenges of change.

Tom has two grown children and three grandsons and lives with his wife of forty-two years, Andrea, a pediatric nurse, in San Rafael, California, along with several animals and one big garden with many flowers.

To receive information about Tom's workshops, consulting, retreats, and pilgrimages or his audio/video recordings, books, and articles, or for more information about Wakan, please contact him by e-mail at thomas@ microweb.com and visit his websites:

www.nierica.com

www.anewvisionofaging.com